Moving Cultures

moving

cultures

Mobile Communication in Everyday Life

André H. Caron | Letizia Caronia

McGILL-QUEEN'S UNIVERSITY PRESS
Montreal & Kingston · London · Ithaca

© McGill-Queen's University Press 2007

ISBN 978-0-7735-3218-2 (cloth)
ISBN 978-0-7735-3203-4 (paper)

Legal deposit second quarter 2007
Bibliothèque nationale du Québec

Printed in Canada on acid-free paper.

This book has been published with the help of
a grant from the Bell Chair in Interdisciplinary
Research on Emerging Technologies at the
Université de Montréal.

McGill-Queen's University Press acknowledges
the support of the Canada Council for the Arts
for our publishing program. We also acknowledge
the financial support of the Government of
Canada through the Book Publishing Industry
Development Program (BPIDP) for our publishing
activities.

**Library and Archives Canada Cataloguing
in Publication**

Caron, André H.
Moving cultures : mobile communication in
everyday life / André H. Caron, Letizia Caronia.
Translation of: Culture mobile.

Includes bibliographical references and index.
ISBN 978-0-7735-3218-2 (bnd)
ISBN 978-0-7735-3203-4 (pbk)

1. Communication and culture.
2. Communication—Social aspects.
3. Communication—Technological innovations—
Social aspects. 4. Mobile communication
systems—Social aspects. 5. Technology and
youth. I. Caronia, Letizia II. Title.

P94.6.C3713 2007   302.2   C2007-900295-1

This book was designed and typeset by studio
oneonone in Sabon 10.5/13.5

Contents

Acknowledgments

The research we undertook was made possible with the support of various entities including the Faculté des arts et des sciences and the Centre for Interdisciplinary Research on Emerging Technologies (CITÉ) of the Université de Montréal, the Facolta' di Scienze della Formazione, the Dipartimento di Science dell'Educazione of Bologna University, the European Marco Polo Program, Canadian Foundation for Innovation, and, not the least, the Bell Chair in Interdisciplinary Research on Emerging Technologies at Université de Montréal.

This book is the collaborative work of both authors. André H. Caron was responsible for the final draft of chapters 1, 3, 4, and 9, and Letizia Caronia for chapters 2, 5, 6, 7, 8, and 10. The introduction is by both authors. The translation and adaptation of this book from its original French version was expertly done by Mary Baker and Karen Sherman, to whom we are extremely indebted.

We would like to express our gratitude to all those who assisted us at the Centre for Youth Media Studies (GRJM) and at CITÉ at the Université de Montréal and especially to Flavie, Mathieu, Laurent, Andrée-Anne, and Olivier.

We would also like to greatly thank Mafalda, Moussa, Simon, Virginia, Alexandre, Raphaëlle, Annie-Josée, Rosalie, and all those of the emerging generation who assisted us in better understanding their "mobile culture."

A.H.C.
L.C.

Transcription Conventions

The transcription conventions used in the extracts are as follows.

[*xxx*]   Italicized text in brackets indicates transcriber's descriptors.

[???]   Question marks in brackets indicate unintelligible words.

[xxxx]   Words in brackets indicate uncertainty on the part of the transcriber.

::   Colons indicate stretching of the preceding sound. The more the colons, the more the sound is stretched.

(.)   A period in parentheses indicates a short pause, whether in the turn of conversation or between turns.

[...]   Periods in square brackets indicate a cut of one or more utterances.

_____   Underlined text indicates emphasis.

xxx   Bold text indicates points relevant to the analysis.

⌈   Left brackets one above another on two successive different
⌊   lines indicate the point where turns of talk overlap.

Moving Cultures

Introduction

In recent decades the information and communication technology universe has witnessed a whirlwind of changes and innovations. Although common sense might argue the contrary, this phenomenon is not particularly new. Over the centuries humans have been repeatedly inventing techniques and supports to enhance communication and information flow. The invention and adoption of writing, printing, photography, and telephony and the shift to the digital age are just a few examples of solutions to the apparently insurmountable problem of overcoming the limits and constraints of face-to-face communication. Each of these communication instruments represented a cultural turning point for its era and for the communities concerned. Constant advancements in communication and information techniques, the ways that technological innovations trigger deep cultural transformations, are evidently far from new phenomena. We may even say that the process of mutual construction of technology and culture is one of the phenomena most studied by social scientists interested in human evolution and cultural development. What invariably lies open for further investigation is the *kind* of innovation proposed each time by a "new generation" of technologies, insofar as it is always after the fact that we can reconstruct the forms of interactions and the ways of life each technology helps to create.

This book explores the social and cultural dimensions of the "mobile turn" in everyday communication and the multiple ways in which these new communication practices participate in the everyday production of culture. How do emerging technologies impart meaning to daily life? How do they create the identities of social actors? How do the actors, in turn, attribute meaning to mobile communication technologies? How do they incorporate these devices into their cultural web of meanings through daily use? These questions will all be addressed in this book.

Emerging Communication Technologies in Daily Life

As communication instruments become part of our daily routine, they free us from most of the spatial and temporal constraints that govern our lives. Significantly, overcoming such constraints has ramifications beyond the ability to effectively manage the multiple, simultaneous tasks that characterize contemporary life. This purely practical function conceals deeper cultural and social issues, because these technologies prompt us to rethink and recreate the cultural aspects of the ways we live together. Even the simplest concepts that make up "everyday knowledge," that is, all of the practical knowledge that enables us to interact in a culturally appropriate way, can no longer be taken for granted. "Being present or absent," "being here" or "being there," and "being alone" or "with someone" are simply lexical labels that require a redefinition, invariably situated, of their meaning each time they arise. The same can be said for everyday interaction rituals, that is, the shared cultural codes that let us participate in social encounters in a coordinated and mutually comprehensible manner.

Consider the example of mobile telephones, the contemporary tool that perhaps most condenses and best represents the cultural challenges of the "mobile turn" in daily communication. Although North Americans mostly refer to this technology as the "cellular phone," the technical aspect is rapidly evolving whereas the mobility-creating function will remain – thus our preference for the descriptor "mobile." When two people keep their mobile phones on when meeting for lunch, one must ask what has become of a simple conversation. The rights and duties, expectations, and even face-to-face manners of participants must now be negotiated with those of *ghost participants* who may join interactants and enter into the occurring conversation. People living "out there" can be "here" at any time, thus changing the participation structure of the event.

By giving rise to new forms of interaction, this technology obliges us to rethink the cultural models of social encounters. Cultural transformations brought about by new communication practices go beyond the participation structure of social events. They also prompt the reconstruction of social links and interpersonal relations. In a world where parents and children can always stay in touch even when far from one another, the mobile phone is much more than a simple technology for coordinating activities. Crucial and somehow paradoxical tasks of parenting such as exercising responsibility and control while fostering children's independence are seemingly being accomplished in new ways. Working as a new *panop-*

tikon, the mobile phone allows for remote parenting, thus forcing us to rethink our cultural model of "being a parent" and "being a child."

These are examples of the many ways that emerging communication technologies impart meaning to daily life. Once they become integrated into our routines, they reformulate possible meanings: places, actors, reciprocal relations, and the typical events that comprise them are thus amenable to new modes of accomplishment and interpretations. Modern avatars of the first tool invented by humans to overcome the limits of face -to-face communication, these devices force us to rethink and reinvent the forms of social life and the cultural models that constitute our everyday knowledge.

The opposite is also true. If individuals are manipulated by technologies, equally they manipulate them. Although they appear to be sovereign masters of our daily life, living objects that can alter the smallest details, technologies are nonetheless influenced by a systematic process of cultural domestication. They acquire or lose functions and are interpreted by individuals according to shared frames of reference. Their uses and meanings are reformulated each time in a situated setting and according to the world of meanings specific to a given community.

When adolescents use text messages (SMS) to chat, flirt, and gossip, when they engage in endless instantaneous written exchanges, they reinterpret the technology to meet the needs of their specific culture. The logic of asynchronous exchanges has been converted into the synchrony of mutual coordination and ongoing adjustment of oral conversation. SMS messaging in teen culture far exceeds sending information in a quick, short manner. Rather, it is a verbal performance through which young people create and maintain their social world. Regardless of the forms of communication suggested by and inscribed in the technology itself, teenagers have radically interpreted its meaning and functions according to their cultural frames of reference.

Situated in a given context, technologies are thus integrated in its constituent dimensions, with their ultimate meaning defined by both the context and the actors therein.

Anatomy of a Process: From Visible Aspects to Hidden Dimensions

Focusing on the relation between mobile communication and cultural creation implies analysing the anatomy of a joint construction process, because if technologies build culture, they are also shaped by culture. There are evidently several ways to analyse a phenomenon of this structural complexity. To go beyond the most visible and general aspects and grasp the more subtle issues and details that often make a difference, research is crucial.

Most of the proposals in this book originate from field research. Given the scope of the phenomenon, our research, carried out over an eight-year period, mapped out a specific area of investigation, with the assumption common to all empirical research that systematic analysis of a well-defined portion of a larger reality can shed light on the characteristics and less visible processes of the "whole" of which it forms a part.

In our empirical investigation of the co-construction process between emerging technologies and daily culture, we began by targeting the convergence of technologies in the home and the role of this convergence in building a family structure and culture. Analysis of this social microcosm effectively revealed the extent to which information and communication technologies can be used to create a structure and culture specific to a family, and further, to define the identities of family members.

As we entered this fascinating world, our investigation cried out to be taken much further. The mobile communication practices of young people and adolescents, their representations of this technology, and its role in daily life then became the subjects of the research projects that followed. These choices deserve justification.

Mobile phones encompass many characteristics of emerging communication technologies. Portable, mobile, cellular, *telefonino* – the names themselves given to the latest incarnation of remote voice communication highlight distinctive features. Although they all designate the same object, each label has different connotations. If "cellular" emphasizes the technological innovation behind this communication tool, *"telefonino"* (little telephone) plays on the morphological aspects that allow the incorporation of the object in the subject. If "portable" shifts the emphasis to the users and their communication practices, "mobile" carries this semantic displacement close to the social dimensions of technology. Relegated to the semantic backdrop, technological innovation is no longer the semantic core: "mobile" emphasizes the new nomadic identity of contemporary social actors.

This rich concentration of characteristics in a single technological object makes the mobile phone a fine example of a category of emerging communication technologies and their social uses. Another factor that motivated our choice of the mobile telephone as a research subject is the speed of its adoption and dissemination in Europe, America, and Asia, astonishing even its designers and manufacturers.

We could have chosen from among a panoply of new technologies or information and communication systems (nano computers, multifunction devises, telephone over Internet (VoIP), voice mail, visual messaging), but the adoption of many of these systems is still in progress, and their dissemination rate would have been less conducive to research that extends beyond the early majority of adopters. Although intriguing, such research would not have addressed as well our interest in technologies as shared cultural resources and communication practices as key components of daily culture. It is this set of traits specific to the mobile telephone and its role in social life that makes this technology – in our view, at least – a good analyser of mobile communication and mobile culture.

Numerous factors motivate this research avenue. In Europe as in America the market and the discourse of advertising more and more target the emerging generation of young people as the best interpreters of this product. After a period in which the target was defined by professional category, age became *the* category of advertising discourse. This preferred relationship between youth and mobile telephones is confirmed by research and also by the general grasp of social phenomena that comes from our everyday experience and understanding. From both perspectives, young people have not only adopted this technology but, more importantly, also harnessed all of its assets by integrating them into their daily life. This adoption was as quick as it was extreme. The remarkable unfolding of the *culturalization* process of this technology makes young people a social category particularly revealing of the issues and characteristics of the process.

As our research confirmed, in their use of new communication technologies, young people are both extremely innovative and extremely conservative. This dual nature of teenagers' approach to technologies creates an effective litmus test – precisely because it is so extreme – for the inescapable relationship between creativity and conservatism, innovation and cultural incorporation, that characterizes the adoption of technologies, although the extent varies with the individual.

The choice of young people as research subjects offers a crucial analytical advantage: like the exception that under certain analytical conditions makes the rule, extreme situations reveal the nature of what they are – precisely – *paroxystic* expressions. A critical analysis of excess is a convenient short cut to shed light on what usually remains moderate and therefore less visible.

From the Users' Point of View: Multiple Interpretations

Evidently, the relationships between youth and technologies can be analysed in many ways. If we had wanted to paint a global picture of the phenomenon and its macro-characteristics, we would have chosen a bird's-eye view typical of large-scale statistical surveys, which would have provided an incomparable overview of all the broad frameworks and general characteristics. The unique advantages of this approach in terms of representativeness and generalizability are well known. However, losses also occur. In contrast, to grasp and tease out the multiple and recursive relationships between language, interaction, culture, and technologies in daily life – which is indeed our goal – it is more fitting to scrutinize the micro-order of daily life. Once the scale of analysis is changed, even the smallest details become significant. Examined through the magnifying glass of the ethnographic perspective, these details reveal the extent that culture is gradually constructed by people throughout their situated interaction. In the ethnographic approach, what is lost through the inability to generalize is compensated by the ability to capture the process of construction of meaning. By posing the crucial ethnographic question – "Why this now and from which viewpoint?" – the strange (or the stranger) becomes familiar, and the familiar becomes sufficiently strange so that we can see its hidden features and processes.

That is why we have retained ethnography and some of its techniques in our analysis here. This choice is not exceptional in itself: researchers interested in communication practices as cultural construction mechanisms have long turned to ethnography to support their analyses and discourse.

That being said, there are certain major consequences of this choice, in that adopting a methodological approach implies more than using certain instruments: it also entails adopting a theoretical paradigm. Readers may be surprised to find this book bereft of certain conventional approaches to social phenomena. For example, there are no explanations of technological behaviours based on concepts such as social origin, gender, or economic status of the actors concerned.

This "absence" harks back to the fundamental assumptions of the ethnographic approach: the researchers are not strictly interested in explaining events through the concepts they create; rather they are mainly concerned with the categories through which the actors themselves interpret their own practices. In our case this implies that we will not necessarily apply concepts such as "social origin," "economic income," or "gender" to explain uses (or non-uses) of technology unless the actors themselves cite this type of explanation to account for their and others' actions. For instance, if Sara explains that she does not have a mobile telephone in terms of "it's only showing off" rather than in economic terms, it is this explanation that we will analyse, namely, the one that informs her understanding of mobile telephones.

Assuredly, we strived to attain an equilibrium between the perspectives of the actor and the researcher, and to advance interpretations rather than explanations. Multiple interpretations may co-exist, often differing according to the viewpoint adopted. This book therefore provides informed readers with an overview of the multiple levels of reading social reality. And like all authors, we hope to establish a contract of trust with the reader as to the writing choices that originate from our approach.

Giving the Actors a Voice: Polyphony and Writing

Opting for field research implies following an approach in which general reflection originates from the analysis of particular cases and the view of singular cases is oriented by theoretical frames of reference. We must therefore "provide the case," which can be achieved in several ways. In ethnography of situated communication practices, providing the case means giving a voice to actors the researcher has met in the field. The next question is: which voices and how?

After the dialogical turn in social sciences and critical reflection on the traditional strategies of representation, we can no longer consider scientific writing as an unproblematic activity. Researchers' descriptions, analyses, and words invariably originate from a number of dialogue practices in which the researcher participates, alongside the informants. However, most often these interactions remain hidden to the reader, who hears only a sovereign monologue. The erasing of the Other in writing is a problem that has both rhetorical and ethical facets, because the apparent lightness of a monologue masks manipulation that can no longer be underestimated. Our goal is therefore to produce a text that can render the full richness of the social encounter between human beings, a text that represents the complementary and sometimes conflicting juxtaposition of several discourses, and that puts several interpretative perspectives at centre stage.

In this book we chose polyphonic writing in which scholarly discourse is combined with the situated and living words of both the people we encountered and ourselves while engaged in dialogues in the field. Actually, these living words are the true source of all the analysis we advance. This is certainly not a representation that purports to be objective, given that any transcription is a translation. Polyphonic writing is rather a rhetorical strategy that purports to (re)produce the polyphony and *heteroglossia* specific to ethnographic research. Moreover, this text will provide readers with more direct access to the scenes observed and the words spoken, which will illustrate how the actors accomplish, represent, interpret and account for their own actions. Below is an example of a typical passage that can be found throughout the book.

ASSOUM: Yeah, what's up?
CHAN: Uh, playing [???], you know.
ASSOUM: Ha, ha. [All game], no life.
CHAN: Yeah, no:
ASSOUM: [*laughing*] Guess where I am?
CHAN: Uhh, Outremont?
ASSOUM: Yeah, dude, you're good. How did you know?
CHAN: Oh, man ... you're always there.

Despite some compromises to make the conversation intelligible, we present a written text that defies the conventions of standard language, especially in its written form. This non-standard writing is the condition for conveying not only the meaning of words but also the social and cultural significance inscribed in the ways people talk together. It is well known that standard language is an abstraction, an extraordinary, necessary invention that, significantly, does not correspond to any of the situated, living communication practices in our daily life. "Reality" offers only historic, social, radically situated variants.

It is important to keep in mind that the challenge of this writing style is not to provide examples of a regional variant of a language. Nor are we aiming to provide a representation of the characteristics of specific, situated usage (that of informal groups of adolescents in a North American urban centre). Rather, we aim to elucidate the interactive and social roots of daily speech, to preserve the traces of its fragmented, apparently incomplete nature, linguistically remote from the standard model. If the products (certain words or expressions, language games, or innovations) are local, the underlying processes lend themselves to a general analysis. This writing style therefore requires the reader's complicity and an effort to avoid being seduced by the siren song of the extremely local. Like a good tale, a single everyday event stands for general issues and demands the reader see the world in a grain of sand.

The choice of avoiding a total purging of the marks of oral communication or paraphrasing the discourse of others was motivated by more than just concern for the enlightened reader. Giving primacy to speech also implies giving actors back their voices and respecting the – virtually untranslatable – richness of all communication practices, technologically mediated or not.

Different Readers, Multiple Readings

The dislocation of the subjects as they go about their modern roving apparently does not imply cultural uprooting or loss of cultural landmarks or information. On the contrary, new technologies purportedly weave a new web of social contacts and guarantee the availability of knowledge. The first chapters contain a critical description of the new social scenarios engendered by emerging technologies (chapter 1); reflection on the technical objects as actors, on a par with people, in the processes of construction of daily culture (chapter 2); and an analysis of the social life of technologies and their role in the definition of users' identities, spaces, and different moments of daily life (chapter 3). Chapter 4 analyses the form of a social discourse that has contributed to the creation of meaning of communication technologies: advertising. By following the gradual unveiling of rhetorical strategies through which companies link young people and mobile phones, readers will be immersed in the universe of the mobile culture of contemporary youth. The following chapters then explore this universe. By closely following the daily life of an informal group of adolescents – young adult couples and a network of youngsters in middle and high school – chapters 5, 6, 7, and 8 explore the heart of a passionate phenomenon: the incorporation of technologies in a community of practices and their role in the creation of the community itself.

Translators of technologies into the terms of their specific culture, young people do not form a closed community. Interpreters and diffusers of this mobile culture, they act as social bridges that link different communities of practices in the urban space, routinely crossing boundaries. Chapter 9, dedicated to trans-generational relations, spotlights a meeting ground between the technological culture of parents and that of their children. Although more discrete than most of the factors that are transforming the traditional family model, the arrival of certain communication and information technologies in the home is certainly a change-driver. The role of technologies in the construction and transformation of what counts as a "family" cannot be underestimated. Not only are these technologies used and represented differently within the same family but they also lend themselves to strategic uses. They are thus used as a powerful tool to transform the practices and cultural models that define parental and other roles.

By underlining the role of emerging communication technologies in the construction of a new awareness of the Other on the public scene, chapter 10 reflects upon the ethical and aesthetic dimensions of technological culture. Among the least visible cultural consequences of the mobile turn in everyday communication, these aspects nonetheless defy most of today's common-sense assumptions. Despite what one might imagine, dissemination of these tools in daily life does not produce an isolated individual oblivious to social constraints, nor has it triggered a process of globalization of standardized social practices. The chapter concludes with a reflection on the role of mobile communication devices in creating the intersubjective dimension of our world.

This book was designed to be read not only linearly but also in a rhizomatic mode. Although the sequence of chapters is meaningful (typically going from general information to particular cases and back), this configuration is not constraining. Each chapter has an internal coherence and autonomy allowing readers to forge their own path through the book.

By tracing the anatomy of the ways in which individuals use certain cultural artifacts, our research clarifies how and to what extent communication technologies play a role in the creation of identities, social links, and daily life. In short, our book illustrates the crucial dimensions of the contemporary mobile culture in which we all participate, whether we like it or not.

Chapter 1

New Social Scenarios

New technological mediation plays a revealing role in our everyday relations to space and time. The changes we have faced since the new millennium raise challenges in more ways than one. New conventions have appeared alongside old ways of seeing and doing that have nonetheless endured. Suddenly, old norms are crumbling, commonplace certainties are being shaken, and things we used to routinely accept as obvious are no longer so evident. Space and time have changed and are suddenly taking on singular importance. *Where* are we when we interact with one another over digital networks? *When* are we when we instantaneously exchange with people in a completely different time zone? We cannot help but wonder about the nature of reality itself: what is real when our relationships increasingly take place in the virtual world? In a society that is becoming more and more interconnected, in which we find ourselves literally submerged by constantly growing and accelerating flows of information, how can we negotiate our relationships with others and technologies, with humans and techno-objects? Is there a risk that the reality of sensory experience could be replaced by the virtual as we are surrounded by more and more screens, which are gradually becoming our main reference to the world? Are we committing ourselves ever more deeply to a world of virtual reality – or real virtuality?

To understand this troubling strangeness that is so much a part of today, and find answers to these questions, our observations have led us to formulate three scenarios that circumscribe the new technological mediations. In this chapter, we discuss alternately the delocalization and multilocalization of one's self, the hybridization of time, and the death of silence.

1.1 Looking for the "Where" and "Who" of Our Communications

Computers and digital networks have of course been indispensable in economic and commercial relations for some time. We need only think of ATMs, office automation, and on-line goods and services. However, society has been digitized not only with respect to economic interactions but in all areas of social life and interactions.

Thus, at least since the 1980s, new forms of media have gradually infiltrated family space. The new media, which many call NICTs (for new information and communication technologies), may in some instances still play some of the roles traditionally belonging to their mass-media predecessors, but they differ from them in a crucial way. Networked personal computers and, since 1994, the Internet have the special feature of being interactive, and therefore of making bi-directional and even multi-directional communication possible. This was never achieved with traditional media. The fact that it no longer surprises us that millions of people have social and commercial relations over digital networks is because we forget that this increasingly occurs with no real territorial anchorage. While our physical bodies do indeed remain in a real environment, "much of our conscious life has already emigrated to the temporal universe of access relations" (Rifkin 2000). Moreover, when we communicate over digital networks, we are generally alone, at least physically.

Some go so far as to assert that in networked society, spatial distances become less relevant and, inversely, that "personal relations acquire very great importance even though no one can be sure of the faithfulness of those with whom relations are established" (Boltanski and Chiapello 1999, 201–2). Indeed, new technologies are often criticized, rightly or wrongly, for being impersonal and for distorting so-called natural communication, which is most often idealized in its face-to-face form. In fact, while networked society, in which remote communication predominates, has borrowed some of the expressions by which the intimate, private domestic world identifies itself (personal relationships, trust, face-to-face), actions and mechanisms with the same name (friendship, affinity, meeting) remain very different in the real and virtual worlds (ibid.).

In traditional society the public sphere can be distinguished clearly from the private. In the public sphere, pre-defined, principle- and duty-bound official and social roles prevail, while personal and intimate relationships are not considered important. The latter remain in the private sphere. On the contrary, in a connectionist society in which networks criss-cross both public and private spheres (to such an extent that they sometimes merge), physical public space loses part of its function as a location for meeting and exchanging, and submits instead to the requirements of circulation and visibility.

The "reality" of new technologies is to allow instant contact with other people, despite the physical distance separating us, and this considerably changes the communications scenarios that used to be the norm. Synchronous interactions by mobile phone or instant messaging, no matter where on earth the people involved are located, are now routine. Our experiences with these new technologies sometimes give the impression that geographical distances are disappearing (Cairncross 1997).

For social actors, while physical distances are temporarily eliminated by new technologies, they do not actually disappear. They remain very real, both materially and mentally. Are we therefore seeing a change in the notion of distance? Parents who receive regular emails and phone calls from their children who are travelling the world feel like they are less far away, but they are still physically separated, and that distance is impossible to ignore. Children and parents occupy a different space, another location, when they communicate synchronously, and this changes the way that they relate to one another.

One might think that the new ease of contact opens fresh possibilities for developing and maintaining human relations. Instantaneous, inexpensive communication with friends living abroad is now part of our reality. Yet it would be a mistake to take for granted that everything has changed and that we are now in a world where everyone is constantly interrelated. Solitude and social isolation still exist: the possibility of communication does not necessarily mean that communication will take place. A young person could have his instant messaging turned on but not necessarily interact with other people who are also connected. Technologies never automatically create strong and permanent relationships among people. The social link usually comes first and is always situated both beyond and outside the technology that makes it possible. Thus, the concept of distance between individuals endures, though it is now seen in a different way.

This change in the notion of distance suggests two interrelated concepts: *delocalization* and *multilocalization* of the individual.

1.2 Delocalization

In a socio-economic context in which travel is frequent and people take portable, mobile new technologies with them, more and more places become potential locations for communications. Space begins to move, and the "where" loses the immobility of a specific location to become a sort of aura that accompanies the user. A real redefinition of both public and private spaces is underway, based on interpenetration, or even apparent blending, of public and private, professional and intimate spaces. We can now be in a public space such as a bus, restaurant, or street and yet have a very personal conversation on a mobile phone. In turn, we can also find ourselves in private times and places, such as an evening among friends, or in a bedroom or a bathroom, and be solicited by the public sphere through outside or work-related communications. This "publicization" of the private sphere and "privatization" of the public sphere is not completely new. After all, telephone communications did not wait to become mobile before invading our private space, for example, through telemarketing. However, with new technologies in general and mobile communications technologies in particular, the interweaving of the private and public is increasingly affecting everywhere we live to the point of creating new tension within the spheres as their outlines become more and more blurred.[1]

In such "moving spaces," we are caught unprepared, and while we may know *whom* we want to contact, we no longer know *where* we are contacting them. Since we are less able to tell in advance where our interlocutor is located, the new stock beginning for telephone calls has become "Where are you?" The answer to the question requires mutual adjustment in the conversation because the two interlocutors are aware that the context will influence the interaction. A mobile phone conversation with a lover in a public location such as a bus will probably not be the same as it would have been if the call had been taken alone in an office. When we call someone on a mobile phone, we often hear expressions like "I'm in a meeting," "I'll call you back," or "I'll tell you later," which are intended to inform us of the situation that the call has interrupted.

The delocalization of wireless communications tools such as the mobile phone enables a teenage boy to be in direct contact from home with his friends or girlfriend without any member of his family acting as an intermediary or filter. He thus has the impression that he is escaping supervision of his communications; he feels more free and independent. The difference is obvious between this personal tool and the land-based telephone that used to be located in a shared room in the house and was often controlled by parents.

Pagers and mobile phones can also, on the other hand, become means of parental supervision that make it possible to locate the child.[2] Indeed, one of the major changes resulting from the mobile phone is that it modifies interactions in the social network and makes possible new forms of mutual coordination. People can end up living a kind of "live theatre" in which the mobile phone acts as a mirror. It is supposed to represent "who is where, when, doing what." This scenario changes the way we structure day-to-day life. Social control and coordinated engagement in joint activities now take place in the "here and now."

However, this change has unexpected consequences. How many parents of teenagers feel frustrated when, to the question "Where are you going tonight?" their child answers, "We don't know. We'll see when we meet together"? While in the past a rendezvous was set and the evening planned in advance, today it is increasingly common among young people for plans to change from minute to minute, depending on what is decided when friends are together and what people feel like doing at the moment.

One of the changes resulting from new technologies is that a meeting place no longer automatically refers to a physical space. In a way, technological mediation becomes the meeting point for individuals communicating with one another.

1.3 Multilocalization

The phenomenon of delocalization discussed above is related to the complementary concept of multilocalization of the individual. By overcoming physical distances thanks to technology that enables delocalized communication, individuals can be in several physical locations at the same time. One of the consequences of this is that an individual can play several different social roles at once in everyday life.

We are getting used to seeing our environment as peopled by ubiquitists. People who use their mobile phones while driving often frustrate other people on the road (and on the sidewalk!). Since they are, in a way, in two places at once (*on* the road and delocalized *in* a conversation with another person), such drivers are perceived as dangerous if they get too absorbed in their conversations.

To be at several places at the same time, virtually at least, we have to manage more information. We pass constantly from one "world" to another, one role to another, and even one identity to another. For example, when we are doing the grocery shopping for the family while speaking to a colleague at the office on a mobile phone, we flip between the private and public spheres and immerse ourselves simultaneously in family and professional roles. It becomes more and more complex to simultaneously manage information pertaining to the two spaces, which are becoming less and less distinct, as are real and virtual interpersonal relations.

Those who are with someone who is speaking on a mobile phone are faced with the fact that the latter sometimes leaves the face-to-face relationship momentarily to focus on another place that is inaccessible to those who are physically present. There is a disconnection from the environment shared by the interlocutors, which breaks the time that they are together. It has been noted that the user's egotistical phase is usually transitional, but since the number of people with mobile phones is growing, this may be a Sisyphean situation (Jaurégurberry, 1998). Despite the importance of communications in their lives, some adolescents admit quite freely that they feel uncomfortable when a friend interrupts a conversation to answer a mobile phone.[3]

A person ignoring the presence of others in a public space because his or her attention is elsewhere thanks to technological mediation can certainly make others nearby feel discontented. Even when people in a public space do not know one another, tacit agreements are established between them to mark a degree of mutual recognition of each other's existence (Goffman 1959). Being next to someone wrapped up in a communicational elsewhere and ignoring our physical presence therefore naturally leads to irritation caused by the loss of the social respect that we expect.

Adjusting to these changes in physical and communicational spaces thus becomes a challenge. Places that were not originally designed for communication become new communicational spaces. Sidewalks, cars, and public transit are being used for new purposes. These places, traditionally reserved for travel, are targeted for new communicational possibilities.

1.4 From Identity to Identification

More than ever today, the question of "where" expands to cover the question of "who"; the logic of localized identity is being juxtaposed with a new logic of delocalized identification. The question of identity cannot be dissociated from the question of location, which is not limited to geography. Since identity is both location and self-representation in the world (Baudry 1999), it is anchored in culture and politics. To a certain extent, by constantly producing random contact with strangers, new technologies eliminate certainties but do not replace them with another reference system. Thus what is specific to virtual communities is not the reality of an identity but an avatar of a self-generating identification (ibid.). Regular use of communications tools that allow individuals to "float" to some degree, to have new mobility in both their travels and communications, supposes the end of set references of identity. Moreover, as identity becomes less certain and as the social, immersed in networks like capital, becomes more fluid, the number of identification mechanisms expands. Access codes, PINS, pseudonyms, passwords – we now spend our time identifying ourselves. However, we have to admit that as means of identification multiply, our identity becomes less determined, or at least we have to deal with a degree of indetermination in this respect.

Thus we become nomads again, but in new ways structured around mobile technologies and resulting in protean identities. Paradoxically, the emergent nomadism is combined with sedentariness that is not in contradiction with and is even exacerbated by NICTs, which initially lead to the cocooning that is so much a part of today (Attali 1994). From home we can access a wide range of services by telephone, television, and computer. With the latter, we can now stay home but receive and send emails, read the newspapers of many countries, watch videos, legally or illegally download our favourite music, take virtual tours of museums and exotic lands, and chat in real time. However, is our transformation into this kind of individual, the archetype of a withdrawn recluse, possible other than metaphorically?

We are thus dealing with dual ubiquity: communications objects are now almost everywhere, in the smallest corners of our daily environment, and, thanks to them, we can be almost everywhere at once, in different places and even in different "times."

1.5 The Chronic Symptoms of Our Time

"Real time" generally designates the "time without space" and instantaneity made possible by the use of NICTs. Indeed, connection speeds are tending to eliminate the time lags that traditionally resulted from distances. There are thus fewer and fewer distances to cover and more and more connections to establish. This feature is obvious to anyone who uses the Internet regularly and makes it possible to create communicational relationships that are based on instantaneity (Bonneville 2001). NICTs thus offer *despatialized* time. The only space that remains is that of the screen. Connections via interfaces make it possible to do precisely what distances naturally prevent: to speak with one another, see one another, and exchange (symbolic) goods, both from a distance and simultaneously.

1.6 Wasting Time to Save Time

Users adopt NICTs from personal computers to the Internet and mobile phones because they hope to save time. We no longer understand delays as transition periods from one state to another. In the case of an electronic transaction, everything is done in real time, without travel: the search for the site, the choice of a good or service, and the purchase itself are compressed into a sole and unique moment. All that may remain, in some cases, is a waiting period equivalent to the delivery time of the good or service.

This is to say that everything is integrated into a single "present moment" that excludes any reference to the past or future. What is highly meaningful is that time is seen in relation to the present instant, in its ability to ensure that a result will be achieved without delay (Bonneville 2001).

However, is the time saved real or illusory? On the one hand, it remains real in that the transmission speed and instantaneous nature of NICTs can indeed allow one to save significant time when performing some kinds of work – for example, when correcting texts and corresponding with clients who are physically far away. On the other hand, NICTs also make us waste precious time by exposing us to growing flows of information that have to be processed, filtered, analysed, and managed. This includes not only correspondence that is really important but joke emails, hoaxes, spam, and other junk mail. The ideology surrounding new technologies associates them with capitalization of postmodernity's most valuable good: time. They guarantee that we will save it and that our actions will be more profitable because we will have to spend less time on them. This idea, the latest embodiment of more-or-less tempered capitalism, is a little suspect. How much time do we spend every day filtering, reading, and answering our email? Is this time wasted or saved?

We are thus living in a world where the new technologies that save time paradoxically give us the impression that they are always taking up our time. Indeed, is it not strange that our anxiety over lack of time seems to grow in proportion to the creation and adoption of new machines for saving it? According to some, speed has even become the cardinal virtue of time, and rest has been lumped with sloth (Fischer 2001, 79). Does this myth of efficiency lead us to sacrifice time for thought on the altar of communication speed?

1.7 Technologies in the Rear-View Mirror

New forms of exchange are also affected in another way. As email use becomes massive, we now give greater importance to traditional letters addressed personally and sent by mail. This phenomenon is neither unique nor new. When a new technology has replaced another and established a new standard for performing a given activity, the previous technology can acquire a new value. As black-and-white photos have been replaced by colour photos in everyday use as souvenirs and in family albums, they have acquired new artistic prestige, as have traditional postcards in relation to virtual cards. As electronic signature becomes more routine, handwritten notes gain added value, as do calligraphic invitations in comparison with electronic ones. What is involved in the granting of new esteem to old means of communication?

In contrast with the ideology of saving time that surrounds new technologies, a handwritten letter intimates the opposite: it both hides and highlights the time spent by its author. The format, paper, and envelope have to be chosen. Time is taken to write, buy stamps, and go to the mailbox. When the letter arrives, it expresses time invested in us, and therefore esteem. This is the ideological background of time as the supreme capital, an ideology incarnated specifically by new technologies, giving new meaning to old ones. Old technologies (apparently) express an approach that is opposite to that of NICTs. They confirm the time–value equation and can thereby express the generosity of a person who is ready to take time for us and spend time on us.

The enhanced values of old technologies bring about other new dimensions. In relation to the depersonalization of technologically mediated communication, old ways of doing things gain value. Now that websites offer an astonishing range of virtual cards for all occasions, stationery stores are becoming more sophisticated. The phenomenon of rarity and the personal and authentic aspects that are rightly or wrongly ascribed to traditional technologies explain in part the new configurations of our tastes and habits in communications.

As electronic writing becomes standard, handwriting becomes the physical sign of individuality and authenticity. It acquires a new aura in the terms of Walter Benjamin (2000 [1935]) who, in his writings on art, noted that every copy was from the point of view of authenticity necessarily a degradation of the original, a pale copy. Yet the aura and authenticity specific to the original occurs only later, as a product of the very possibility of reproducing the work. For there to be an authentic work, there must be a non-authentic object to which the work can be compared in order to acquire originality. Thus reproducibility itself creates the original (Hennion and Latour 1996) and allows it to be called unique.

Handwritten letters gain their aura and specialness in the same manner: in their newly acquired difference with typed and, more recently, email letters. While less efficient and functional than email, which has gradually become the standard for correspondence, handwritten letters have acquired a symmetrical symbolic worth: they are seen as more authentic. No one writes like anyone else, and handwriting is thus a sign of Self.

We now live in a world where a growing number of identities are possible, and the ability to send the same email to many different people and the possibility of writing as if one were someone else are a new reality. In reaction to this depersonalization of electronic writing and standardization of virtual cards, handwriting and hand signature re-establish the appearance of the author's authentic identity, the unity of the message, and the uniqueness of the person to whom it is sent.

The gain in value can be applied to a wide range of traditional technologies gradually being disqualified by new technologies in everyday uses. For example, some young people today search for old turntables to reinvent new ways to play music, valuing the scratching of LPs.

Users of new technologies may also use them in somewhat unorthodox manners, for example, in ways that could be considered to the detriment of the economic interests of the technology's designers. This is the case of mobile phone Short Message Services (SMS), which, for economic or strategic reasons, young people sometimes use to communicate with one another instead of talking on the phone. Indeed, SMS belongs to a form of communication that could be considered old-fashioned because it involves very basic written and coded messages.[4]

1.8 Synchrony, Asynchrony, Polychrony

The instantaneity effect present in new communication technology must be seen in relation to other elements. The immediacy of the contacts and exchanges the technology makes possible can also be associated with new synchrony and asynchrony, in particular with respect to the Internet. Indeed, the Internet's asynchrony can be even better than real time. It gives others the time to organize and process available information, and the possibility of taking one's time in turn (Hafner and Lyon 1999). This is the case with forms such as email, newsgroups, databanks, and SMS.

In contrast, communication mechanisms that make it possible to discuss online – in other words, to have a conversation in real time without any lapse in the exchange (for example, chat rooms, networked games, webcam-to-webcam communications, and instant messaging) – instead provide the medium with an immediate, synchronous temporal dimension that also seems to be attractive to young people.

Of course the instantaneous nature of communications is not new (we need think only of the telephone or even the telegraph), but with NICTs it is available in an increasingly broad range of activities and combined with other new aspects such as portability. While much attention is paid to the instantaneity of NICTs, that is, the establishment of real time, a present with neither past nor future, we should not overlook the asynchronous features of the medium, which may be less celebrated but are undoubtedly used more often.

New technologies, in particular personal computers and the Internet, allow and to a certain extent force us to operate in multiple times simultaneously. This could be called polychronicity, and it is how we should understand the novelty of multi-tasking environments, where one can perform several tasks both in succession and simultaneously (that is, several activities performed simultaneously in "real time" follow several others that are also performed at the same time, and so on). Such simultaneous polyvalence is very frequent among young Internet users, though often they do not themselves perceive the novelty or originality of the activity. Indeed, it is not unusual for a young person to visit several websites at the same time by opening a number of different windows, while also downloading a piece of music, chatting with friends, and watching television.

As time becomes a notion that is more than variable, in which changes, economic events, transactions, and the circulation of information accelerate, it is not certain whether people and organizations can handle the speed. Clearly many have difficulty dealing with it. Since the world of media is saturated with information, there seem to be no limits to its production and publication; however, there may well be a limit to reception.

1.9 The Death of Silence?

Silence is a notion spontaneously associated with emptiness and nothing-ness. It is thus often defined as a simple absence of noise. However, the generic meaning of the word can be extended to other areas such as the arts, in which silence can be seen as a form of expression. Thus, what is left unsaid in poetry and silences in monologues at the theatre may be empty of sound but not of meaning. Roman mythology provides us with various illustrations of seeing silence as meaningful non-action linked to speech. Lara, also known as Muta or Tacita, is generally acknowledged as the Roman goddess of silence. Since her tongue was cut out for having talked too much, she is also considered the goddess of gossip. The goddess Angerona, the guardian of Rome's secret name, is represented with a finger on her lips and her mouth banded. She has been silenced, but she also demands silence. In both cases the way that silence is personified indicates that silence is sometimes preferable to speech.

Linguists study the role of silence as a powerful tool in human communication. By not opposing silence and speech but instead seeing them as complementary, we can view silence as an eloquent means of communication. For example, answering a question with silence can be very meaningful. However, it may also be ambiguous, because it can be interpreted in different ways. The context surrounding silence thus has to be taken into consideration. Just as every culture has its own rules to govern speech, these apply as well to silence.

As a notion, silence can thus be *heard* in a complex, multifaceted manner, and not only as an absence of sound. When we stop to listen to what people feel about new technologies in their lives, we find evidence of negotiations between points when they engage in communication and other times. The evocative expression "the death of silence" seems apt to describe the feelings of many people.

1.10 Seeking Noise

Today's adolescents often see silence as a difficulty to be overcome. Having grown up with the Internet and mobile phones, that is how they have constructed their relationships to communications. This is probably why as a group they are generally the most enthusiastic about the many possibilities for communication that are offered by new technologies. Judy and Jennifer, met during our fieldwork, aged seventeen and fifteen respectively, concur:

JUDY: New technologies make communication between people easier. Everyone can express themselves easily.

JENNIFER: The "death of silence" means that everyone needs to communicate with someone at some time or another, and that today, with new technologies, it's become simple and easy.

NICTs are seen as ways of breaking the silence that is often related to the solitude and isolation that adolescents fear. Thus for them the "death of silence" is linked positively with belonging to a broad network of acquaintances. Judy makes this relationship clear: "Before, everyone stayed in their corner and had no way of communicating to unwind, express themselves ... now, if you need to talk, you can talk to a friend by phone or send an email. In short, people are less isolated."

While, as we will see later, young adults often seem to associate silence with peace and quiet, many adolescents see it as synonymous with boredom and downtime. The preference for noise over silence reflects the tendency of adolescents to get carried away by a kind of communicational euphoria that sometimes turns into "technological fetishism" (Fischer 2001, 101). Silence has to be covered by communicating, and by engaging in leisure activities like online games that technologies make possible. Many adolescents admit they use communications technologies in this way: whether they are chatting on the Internet or on a mobile phone, the primary and acknowledged purpose is to pass time. Short and to the point, Chantal's words express this idea: "When I've got nothing to do, I call my best friend and then we find something to talk about." For teenagers, communicating has very positive connotations and is for them a central value in society. As Jennifer says, "Society is always communicating, and that's going to continue for a long time."

Adolescence is a period characterized by the desire and need to socialize with peers. Thus is it easy to understand how a concept like the death of silence could be seen as an ideal situation, up to a certain point. For example, if every telephone call is considered a sign of belonging to a social network, a life without silence can be seen as a symbol of social prestige. Indeed, our field research showed an urgency to communicate among many adolescent NICT users.[5] They often differed from their parents in that they believed that it is essential to be able to contact others and be contacted at all times and everywhere. Being constantly available to other members of one's community is seen as one of the crucial values of adolescent culture. However, this can result in a relative constraint when the immediate communication that mobile phones make possible turns into a kind of obsession to always be in contact with everyone and stay up to date about everything. While there may never be any real emergency, there is always the impression of an urgent need for contact.

Adolescents thus already seem confronted with the fact that ease of communication can become counter-productive. Faced with a multitude of tools offering ever more convenient and cheaper means of communication, users of new technologies have to deal with problems in the organization of their social contacts. Adolescents feel the need to manage their contacts in order to avoid invasion. Some expressed difficulty in organizing lists of electronic contacts. They had to decide who deserved to be on the list and how they should be ordered, and then how priorities should be assigned and exchanges managed. This is well described in the following discussion between Robert and Jessica.

ROBERT: But before, I used to just go on the Internet and all that, I used to chat, I let anyone who wanted join, but then I didn't know anyone there anymore. There were so many people that I deleted everything.
JESSICA: That's the problem. It's too difficult to know and judge, there are too many people. You have to cut the number down.
INTERVIEWER: Is that in a chat room or on MSN?
JESSICA: MSN.

Silences in instant electronic exchanges have meanings that have to be defined. For example, would a silence caused by giving priority to a telephone call while conversing by instant messaging be perceived negatively by your on-line partner? Is it polite to conduct several conversations simultaneously and therefore produce delays in one's response time? The newness of some technologies results in uses in which the rules and codes are not yet well defined.[6] Nonetheless, the increase in communications possibilities contributes to defining silence as a choice, as a deliberate action of non-exchange (and in this sense it is indeed a form of communication). Jenny, aged 15, was clear on this: "Means of communication make it that people no longer have an excuse for not talking to one another. Mobile phones, pagers, and email are now more or less portable, which makes it possible to communicate at all times."

Priscilla, a teenager who felt obligated to answer when people were trying to contact her, explained that a person who chooses or even involuntarily creates silence has to accept the responsibility of refusing to accept the other's communication: "Say your friend calls you and it's turned off, you know, it's like, it's hard to find an excuse, to say it was turned off and I didn't feel like talking. With the displays now, you know it's your friend and that you don't feel like talking."

1.11 Seeking Silence

Among young adults who have lived through the emergence and proliferation of NICTs but who have also therefore experienced relative silence in the past, talk of the disappearance of silence provokes more complex reactions. Yet their perceptions are often coloured by a degree of technological determinism or even defeatism about the user's power to resist the invasion of technology. The concept of noise (seen as the primary enemy of silence) is often used to describe everyday situations disturbed by an incessant flow of communications. Silence is seen as a rare commodity in a social space invaded by noise. As Matthew said:

When people talk about the death of silence caused by new technologies, we can think first about the freedom of expression that they have made possible ... It's true that the Internet democratizes writing by giving a voice and ears to anyone who wants ... Silence as the "attitude of a person who cannot express himself" is finally a thing of the past. But silence is also the "absence of noise and agitation." From this point of view, new technologies inspire less optimism. Their extreme availability and invasion of privacy tend to saturate our lives, which is contrary to notions of calm and peace.

Like many adolescents, a number of young adults believe the extinction of silence results from the possibility of being contacted at all times. New technologies link individuals who then find themselves in a permanent state of availability to communicate. Young adults acknowledge that the portability and mobility of communications tools make possible greater flexibility and freedom of movement. However, a redefinition, in the sense of a reduction, of what are considered reasonable response times goes hand in hand with constant availability, and the traditional conception of time is thus changed. Silences, threatened with extinction, acquire new meanings.

Before examining these meanings, we have to note that imagination finds raw material in many different things, and thus that perceptions of silence and communication are not the products of solitary attitudes. On the contrary, they are fed by the various different discourses in social space. One of the largest contributors to the collective and individual imagination is advertising discourse.[7]

A goal of the advertising discourse surrounding mobile phones, for example, is to show how to fill as many silences as possible by using a wide variety of technological means to facilitate exchanges. Implicitly painted as hostile to communication and social links, silence can thus become a real source of worry. Shana described her discomfort with the enforced silence resulting from a day without her mobile phone:[8] "I had the impression that I was missing important phone calls, and I was angry with myself for forgetting something that I never go anywhere without."

Some said that if an individual is silent, he or she is considered reclusive and withdrawn. According to Sarah, "Since silences can be technically eliminated, a person's silence is considered intentional behaviour."

Many young adults worry that the increase in connectivity among individuals could have unfortunate consequences. There is a palpable fear of dependency on communication. Doing one's grocery shopping while talking on the phone, or turning on the email software every time one starts up the computer, gives the impression that other people's presence is necessary at all times. Sylvia finds that people seem caught in an "inability to stand a moment of rest, a moment of reflection, a meaningful moment, a moment for oneself ... a silence." Since silence is often associated with collecting one's thoughts and introspection, young adults wonder whether the growth of means of communication will inevitably lead to the elimination of time for oneself. Since new means of communication are already operational, will it become more and more difficult to take full advantage of the empty spaces that used to be normal parts of communication?

1.12 Communication: Between Noise and Silence

In addition to the tendency to fill downtime with flows of exchange, many young adults also note the use of mass media as a background for routine activities. The fact that people watch television or listen to the radio while doing other things gives the impression that silence is difficult to tolerate. A number of interviewees suggested that people use media to fill in silences in their daily lives because they fear being alone. Media comfort them like a human presence. Reflecting on her media consumption in a typical week, Maria became aware of the role played by media and new technologies in her daily life:[9] "It seemed to me that a kind of unconscious routine has been established in my media consumption. Some repeated actions seemed to have become automatic, particularly with respect to the television and computer. The first thing I do every day is turn on the computer and the television."

Moreover, the constant communication flow is often associated with disorder, as Matthew noted: "The Internet is a huge field of free expression. But you have to admit that the space for free discussion has also created an incredible cacophony."

The new technologies can produce the impression of a social universe saturated with information. It can thus be disturbing to feel the pressure of always having to be informed as quickly as possible. Individuals are sometimes compared to passive spectators in social spaces where they are constantly exposed to stimulation from all sides. Overwhelmed by the situation, many seem to have no choice but to take refuge in silence. According to Julia, for example: "Having a say in things becomes difficult for modern citizens faced with the speed and exceptional quantity of information. They are often reduced to silence and anonymity."

Silence can imply passivity, when we think of the attitude of a silent individual. Breaking down the wall of silence is thus linked with freedom of expression. According to Kevin, "The death of silence also lies in the fact that with the Internet, everyone, no matter what their status, opinions, political party, reputation or geographical location, has the possibility of expressing themselves on the Internet as a single individual, group or minority, and of being potentially read or heard by millions of people in the world." From this point of view, media allow people to get information easily and quickly about issues and problems that concern and interest them. Silence as an answer to a request or question is no longer acceptable, because technology has greatly facilitated access to resources. Thus, young adults think that technological developments can encourage a profusion of points of view. This line of thinking often leads to seeing the Internet as a powerful democratic space.

For some, like Roberto, new technologies finally make it possible to break free of silence and even to promote, in a way, the very essence of humanity, which they see as communicational: "They say 'silence is golden,' but it seems things are the other way around today. We are living in a society that is so complex that being resigned or staying silent in a corner cannot really provide peace and comfort and even less gold. Communicating is living. Instead of committing suicide, people have decided to kill silence ... People have become supporters of speech, or rather of communication, and that tends to condemn silence to extinction."

Traditional technologies such as radio and television have been observed as helping the elderly to deal with solitude and isolation; perhaps an analogous phenomenon is now being seen among adolescents with the Internet (email, chatrooms, instant messaging), mobile phones, and other multifunctional devices. Naturally, when adolescents communicate using new technologies in interactive ways, they communicate with people, communicating beings who interact with them at the other end of the keyboard or mobile phone. However, it is sometimes the same fear of solitude, isolation, and boredom that leads them to fill silence up in this way and that makes them feel uneasy when silences nonetheless occur. In this sense, escaping silence by chatting on the Internet is perhaps not so different from avoiding isolation with television.

In any case, there is a striking intergenerational difference with respect to the notion of the death of silence. The perceptions and representations are more or less opposite. On one hand, hyperconnected adolescents seem not to suffer from the apparent loss of time for oneself and even perceive silences as holes that need to be filled. For them, communications technologies are means of killing solitude and boredom. On the other hand, those who are a few years older seem to see silence in communication either as an admission that one is powerless to make oneself heard or as a valuable commodity that should be cultivated because of its rarity. For this latter group, NICTs allow silence to be broken in some cases, but they may also replace it with noise and chaos, preventing reflection.

We have to wonder whether adolescents' urgent need to communicate and their tendency to flee silences will follow them into the workplace. We will leave the last word to Gary, a graduate student soon to be employed:

From morning to night, people hear their alarm clocks, the television, the radio, the telephone ringing, the mobile phone ringing, the roar of thousands of cars, elevator music (or music from the next person's Walkman), the "ding" of the microwave, the "beep" of the computer (desktop or laptop). What does this mean? The individual is not exposed to silence at any point in the day. I don't mean the false silence of the city dweller, which is only apparent and never free of the hum of the city, but real silence ... the silence that creates anxiety because it is unfamiliar, and that plunges one into isolation. The silence that provides no escape and forces one to examine one's conscience ... As it pulls one ever deeper into introspection and begins to raise primordial questions of existence, a distant sound is heard. It's the pager, that joyful friend, who reminds us that, happily, we are not alone in the world. After the friendly "beep beep," everything goes back to normal. Silence is dead again.

1.13 Social Actors: Locations and Links

Merging spaces, fluctuating time, and extinction of silence: new technologies are inviting us to embrace strange scenarios. However, we should not conclude from this that, caught in an incessant techno-media whirlpool, the social actors in the new scenarios do not know which way to turn. On the contrary, as we will see in the following chapters, people are constantly inventing new answers, both with respect to their relationships with others and their relationships to technology itself. Thus, at the very heart of everyday life, individuals, particularly younger people, are not only the subjects but also and above all the co-creators of both technological challenges and related social stakes.

In the next chapter we will try to formulate a more theoretical approach to these empirical observations. A few conceptual foundations will be useful for understanding the process of scenario co-creation that links technological objects with individuals and that, reciprocally, forms the raw material of everyday life. By looking at how communications practices are constructed today, and the way we construct ourselves through them, we will try to show the importance and immanence of technologies as veritable seats of social meaning. They are places, and relationships, peopled by many social actors, both human – all too human – and non-human.

Chapter 2

Speaking Objects, Acting Words:
New Communication Practices

2.1 Technologies and Everyday Construction of Culture

Technologies are both products and producers of culture. Human made, they construct humans' daily environment. Historical products of a given society, they in turn transform society and its history. Grasping this circularity and accounting for it are essential, because the mutual construction among technologies, culture, and society is precisely where the game unfolds.

According to a phenomenological theoretical approach to culture and everyday life, people are constantly engaged in constructing the meaningful dimensions of the world they live in. Through their situated and object-mediated actions, through their ways of speaking about and referring to those actions, contexts, objects, and characters that inhabit their social world, individuals constitute the cultural forms of living their social lives.[1]

According to this approach, everyday life is conceived as a never-ending cultural work through which individuals constantly produce the meanings, structures, and social organization of the world they live in, as well as their social identities and those of the people they interact with or talk about.

The social world where this work of everyday culture construction is performed is not constituted solely by people who interact reciprocally. As renewed attention to the material aspect of social life indicates (De Certau 1980, Appadurai 1986, Latour 1992, Gras, Jorges, and Scardigli 1992, Semprini 1995, 1999), the *artifactual* dimension of daily life is a crucial component that affects and is affected by interactions, social organizations, and cultural frames of reference. Things, whether technological or not, are more than an inert background for people's everyday lives. Insofar as people establish meaningful interactions with objects and artifacts, they make them exist in their social world, making sense of and involving them in a mutual co-construction process (Livingstone 1992, Semprini 1995, Caron and Caronia 2001, Lally 2002).

Literature on the social uses of media and cultural ways of coping with a technological environment has shown how these uses, like other social practices, may be considered *semiotic actions* in the strict sense of the term – that is, actions in which performance is both a way of communicating and a tool for constructing meanings and social realities.

The available technologies, the material features of the objects that support them, and the daily routines they create or are integrated in are all tools for the everyday production of culture and identities. Through media-related practices, individuals construct themselves in specific ways and produce the forms of their social participation (Caronia 2002). Simply put, through our uses of media, through the way we act out these uses, we define (at least locally) our belongings and our identities.

We define, but we are also defined. Insofar as face-to-face interaction and talk may still be considered the basic forms of socialization (Boden and Molotch 1994), the ways in which media uses become candidate topics of everyday conversation are powerful tools to construct their meanings and the identities of those who use them. People's ways of using media, real or imagined, enter into everyday conversations as parts of the narratives through which people constantly construct who they are and who are the people they talk about (Ochs and Capps 1996).

The progressive, never-ending introduction of new technologies into people's everyday lives, the multiplication of available new courses of action and ways of communicating and getting information, hypothetically expand the range of the tools through which people construct everyday culture and identities.

How do objects produce meaning? By which modes do communication technologies, both new and old, perform this human job of producing culture? Our hypotheses can be summarized as follows: Communication technologies contribute to the construction of culture and society in two ways. First, they make *us* communicate. This may appear obvious, but communication is invariably the primary practice of any cultural construction. Second, they create culture because they are *texts* that talk and make sense of what they talk about. As Wittgenstein notes, speaking entails creating forms of life and therefore culture. We may rightly ask how these technologies speak and what do they say.

Technologies speak through their material components, design, and engineering and enounce specific cultural models of things, people, and contexts.

By moving the image from the permanence of the analogical universe to the ephemeral digital world, the digital camera demands and proposes a radical, non-realistic ontology for photography. Even the social perception of the photographer's work and identity has changed. The digital camera has definitively legitimated photography as a manipulation of reality through iconic representation. Whereas the non-referential nature of documentary images has always been a taken-for-granted assumption among epistemologists and philosophers, the digital camera has integrated this nature into the layman's culture. In allowing people to make, re-make, and un-make iconic representations of reality, the digital camera has produced a new everyday culture of photography.

The shapes, aesthetic properties, and uses inscribed in the engineering of technologies allow them to function as *objectual narratives*, their main character being the intended user, their location, the contexts of everyday life. Beyond the story told through their design, technologies contribute to the meaning-creation process when they enter a social scene. Working as active actors, they make sense of the scene. Indeed, a family, company, or group of adolescents builds their lifestyle around the techno-material tools in their environment. The available objects open and close possible courses of action, suggest possible interpretations of social encounters, and create new identities for individuals. They literally create the contexts of social life.

A lunch between friends where each person has placed a mobile phone in "on" mode on the table is no longer the same social context as it was before the mobile phone appeared. The objects work as communicative cues, signalling the owners' stances within the ongoing situation. The mobile phones on the table say that the owners are ready to leave the face-to-face conversation to engage in external telephone communication, while remaining in place. The social context is thus redefined by these techno-objects that introduce a new pattern of meaning: *the absent presence* of human subjects (Gergen 2002).

The cultural work of this technology does not end there. The presence of mobile phones on the table calls into question the relevance of the canonical script of the event. As Goffman has asserted (1974), the members of a given community share canonical models of the routine activities of everyday life. Participants in these events refer to these shared models of the situations to define what is going on and to behave accordingly in a mutually coordinated manner. The mobile phones on the table break the relevance of the shared frame of the event and suspend the conventional roles and rules that bind the members: the *stand-by* status of the subject at the table is ratified and becomes an official, albeit local, identity.

When a mobile phone is present "at lunch," the prototypical model of this social event no longer applies: the stand-by status of some participants is now ratified as a way of participating in this social encounter. Suddenly exiting the face-to-face interaction becomes a possible social behaviour, and the code of etiquette needs to be renegotiated.

The sociocultural construction task performed by this techno-object is even more multifaceted. It not only introduces new possibilities of behaviour (such as talking on the telephone when seated at a table with other people), but it also engenders new forms of social participation. What happens, in effect, when a group of people seated together at a table must contend with potential interlocutors who can join them at any time and interrupt their dialogue? Given the constant, imminent presence of these *ghost participants*, new characters must be constructed: the interlocutor suddenly thrust into stand-by position must invent the gestures of this new role.

Moreover, new forms of interaction must be devised to enable the actors to manage the imminent presence of ghost participants, to cope with the rupture of the ongoing interaction and to re-establish the face-to-face relationship after the disruption. It is therefore the very repertoire of the established *interaction rituals* (Goffman 1967) that must be reinvented. Even in a ritual as common as being at the table, the presence of a technological object creates new cultural models for the context and the participants' behaviour.

The appearance of these techno-objects casts new light on the forms of social life. The case of the mobile telephone as a friendly partner in a gathering around a table is just one of many examples of the role of these non-human actors. As soon as they surface in a given social context, they impart forms of unforeseen significance and create conditions for novel behaviours.

Their influence extends far beyond these types of social situations. Technologies act in many other domains of our social and daily life and can alter the current definitions of those situations dramatically.

Since the generalization of the mobile telephone and hands-free models, seeing a person apparently talking to himself in the street is no longer interpreted as unequivocally as before. Until recently, talking to oneself in the street was a well-established sign of mental illness. Today this behaviour no longer lends itself to as simplistic and automatic an interpretation.

The emergence of the mobile telephone has created a broader interpretive repertoire for such a categorization device; attributing an identity to a man talking to himself in the street is no longer as mechanistic a process.

By creating new behaviours or new meanings for pre-existing behaviours, new communication technologies dispel the automatism of ordinary understandings of social life. Like Garfinkel's breaching experiments, they disclose the operating but unnoticed cultural rules that govern everyday understanding of social life (Garfinkel 1967).

2.2 Technologies as Statements: The Performative Force of Social Objects

The production of new courses of action (speaking on the phone at dinnertime), the creation of new actors (the ghost participant, the stand-by interlocutor) and the construction of new interpretive repertoires for human behaviour all illuminate the process of cultural construction performed by techno-objects. Nonetheless, this process goes much further. Places and times are also components of daily life that are subject to the influence of techno-objects, which they tend to endow with new meanings.[2]

One example of this making-sense process is the *migration of technological objects* (Caron and Caronia 2001). During their life cycle technologies often change locations. Such migrations create new significance for the various places involved. When the old television is moved from the living room to the children's bedroom, the bedroom is no longer a space reserved for sleep and related activities. It also becomes a place where children enact the rituals of a very specific and private *bedroom culture* (Livingston and Bovill 2001). The presence of a television set transforms the bedroom into a cultural space and, conversely, this space defines the use of this technology as a private activity. Such migrations therefore reformulate the significance of household places and, by changing the definition of what may or may not be shared by family members, they establish new cultural frontiers between daily activities (ibid. 2001).

Social actors are not oblivious to this phenomenon, and do not act as if they were over-determined by the redefinition of places triggered by technological objects in the home. On the contrary, they often resist this meaning-making process, thus entering into conflict with the technologies. In one family encountered during our research, the father insisted that the computer remain in the kitchen rather than migrating to the basement, where his son would use it on his own. The kitchen formulated the *computer-in-the-kitchen* as a collective technology, and inversely, the *computer-*

in-the-kitchen redefined this context as a space of family control, as a place for meeting and sharing the activities of the family members. The decision to prohibit the migration of the computer from the kitchen to the basement thus represented a true form of resistance to the performative force of the technology: the computer would not reinforce the significance of the basement as a private place where one could isolate oneself and withdraw from the control of others, whereas the kitchen, like Jeremy Bentham's panoptikon, would remain a space of invisible but constant control.

By reformulating the use of spaces and their meanings, technologies participate in the transformation of physical places into *lived spaces*. This process did not go unnoticed in this family. The members were involved in a conflict between two possible enunciations of the significance of family space. In response to the discourse of the object, the parents produced a counter-discourse and, to impose their definition, had to neutralize the technological interlocutor.

In our informants' descriptions of their domestic practices, we observed that communication and information technologies reflect not only a pre-existing culture and family organization but also modify this family culture profoundly (Caron and Caronia 2000, 2001). What applies to lived space also applies to time, because techno-objects also enounce the meaning of the moments of daily life. A mother told us, "For my child, the telephone is for after supper. During supper, it's me that answers: 'We are eating right now. Please call back later.'" The telephone is strategically placed right in front of her – the child said, "And even if you get up and you stretch your arm out to try to answer it before she does – Too late!" The mother interrupted, "I am much quicker!" The same is true for television. In this family as in others, the parents impose strict rules: during mealtimes there is no TV, "because it's the only time we can talk together, the four of us."

In fact, making rules implies recognition of the performative power of technologies. The telephone suggests the opening to the outside world as one of the possible meanings of mealtimes. It enounces the possibility of leaving the conversation among the family members to enter another communication that includes an absent party and excludes those present. Similarly, television, if it remains on during the meal, redefines the meal as a time of entertainment or information, or a family's collective reception of a message conveyed by strangers. Regardless, to impose on family moments a different meaning from the one proposed by the techno-objects, the actor must issue a counter-enunciation. The rules are as simple as that.

These conflicting interpretations that redefine the moments of daily life are, like any interaction, ways of culture making. The conflict interaction in which human enunciators confront their non-human counterparts tends to definitively establish what counts as "being a family": the boundaries of the public and private spheres are negotiated, to produce – at least locally – a specific culture and social organization.

Far from *fixing* the significance of time and places of daily life, technologies state possible meanings that can be affirmed or challenged by individuals. As we have seen, people actively re-make the various meanings at stake and negotiate with non-human actors the significance of their behaviour, moments, and living spaces.

In one of our recent studies (Caronia 2005), we observed another phenomenon that clearly confirms the role of techno-objects in creating the forms of everyday life. It concerns the signification that is attributed to *nowhere places* (Augé 1992) and *no-when times*. Nowhere places are crossing places devoid of any social or idiosyncratic significance, places that seem to exist only to be passed through and allow the individual to get to a more significant "where." Symmetrically, "no-when times" are stand-by moments that cannot be defined through reference to any specific activity, times of the day where the actor is simply waiting for someone to come or something to happen. It is fascinating to observe how certain techno-objects can suddenly endow these times or places with meaning.

Assoum,[3] one of our teenaged informants, made and received about 20 per cent of the calls on his mobile phone during *no-when times* and in *nowhere places*: waiting for the bus, walking to get from one place to another, in the street, or in other "anywheres" that he could not define in greater detail, precisely because of their neutral nature. Since Assoum has integrated his mobile phone into his daily life, these *non-times* and *non-places* have gained a function: he uses them to make phone calls and fills them with technological practices intended to maintain social contacts. In fact, most of the mobile conversations that occurred in these contexts were not informative at all. Through them Assoum confirmed his belonging to a community of peers and confirmed that others are also there.

During his bus-ride home, Assoum calls his friend Marc:

ASSOUM: Yeah.
MARC: Yeah.
ASSOUM: Uhh, eight, six, five.
MARC: Eight, six, five.
ASSOUM: Six, eight.

MARC: Six, eight.
ASSOUM: Five, five.
MARC: Five, five.
ASSOUM: Okay?
MARC: Yeah.
ASSOUM: Well, call me back this evening.
MARC: Okay. What time sh'd I call you?
ASSOUM: Anytime, man.
MARC: Anytime?
ASSOUM: Yeah, me, I'll be outside with my friends and –
MARC: Okay, yeah.
ASSOUM: Okay.
MARC: 'll call you, yeah.
ASSOUM: Okay, ciao.
MARC: Bye.

The mobile phone has given sense to these meaningless times and places, transforming them into social situations dedicated to the construction and the empowerment of interpersonal relationships. Dedicated to a social activity, they are now identified moments and meaningful situations: times and places where teenagers tell each other that they are there, where they confirm the validity of their friendship contract which assumes that members have to be in "perpetual contact" (Katz and Aakhus 2002) and that they are allowed to seek each other out.

Let us reflect upon another scene observed during our ethnographic studies. Some students are outside their school waiting for their classes to begin. Some are talking with each other according to the social rules of informal groups, but others are alone, excluded from any of the ongoing conversations, not part of any of the groups around them. They do not speak to anybody else but they are using their mobile phones. Armed with video games, with constantly changeable configurations, and, importantly, with the opportunity to communicate via SMS, this technology allows them to give sense to this "waiting time" and redefines their identity. They no longer feel or are perceived as someone alone, as an outsider with respect to the other groups around them. Nor are they wasting their time, just waiting for their classes to begin: they are *doing* something. Opening up a course of action in this social scene, the mobile phone has accomplished *face work* (Goffman 1967), providing a new identity for the users and a new meaning for this – otherwise socially embarrassing – moment of their day life.

As this scene demonstrates, the sense-making work accomplished by technologies, their role in constructing meanings and social realities, in building people's identities, seems to be a widespread process that affects the details of our everyday life.

2.3 Technologies That Make Us Do

The objection here is self-evident: is it not the human subject that endows things with their competencies? Does not the individual construct technologies as actors able to construct forms of life? Do not individuals situate them in "nowhere places" and use them in "no-when times," making them work as meaning-creating tools?

The answer can only be yes. Upstream of the social life of things (Appadurai 1986), there is the human. Humans generate technologies, grant them a life, a language, and a performative power. As we know, ideation, conception, and design are nothing more than the inscription of culture in an object.

However, once we have conceived them and allotted them cognitive and pragmatic competencies, things acquire de facto (relative) autonomy from human beings. Generated by the meaning that we choose to give them, they in turn generate meaning. Created by culture, they create culture and social reality.

Latour's example of the shepherd, the sheep, and the fence clearly illustrates this point (Latour 2002). Obviously, the shepherd conceives of or at least installs the fence that prevents the sheep from escaping. He gives concrete form to this intention, the fence he builds. Yet once the function is delegated to the fence object, once this result is achieved, the fence takes on a life of its own. It becomes a specific actor that is now part of the social world of both the sheep and the shepherd. It is neither an instrument nor a prosthesis but an actor that produces a reality (the enclosed terrain) that did not previously exist for the shepherd or the sheep. The fence has transformed the context, opening a field of possible actions and setting limits of another order: the shepherd can sleep, the sheep can no longer escape.

This example raises another issue. As we saw, technologies are actors that "do" by stating discourse and building contexts. But they are also actors that "make us do." Studies of the telephone have shown that almost throughout Europe and America, a ringing telephone triggers an obligation to answer. As Schegloff pointed out (1968, 1080–1), the ring of the telephone could be regarded as a summons that is the first part of a two-part sequence. The action of answering is the second part. Similar to the questions that we ask, excuses we make, and greetings we utter, or any other first part of a socially organized interaction, the ringing phone obliges us to perform an action in return.

The telephone therefore acts as a real social actor. It plays the basic role of generating an action that is a relevant condition[4] for the occurrence of a specific reply. The basic structure of any social interaction – *the adjacency pair* – is operative here, except that in this case the first move is not performed by a human actor. The telephone plays the role of an outsider, a potential first partner of an imminent interaction that has the privilege of joining people at any time, of interrupting the ongoing course of action by involving the call recipient in a side conversation (Hopper 1991, Schegloff 2002).

Mobile phones have magnified this interactive role of the telephone. Because of its design, the mobile phone is endowed with the technical possibility of being put in "out of service" position, yet this function is less and less exploited as the use of the mobile phone has become generalized. Among young people, for example, the "off" position has been deleted from their cultural model of the mobile phone. From a phenomenological point of view, it simply no longer exists. Answering almost anywhere, anytime, has become vital: adolescents invariably reply to the mobile phone summons, which they consider the first part of a constraining adjacency pair.

It is also to escape the tyranny of the telephone ring that the answering machine was invented, originally for conventional telephones. We now recognize that these devices manipulate people equally well. When people come home in the evening and the answering machine is flashing, once, twice, up to ten times, they know that they *must* listen to the messages and return the calls (as promised in the recorded message). These flashing lights are signals that force us to act. Of course we can choose not do so, but then a vague feeling of guilt will gnaw at us, a clear sensation of having failed in a duty. The excuses – even the lies – that we concoct to justify our missed actions are nothing more than social repair strategies: a response to violation, they certify that we have failed to meet an obligation, to deliver on a promise.

It is precisely the awareness that the techno-object is able to manipulate us that at times prompts individuals to revolt against this performative power of objects. Yet, emancipating ourselves may be almost more difficult than letting ourselves be manipulated: we must thus accept feeling guilty for having deliberately ignored the flurry of messages or having lowered the ring volume. We must offer excuses for turning off a mobile phone or not having read an email. In short, we have to repair a social offence.

As Landowski notes, technologies do not simply organize our ways of experiencing time and space for practical purposes. They also contribute to defining our ways of relating to others (Landowski 2002). Formulating excuses, inventing plausible lies, creating rituals of courtesy that let us leave the person in front of us on "stand-by" to give our telephone interlocutor precedence – the list of forms of social life derived from our manipulation by objects is nearly unlimited.

Like Latour's shepherd's fence, technologies, because of the manipulative competencies we attribute to them, make us *act*. Even if we decide to oppose this form of tyranny, we must *do* something, we must engage in actions that let us *not act* and that legitimize our missed actions. Revolting against the manipulation of technologies or letting them make us act is a choice, and regardless of our reaction, it will have consequences – at least locally – on our life and on that of others.

2.4 The Contemporary "Nutcracker": The Cascade Effect and the Interrelation of Technologies

We have already discussed the mutual constitutive relations between technologies, individuals, and contexts. Yet this co-construction of meaning also occurs among objects. The location of techno-objects in space, their complementary functions, the obsolescence of existing technologies caused by their newer counterparts, the mechanisms inscribed in a technology to prepare it to welcome the next avatars of itself – this chain of reciprocal references produces a specific world animated by the techno-objects themselves.

The semiotics of objects calls this world *interobjectivity* (Landowksi 2002, Maronne 2002), a label that emphasizes the negotiation of meaning that takes place in the world of things. This concept concerns us directly as human actors. The phenomenon of the migration of objects, described above, also educes how things make sense of each other. What happens when a technology encounters other technologies along its migratory path? Consider the arrival of the first mobile telephone in one of the families that participated in our research (Caron and Caronia 2001). Initially purchased as a piece of emergency equipment for the car, it was entering the home more and more often because the telephone line was being used by one of the children who was always connected to the Internet. The encounter of two communication technologies therefore modified the meaning of one of them. As soon as the mobile phone – which had migrated from the car to the home – met the Internet, it no longer simply fulfilled an emergency function but took on a new significance, as a tool to maintain social ties. This case exemplifies minimal interobjectivity: one technology – in this case the Internet – modifies the significance of another – mobile phone – by simple juxtaposition.

Our research brought to light another phenomenon that clearly illustrates the construction of a world of objects by objects themselves, a phenomenon we dub *cascading adoption.*⁵ In several families, the arrival of a technology has created repercussions that the members themselves often describe as "unforeseen": the arrival of the Internet makes the existing computer obsolete and calls for a new one; a single telephone line no longer suffices, and along comes the mobile phone. The mobile telephone in turn often becomes too immediate and invasive, and thus the pager is added to allow asynchronous communication. The burgeoning, unmanageable volume of messages received on the pager has led one of the adolescents encountered in our research to subscribe to a voice-mail service. Our informants repeatedly told us, "We didn't expect this."

Technologies seem to be linked together in a process constructed according to its own logic. Although the process is engendered by humans, it can overwhelm us. Beyond any references to a world out there, the concept of interobjectivity captures our everyday perception of our technological environment: technologies are overtaking and controlling us (Lally 2002).

Like words in a sentence, technologies are inherently redundant: each makes it possible to foresee the next one (even if unforeseen), each object dictates the appropriateness of the next generation in the paradigm of possible technologies. Through its functions and mechanisms, each technology implicitly projects the next (even if not strictly required), and in so doing it accomplishes a veritable interactive structure: each becomes a move that is in itself a condition for the arrival of the next. Technologies are not linked together by chance and often do not necessarily follow the intentions of the human actors. Rather, they are structured according to the rule of *conditional relevance* (Schegloff 1968). This basic form of social organization also seems to govern the interaction of objects among themselves.

Interobjectivity is thus a fundamental characteristic of the world of things, of this material universe in which the juxtaposition of things and the logic of their linkage produces meaning. Objects redefine the uses and significance of their counterparts, shed light on and even create each other's limits, and change their status and value *for* people. Like human actors, objects make sense as a practical, emergent, and local accomplishment.

Once in the social world of people, technologies do more than simply lay anchors. Domesticated by a pre-existing *moral economy* (Silverstone, Hirsch, and Morley 1992), they actively participate in the redefinition of this economy of actions and meanings. Once granted skills by humans, the object becomes an actor in itself, able to do, to say, to make us do, to make us say; and it does this with us, despite or thanks to us. In other words, objects become capable of introducing significant interactions with the other actors that inhabit the same social world: human, non-human, and hybrid (Latour 2002).

2.5 Reflexivity at Play: The Interaction between Technology and Culture

As we saw, technologies create meanings: a table on which friends have laid their mobile phones is no longer the same object. The nature of the social encounter changes, if only because the actors concerned are multiplied beyond the visible. Now the parties must contend with interlocutors present in the face-to-face gathering, ghost participants and "human-mobile" hybrids (Maronne 1999, 2002). A small technological object (designed and manufactured by people) redefines the modalities of social participation, changes the paradigm of possible actions, the meaning of an event. Our informant Assoum is no longer the same leader of his network of friends as he was before getting a mobile phone. This Assoum-with-a-mobile is a new actor, because of the identity and added possibilities this object grants.

Building fields of action, constructing identities, creating potential paths, setting limits and possibilities, generating the significance of things, places, and time amounts to producing culture. In this sense, technologies fabricate culture. However – and this question is central to our proposition – although it is legitimated by solid theoretical frameworks, backed by empirical data, and argued by rigorous analysis, can we accept this affirmation as stated?

We think not. This assertion is only half of a more complex statement, the first part of a more dialectic view of the processes at play. In this techno-human universe, the frontier between what "does" and "what makes us do," the ontological rupture between the intentional subject and intentioned object that an overly humanistic phenomenology would dictate seems impossible to posit. Who or what constructed the new identities surrounding our dinner table? Who or what delimited new possible fields of action? The mobile telephone with its technological mechanisms, or the person who designed it? The designer, by foreseeing an "off" position, or the user, who pretends that this technical possibility does not exist?

Technologies manufacture *potential* fields of action, *possible* narrative programs; they expand the field of possibilities of human subjects. It is in this sense and only in this sense that we can affirm that *technologies fabricate culture.*

It is precisely this notion of possibility that differentiates the determinism that surreptitiously underlies this assertion and the dialectic perspective that we have adopted. The relationship between technological objects and culture is not conceived solely in terms of *technologies as producers of culture,* because if they do and they make us do, if they say and make us say, they are nonetheless done and said.

We will attempt to rethink the relationship between technologies and culture in terms of *reflexivity,* that is, as mutual construction.[6]

We cannot define culture solely as a system of ideas, a repertoire of interpretations that is stored in people's minds. As we have seen, culture is incarnated in objects, distributed between human and non-human actors, and performed through their practices. What does thinking in terms of the reflexivity of the relationship between culture and technologies imply?

To this point, we have seen how technologies work as actors and how they contribute to producing meaning in daily life. But how does the routine of everyday life, the social interaction between individuals, their uses of technologies in context, generate the meaning of technologies? To grasp this process, we must situate technologies in a network of social interactions and related communication activities, which means taking into account people's practices and their role in constructing the meaning of things.

This research field has been explored extensively and is better known than the previous one. The phenomenological approach, on the one hand, and empirical analysis of the reception of technology, on the other hand, converge on at least one idea: things, technical objects, technologies, and their functions have a profoundly social nature. Not only do they have an intersubjective genesis and destiny, but their daily life, their functions and meanings, are constantly defined and redefined by the practices associated with them, by the discursive fabric in which they are situated, by their becoming detonators of ordinary conversations and the topic of people's everyday narratives.

2.6 The Discursive Origin of the Meaning of Things

"Him? He's always watching TV." "Can you get off the Internet, there're other people here too!" "We're at the table. Turn off your mobile phone, please." "You know, I turn it on only to make calls, I don't want to be bothered all the time, but the kids, it's crazy, they can't do without it." "I have a lot of emails, I have to reply – I get it. Come to my office soon, okay?" "Robert? He's the techie guy."

In the evening at home, in the train, at the café, at work – in short, in nearly all the places of daily life – we constantly participate, even simply by listening, in exchanges of this type. It is through a subtle weave of everyday practices and discourses, of activities and words, that individuals confer meaning, value, roles, and functions on technologies. By the most invasive, most everyday, most widespread of all communication tools – ordinary conversation – individuals negotiate and share visions and versions of technologies, interpretations of their uses, and definitions of themselves and others as users (Caronia 2002).

Beyond any meaning inscribed in the objects themselves, it is in fact through daily exchanges, ephemeral conversations, through the micro-narratives of everyday life, that technologies are connected to emerging dimensions of our social world: the identity of actors, the norms of everyday life, the constraints of social structure, gender, and age differences, and so on. Communication and information media are therefore access routes to common, locally shared worlds. Not only do they inform us and let us communicate but more importantly, they anchor our conversations, they establish communications, because they facilitate our social encounters, and they become pretexts for acting and speaking with others. In other words, communication and information technologies are not merely material objects but also *discursive objects*. By situating them in relation to the broad narrative categories that account for the forms of social life – knowledge and power, will and duty – we inscribe technologies in our social and cultural world.

It is not sufficient for the technologies to enter the objectual universe. To become a significant component of our daily culture, they must be grasped and formulated by language. Technologies – the representations of the world and of people that they convey – are presented to us as *possible* cultural objects. They *may* become relevant presences in the social world that we construct and deconstruct through our daily interactions. Yet this integration is not an accomplishment that should be taken for granted. To become social objects, these things awaiting meaning must become topics of discourse, a focus of joint attention, or objects of practices by human actors.

Technologies become an integral part of our culture when they enter the culture as influential characters in our daily stories, as things that we talk about and that we have to know how to talk about, as subjects of these micro-narratives of daily life through which we construct and deconstruct the sense of things. The meaning that we grant to technologies, their crucial influence on our social life, their capacity to enounce our social life – in short, their *cultural and social power* – indeed emerges from the culture of daily life that is constantly constructed through everyday talk.

In this sense, our encounter with technology, the experience that we construct with a techno-object, is no different from any other experience: it is mediated by language, by the subtle framework of discourse that determines the meaning of things, by the words (said and heard) that confer value on objects and that link them to us and to our daily practices.

2.7 Common Sense, Technologies, and Daily Life

The phenomenological tradition clearly illuminates the relationship between subject and object. This perspective maintains that any encounter, any action, any reaction of an individual to an object, whether it be material, conceptual, or technological, is mediated by all the commonly transmitted and accepted discourse, beliefs, and shared knowledge that constitute people's everyday culture.

The object is therefore always "lived" in a mediated form and is *constructed* by the human actor according to schemas, frames of relevance, conventions of meaning, and typified interpretations that we share and master as a member of a human community. The encounter with an object – technologies included – is situated in what phenomenology calls the *lifeworld*: a backdrop of references taken for granted and shared by all, which constitute the basis of all experience, including our experiences with material objects. It is precisely this invisible but operative dimension of human culture that causes us to never experience brute facts or objects but rather social events or objects, that is, scenes and objects that circulate, paired with socially shared interpretations. This transformation from brute things to social objects is performed mainly by the language that gives reality a social existence.

One might protest that this idea of construction of the object is counterintuitive, because the objects that surround us appear to truly be there, well constituted with their forms, functions, colours, textures, and the robustness of their materiality and range of possible actions that are already inscribed in their design and their technology. As we have seen, objects have a performative force: they do, they make us, and they make us do.

Yes, the object is indeed there, and it is indeed given to us, but our *experience* of the object, what we will do with its technological possibilities, the significance we impart to its acquisition or rejection, its social uses, and practices in which it becomes an actor, all concern the order of knowledge, beliefs, desires, values, and shared meanings that are part of the specific cultural universe that we call "common sense" (Geertz 1977, Schutz 1967).

As is the case for almost anything, there is a "technological common sense," and people's uses of technologies are constantly situated in – and mediated by – this set of theories, models, and shared ideas constantly made and remade during daily interactions. This is because, as we well know, *common sense* is constructed with language and speech of everyday talk, through media discourses and urban legends, through scientific and lay discourses. All of these fields of enunciation simply weave the discursive framework that lets us think about technologies and use them in a culturally specific way.

Complaining of the number of emails that we must manage or a mobile phone that rings all the time, becoming annoyed, conversely, because another person's phone is always turned off, flatly stating that a book does not exist because we cannot find it on the Internet, daring to comment on the effect of video games in the life of young people, running to answer the phone, mentioning in a conversation the appearance of a new computer virus – these are all elements that ultimately constitute social discourse surrounding technologies. They contribute to creating ideas and transforming human behaviours related to technology. It is then that the current ways of thinking and taken for granted ways of acting emerge and become natural.

This process has less to do with the techno-objects themselves than with their becoming objects of discourse and practices. To grasp the cultural role of technologies and the complex relations they maintain with human actors, we must analyse not only the meaning, actions, and representations of the world, or even the discourses that technologies state, but also the discourses that talk *about* them.

As Duranti noted, it is mainly through the ways of speaking, the ways of being in the world inscribed in the ways we talk about the world and in the world, that we construct the fundamental dimensions of our experience and of those around us. Language is a form of life because it traces models of actions and modes of relationships with things and people (Duranti 1997). Each of us apprehends communication and information technologies according to received ideas, recurrent statements, and ways of speaking that suggest ways of being-in-relation-to-technologies. Words – in this case as in any other – are never neutral. It is through words that speakers express their stance regarding what they are talking about and contribute to circulating a cultural model of understanding reality. In the social world, words "make" things by building consensus that establishes the existence and meaning of things. They fabricate the canonical versions of reality and allow their circulation. Even the most banal of language operations – naming objects – is a practice of constructing their meaning.

Words that grasp objects or that connote them (including sociologists' words) are acts of meaning that contribute to transforming things into cultural objects: "*telefonino*," "portable," "mobile phone," "perpetual contact," "nomad communication," "virtual reality," "network," "World Wide Web." No matter how technological objects and their uses are named, it is also through these *designation practices* that their cultural dimensions are established. The names given to things do more than refer to them: giving relevance to some features while ignoring others, they circulate in the form of condensed descriptions that do not convey a brute object but rather one that is culturally grasped.

The relationship we maintain with communication and information technologies is therefore a cultural practice in at least two respects. First, these technologies locally induce specific cultures, particular *know-how* and *know-what*, implying forms of participation and social organizations that are quite new and directly linked to objectual mechanisms. Second, technologies are anchored in the beliefs and cultural representations that we share, reconstruct, and transmit through the ways we talk about technologies and use them from day to day. Admitting that technologies are social objects that create meaning, and at the same time objects of practices and discourse that determine their meaning, has several consequences. First, we must reject any one-way interpretation. If technologies *make* (we have seen how) human actors, people *make* something of them. Second, if we consider our relations with technologies as a social practice, we must avoid isolating techno-objects from the social and cultural context in which they become objects of discourse and usages.

If we accept that we become a member of a community of ideas and practices largely through the use of language (Duranti 1997), then we must admit that it is also and mainly through language practices that we appropriate technologies. Living in a technological world implies experiencing it through the mediation of discourse and cultural practices that characterize it. We will therefore attempt to clarify the constitutive role of language and social interaction in the construction of a technological culture.

2.8 Doing with Words: Language, Interaction, and Culture

Since Vygostski and Wittgenstein, it is now commonly accepted that language is a system that allows production of meaning, a social tool to construct what counts as reality, a performative instrument to coordinate activities consensually. It is in the *uses* of language (rather than in its grammar) that one can observe its primary functions, that of representing *and* producing social organization and culture. If language practices are organized by the world views of a given community, the opposite is also true: language practices create canonical versions of the world for those who share these practices (Ochs 1988). As Bruner noted, "How one talks comes eventually to be how one represents what one talks about" (1986, 131).

This principle is more important than it initially appears. It stipulates that language is a system to represent *and* produce meaning, but especially that speech – that is, the situational use of language – is an action that presumes meaning at the same time as it constructs it. In effect, speaking and listening are *inter*actions. For these interactions to be effective and mutually intelligible for the partners, they necessitate a background of shared knowledge, a set of taken-for-granteds, agreement on the functioning rules, sharing (at least partial) of conventions and communicative strategies. In short, mutual understanding is supported by this common world of shared meanings that we call (at least by convention) "culture."

Therefore, speaking and listening must also be considered *actions*, in that they constitute a fabric of intersubjectivity. As forms of communication, they allow at least the circulation of the version of reality as it is conceived, defined, and shared by the members of a community and inscribed in discourse. Yet speaking and listening are actions also in a stronger sense: they enable individuals to (re)construct, negotiate, reinvent, and constantly transform this canonical version of reality.

As advertising copywriters know, words can trigger behaviours and create things. Without even considering the extreme case of a well-constructed lie, it is evident that the briefest and simplest verbal exchanges contain an element of cultural creation. Imagine the following scene: Someone answers her mobile phone that rings during a family meal. Another family member slides in a small comment, anodyne yet sharp: "You always have to be available!" In this banal exchange there are traces of nearly all the aspects to which we are referring. The gesture of the first person abides by one of the now taken-for-granted cultural definitions of this technology: that of *perpetual contact* (Katz and Aakhus 2002). This acquired definition appears to determine behaviour. However, it is this public gesture (along with similar ones) that defines the mobile telephone as a perpetual contact. Rather than as a guide for the action, the cultural model of mobile phone is an emergent practical accomplishment by the individual. By her behaviour, the actor incarnates it in her gestures and confirms its relevance. In the act of answering, performed before other subjects, there is construction and communication of meaning, because confirming the validity of canonical versions of things means producing meaning. The person could have not answered. She would have then defied the socially established definition of the mobile telephone.

The second character in our story could have remained silent, recognizing the cultural legitimacy of perpetual contact. Instead he utters a comment that refers to the shared definition of the mobile phone, while calling it into question.

The interaction unfolds in this manner not only because of the existence of an object but also because of the *patterns* of action inscribed in its design and the meaning given to the object. Culture organizes and allows this interaction, yet the exchange is also an opportunity to call the culture into question. In this case the two partners negotiate the use of the mobile telephone: one confirms its established definition, the other defies it. These two contrasting attitudes also contribute to establishing the interpretative repertoire surrounding this techno-object that is constantly confirmed, expanded, and renewed by language and interaction.

It is therefore in social interaction that the reciprocal links between language and culture are woven. If culture organizes actions and language, language dialogue and everyday interactions constantly produce culture.

2.9 Individual Sense-Making and Dominant Discourses

As we have seen, language practices are – literally – ways of world making (Goodman 1978). Nonetheless, if we do not want to drift into radical situationism, we must also clarify the sociohistorical side of this process: language and daily interactions construct culture, but they are also constructed by culture. The creative, constantly emerging nature of social life, local construction of meaning, and everyday practical action are in effect inscribed in broader logics. We have tried to trace the logic of things in forming phenomenological fields. We must also recognize the role of *orders of discourse*, which Foucault (1981) avers delineate the repertoire of what we can do or say in a given situation. According to Foucault, any *historical episteme* is characterized by dominant discourses that establish the conditions of possibility for what counts as reality. Individuals' actions, thoughts, and interactions are constrained by overall *discursive formations* that are systems of thoughts, networks of concepts or frames structuring experience (Lynch 1993, 130). This historically layered field of legitimate meanings and actions undermines a radical argument for a locally constructed knowledge and "problematizes any notion of a naked existential grounding of action and perception" (ibid.). After Foucault and Bourdieu,[7] it would be hard to deny the power of history and dominant discourses in delineating the field of what may be thought, said, and done by individuals. Nevertheless, just as we cannot talk about the total determining power of techno-objects or their logic, we cannot attribute to the orders of discourse a power of total determination over individuals.

In any social community there are several concurrent orders of discourse that constitute a vast repertoire of possibilities for (re)constructing culture in daily life. The discourse of design is not necessarily the same as that of advertising. Scholarly discourse and that of the layperson are constantly intersecting with media discourse, and all these discursive formations must be situated relative to the forces and logic of the market.

People's everyday actions and interactions are not situated within a unique discourse. On the contrary, they occur in an interdiscursive ground made up of different voices. As Bakhtin noted, this inherent polyphony of social discourse refers to a fragmentation of cultural perspectives that echo the multiple voices of the different enunciators at hand. Social actors may build their ways of acting, feeling, and thinking upon different perspectives, using and referring to available concurrent and alternative discourses (Lindstrom 1992, 103).

Moreover, we cannot invoke an imperative or coercive power of overdetermination of the discourse established, because of the transgressive and even revolutionary nature of the micro-order of daily life. As we saw in the case of the mobile telephone that rings during a family meal, social actors feel free to seize any opportunity to create, propose, or defend an alternative, competitive, or unforeseen discourse.

In the cultural game, the players on one side are the power of things, the social field, the cultural *habitus*, and the orders of discourse; on the other side they are the resistance of the actors and their sense-making attitudes. When they invoke (sometimes with intentional impertinence) concurrent orders of discourse, or create alternative ways of using technologies, they are acting out a form of silent resistance to what has been established by hegemonic cultural models.

Husserl's notion of *intentionality* clarifies this issue. *Intentionality* does not refer to a cognitive disposition related to a goal but rather to the human interpretive approach to reality. By seeing an object or a given idea according to his or her own perspective, by reformulating established meanings, the subject may attribute alternative interpretations and construct unpredictable ways of life.

In this sense, human intentionality allows resistance to objectual and cultural constraints and enables people to overcome social and historical determinism. Thus, the subject and the subject's *agency* are situated between the logic of things and the logic of discourse (Giddens 1979, 1984). This refers to the capacity to exercise power over the social structure and culture, just as culture and social structure exert a power over the individual. The relationship between the actor and the social, cultural, and technological world is therefore the constantly renewable product of circular interaction. It is then, in his or her very intentionality, that individual actors discover the range of their responsibility. Because where there is choice, there is responsibility.

The theories based on technological and cultural determinism, which in essence deny the subject's capacity to resist the logics inscribed in the objects and social discourses, depict a passive subject stripped of any ability to think and act in alternative ways. Beyond their epistemological weaknesses, these theories leave no room for human responsibility in the construction of the world that humans inhabit.

2.10 Discourse on Technologies as a Meaning-Making Device

The construction of the meaning of things, situations, technological mechanisms, and their assets and functions is a primordially social process resulting from a practice that unfolds through daily conversations, everyday speech, and local micro-negotiations. By evoking a thing, by naming it one way or another, individuals project, even construct, the emerging dimensions of the object they discuss.

In our view, the discourse on information and communication technologies goes further: "Tell me how you speak and I will tell you who you are." This saying aptly summarizes one of the most robust theories of contemporary sociolinguistics: the social characteristics of the speaker are integrated in his or her way of speaking, along with the speaker's stances on the subjects discussed and on the addressees (Gumperz 1982).

However, there are at least two frames of reference for conceptualizing this relationship between language and projection of the individual's identities.

According to a variationistic approach, ways of speaking are determined by social structure. Fundamental characteristics such as sex, age, social class, and ethnic origin determine how individuals speak; they explain their linguistic register, the language variations they adopt, and even what they say (Wilson 1991). According to this approach, the key elements of social structure (identity, status, role, socioeconomic level of the members) determine social behaviours, including self-expression. Expression is then a simple dependent variable of the forces that largely exceed the individual. In an extreme case, it is a signal that enables us to situate the position of each individual in relation to broad conventional sociological categories.

Drawing from the phenomenological tradition, the interactionist approach proposes a quite different and less mechanistic hypothesis. Identities and membership in social groups are conceived as constituted through social practices and language interactions where human actors negotiate their position (Zimmerman and Boden 1991). The traditional hypothesis that individuals speak and act in a certain way *because* they are adolescents, women, men, or marginal people needs to be reversed. According to Sacks, we need to ask *how* individuals *construct* themselves as adolescent, father, child, woman, man, marginal person, gamer, *bollé*, or geek by their forms of talk and behaviour. Far from determining people's ways of speaking, social categories and social identities originate from the (often strategic) uses of everyday language.

As Ochs pointed out, it is mainly through language practices that people construct their culture, identities, and sense of belonging (1988). This theoretical frame delineates a field of inquiry for studies in technologies and everyday culture. Beyond the uses of technologies (who uses what, when, and how), it is important to consider *what* people say and *how* they talk *about* technologies in the different scenarios of their daily life. The following scene from the field clearly shows the extent that talking-about-technologies is an identity-and culture-making device.

It is Sunday evening. Assoum is on the computer. He does not feel like getting up to reach for the land telephone. He picks up his mobile to call his friend.

ASSOUM: Yeah.

CHAN: Oh God!

ASSOUM: Yeah?

CHAN: Alien attack!

ASSOUM: Okay, are you getting dressed?

CHAN: Not really. No, I'm −

ASSOUM: We're going to Karim's and watching *JackAss*.

CHAN: Uhh, okay, I'm not going then.

ASSOUM: What do you mean, you're not going?

CHAN: I ain't gonna watch *JackAss*.

ASSOUM: Come on, bud. [*Silence*] Okay, boring, but anyway, not necessarily *JackAss*, but me, I wanted *JackAss*. Can ya come or no?

CHAN: No no. Not a movie person.

ASSOUM: Okay. I'm gonna remember this tomorrow.

CHAN: Okay. You better.

ASSOUM: No, no, you better. Okay!

CHAN: [???]

ASSOUM: I could have done this like six hours ago, but I was waiting for you guys and this is what I get?

CHAN: Ah, well, I didn't think we were gonna watch a movie.

ASSOUM: Uh, you wanna go get a coffee or something, what do you wanna do?

CHAN: Nah! I don't know.

ASSOUM: You wanna sit at home and play games?

CHAN: Probably. Do you have NS?

ASSOUM: What?!

CHAN: Ah, okay, you don't.

ASSOUM: What the hell's NS?

CHAN: NS is good.

ASSOUM: What is NS?

CHAN: Natural Selection.

ASSOUM: Okay, well, you be the geek. Later.

CHAN: Later.

Immediately following this conversation, Assoum calls another friend to inform him of the evening's agenda:

ASSOUM: Hello.

KARIM: Yeah, yeah.

ASSOUM: Me ... well, he said so [that he's not coming].

KARIM: Why?

ASSOUM: He's playing games.

KARIM: Oh, God, that's dumb!

ASSOUM: I know, that's what I said. Anyway.

KARIM: Oh, God, he's playing a game.

ASSOUM: He said, "I don't feel like it, I'm not a movie person." I said to him, "Are you playing a game?" He said, "Yeah," I said, "Okay."

KARIM: Okay, but you you wanna come?

ASSOUM: Well, it don't bother me.

KARIM: Bring my [???].

ASSOUM: Okay.

KARIM: Okay, I'm waiting, okay?

ASSOUM: Okay.

KARIM: Yo, Assoum, Assoum.

ASSOUM: Yeah.

KARIM: Do you have uh ... Maybe you'll be in the shower [???] call me [???] will call me, okay?

ASSOUM: Okay.

KARIM: Okay, Bye, then.

ASSOUM: Bye.

Through these telephone conversations, through the way they act and speak, these adolescents accomplish the cultural work of "being adolescents." Consider, first, the gesture: calling with the mobile phone because

"I didn't feel like getting up." Accounting for this use, Assoum confers a specific meaning on the mobile phone: a communication technology that is consistent with this form of "cultural laziness" that he claims is typical of people his age.[8]

Now consider the actual words. In their exchanges, the speakers establish relevant dimensions of their specific life world: they confirm the "evening" as a crucial time of the day, they affirm the precedence of "being there" over "what we're doing." They negotiate – at least locally – the cultural place allotted to the uses of technologies compared with other social activities. Moreover, references to technologies and their uses also become cultural tools to define who adolescents are and who the others are: "not being a movie person," "being dumb," being a geek." Through their words on technologies, young people define themselves and are defined by others.

As these exchanges clearly show, it is precisely through these specific forms of discourse that people manufacture their world and identities and negotiate the significance of technologies in their life. Analysis of this type of seemingly anodyne conversation reveals a microcosm of immense richness. It quickly becomes apparent that an in-depth look at the ways people talk about technologies can become an access route to much more far-reaching phenomena. What appear to be merely "speech data" (mobile conversations, informants' accounts of their technological practices, messages written on a screen, family discussions) in fact provide extraordinary insight not only into the social life of technologies but also and especially into the role of human intentionality and of daily practices in the creation of identities and the construction of meaning.

In the coming chapters we will closely follow this recurrent and circular process through which technologies create the meaning of contexts where they are situated, while concomitantly being domesticated by these contexts, which ultimately attribute often unforeseen meanings. We will see how technologies participate in the construction of our identity while they too are altered by a strategic usage entailing constant redefinition. These objects thus confer new significance on actions that they allow us to perform, at the same time as they are constantly being defined by our actions.

Chapter 3

Life Stories of Technologies in Everyday Life

Everyday objects are clearly important to understanding day-to-day life in the ordinary, classical sense. Objects can reveal places' hidden meanings, shed light on the secret issues involved in social practices, and make explicit the implicit meaning of different points in routine life that we rarely think about and that certainly cannot be summarized by our interactions with other people. The social and cultural dimensions of everyday life are intimately linked to objects, the spaces they occupy, and the moments when they are used. Yet most of the time we do not even notice them.

The refrigerator, which is at the heart of almost every home, in the kitchen, is a typical example of a banal everyday object. Its primary function is to keep food cool, but observation of domestic practices shows that it has many other meanings. For example, its door makes it suitable as a place to post reminders or exchange written messages with other household members (Lally 2002). Sometimes it becomes a concrete meeting place when children are choosing their snacks after school. It symbolizes forbidden fruit when it is opened to take secret midnight snacks. These are all peripheral meanings associated with an object with an apparently strictly utilitarian purpose. This type of household object, which is part of a kind of invisible background or backdrop to our daily life, has in fact many meanings that go beyond its strictly technical function.

Given elements such as their shapes, measurements, colours, and composition, these objects are first and foremost material. They occupy space and move and change over time. They also interact with other objects and establish meaningful relationships with the individuals with whom they are in contact. Technological objects thus become much more than simple "things," and we propose to consider them as actors in their own right in everyday life.[1] They behave like de facto partners generating interactions with concrete, recognized functions. For example, an object such as a computer, occupying a specific space in the home, integrates itself into the family dynamic, changes that dynamic, and itself changes as time goes by.

Technologies play an implicit role by operating like signs that speak and reveal things about family members' habits, practices, relations, positions, and statuses. Beyond their functional utility, such objects have an important symbolic dimension. If you tell others that you have a mobile, you are implying that you can be reached at any time. This reveals a desire for communication and the intention to be available. An adolescent might hesitate to acquire a mobile for fear of not being called.

Indeed, a mobile that never rings could confirm the unpopularity of its owner. Thus, objects "speak" to us. The way we use them is just as revealing: carrying one's mobile everywhere, keeping it turned off most of the time, or putting it on a table in a restaurant are all clear forms of behaviour that reveal things about the users and their relations with their social circles. Such examples show that objects are not neutral. At home, school, and the office and in public places, the relations we have with others are influenced by the presence of these technologies.

Understanding objects is fundamental to understanding household practices, but the complexity of the task increases in the case of information and communication technologies because they involve media that have the special feature of creating links by exchanging messages among individuals and institutions (Silverstone, Hirsh, and Morley 1992). As we have seen,[2] such media also create links between our private and public spheres, which leads us to study the permeability of the borders between these two spheres.

With technological innovation, the material context of our everyday lives becomes more complex. As more technological objects enter our homes, several generations of technology end up living together. Of course, most homes have had more than one television and one radio for many years, but only recently has there been more than one computer or a variety of forms of telephony equipment. The amalgamation of these techno-objects, both old and new, changes practices. The objects' integration into daily life cannot be reduced to simple additions of equipment, for they lead to changes in the way space is organized and require users to adapt to the environment. We therefore have to study the redefinition of the relations among traditional domestic technology (like the television and telephone), new technologies (like the Internet and mobile phone), and users.

Technologies are linked to a system of techno-objects with its own dynamics and equilibrium. This can be called a *domestic ecology* (Lally 2002), and exploring it requires an analysis of the interactions of all the technologies in the home.

3.1 How to Domesticate Technology

When a new technology enters the ecology of a home, it is subject to a domestication process (Silverstone, Hirsh, and Morley 1992, Caron and Berre 1995). Domestication involves several stages, from acquisition of the object to its integration into household schedules and routines. Through this process, the technology acquires (or loses) meanings, functions, and values. A number of authors (Kopytoff 1986, Silverstone, Hirsh, and Morley 1992, Caron and Caronia 2001) use an economic metaphor to describe the domestication process. The "economy of meaning" refers to the specific processes that govern the attribution of meaning to household objects. First, it has to be understood that a home is organized around rules and structures that are specific to it and constitute its own culture. While remaining related to the general economy of the society in which it is situated, a household develops its own parallel economy of meaning – in other words, its own system of value attribution. The value may be monetary, social, or affective. In the last case, a number of studies have shown that telephone access in a home is above all, and independent of real needs, an object of emotional security related to the possibility of having contact with the world outside.

A home's economy of meaning results from the everyday practices of household members, who thereby give meaning to the objects with which they share their environment. For example, the mobile phone is part of the general economy of a society because it has a set range of prices, officially recognized functions, and a value that is more or less shared collectively. These aspects accompany the techno-object when it is integrated into a family system, but they are also confronted with the economic principles of the existing domestic ecology. Thus, the mobile phone is at the heart of the daily interactions of a family or couple because it allows members to contact one another at any time. The techno-object fits into existing dynamics such as autonomy versus dependency, individual freedom versus membership in a couple, and private versus shared space. However, it may also assist the dynamics. Thus, if a father's mobile rings constantly for work reasons, his children may give it a negative connotation. This economy of values helps to define the foundations of the family culture. Patricia, a young girl we met while doing a survey, described a family dynamic with her father and his mobile:

PATRICIA: Well, you know, let's say it's with my dad there, like he, he comes and picks me up in the car, and then he spends the whole time talking on his mobile. It's like, "Dad, I'm here too, you know, [*laughs*] right beside you," you know!
INTERVIEWER: So he's somewhere else.
PATRICIA: Yeah. It's no fun.

The synergy between a family and the various technologies that it routinely uses in the home is a very fertile field for research. Too often we tend to see NICTS as unidirectional actors in society. Instead, we should ask up to what point do they help to create, maintain, and change the specific culture and social organization of the family.

Among other things, home life covers more than private life, the private sphere, intra-family relations, and individual use of technology. Today it is difficult if not impossible to exclude use of technology for work from the home. The private and public spheres are merging and intertwined. The home environment is now open to a wide range of uses far beyond the private sphere.

3.2 Life Stories of Technological Objects

In order to understand the links uniting human and material actors, we have to go beyond learned discourse and understand the meanings that individuals themselves give to their own practices. One of the ways to do this is to ask people to tell the "life stories" of the technologies in their homes. Anthropological research often uses life stories to understand the hierarchy of values in a society. Like people, objects have biographies and idealized career paths (Kopytoff 1986) that allow us to understand the cultural meaning given to those objects and to grasp the economy of meaning that governs the home in which they are located.

We probably all remember the arrival of the first computer into our environment. When was it bought? By whom? Why? Who actually used it? Where and when? Since new technologies are actors in the home, it is often possible to write their life stories by following their paths in the family environment. Techno-objects have a life, and they can almost become members of the family, or at least significant partners in interactions.

Yet they do not have only one story. They have several, for every member of the family creates and constructs his or her narrative according to aspects that are specific to him or her. These subjective stories also reveal the symbolic dimensions of techno-objects and our commitment to them. Family members' memories of the adoption cycle of, for example, a television set in the home are sometimes contradictory, and it is fascinating to confront their points of view and see the dynamics of the relations that each person has with his or her memory of the object. The memory becomes collective as family members weave their individual memories together. We asked Beatrice and Stephan, parents in their fifties, and their twenty-year-old son Xavier to talk about technologies in their home. The following shows how combined perspectives can create a narrative in which the story of the object is also the story of a family:

INTERVIEWER: When you decided to put another TV in that room, how did you make the decision. What made you decide to change TVs?
BEATRICE: Oh, yes, I remember! [*laughs*]
STEPHAN: I don't remember anymore.
BEATRICE: TVs came out.
STEPHAN: No, no, we bought the Special Vision ...
BEATRICE: Yes, but after that.
STEPHAN: Oh, oh, the next one. The one upstairs there, we said we'd put it, we'd put it downstairs for the kids and then buy a new one for us. Uh, but ...
BEATRICE: But, no, you're missing one!
STEPHAN: Which did I miss?
XAVIER: The Special Vision, when we put it upstairs, why did you buy the other?
STEPHAN: When I bought that one, the Special Vision, it went downstairs.
XAVIER: Oh, yeah, that's right.
BEATRICE: Yeah.
INTERVIEWER: Okay, it didn't go upstairs because ...?

The life stories of techno-objects confirm that, beyond their material nature and function, they change the meaning of space and time in our daily lives. However, these changes should be seen from the point of view of a process of reciprocal construction involving people and technologies. In particular, four elements generally appear in the life stories created by users: *geographical migration of technologies, unexpected uses, a cascade of adoption and communication, and reasons for adoption and anticipated uses.*

3.3 Geographically Migrating Technologies

Changes in our uses of a technology often go hand in hand with a physical move of the objects within the family space. We have called this displacement a *geographical migration*,[3] because it entails more than just a move; it involves a real life cycle.

In the 1990s the first major technological migration was often from the office to the home, for example, when employers replaced their computers and allowed employees to take the old ones home. Today transfers between the two environments are often bi-directional, in that personal communication technologies also enter the work world. Through this bi-directional movement, many objects become bi-functional, since they are often used for both personal and work purposes. The portable office of an independent worker with a laptop computer is an interesting illustration of the bi-functionality of objects oscillating between the two spheres.

Mobiles also travel between the office and home. While some people have two mobiles, one for their private life and one for work, in most cases the same object plays both roles. Such doubling-up could become even more common since in Europe some people have two or three chips with different numbers that they use, depending on the call they are making. Some mobile phone companies even offer subscribers two different numbers on the same chip to make it easier for them to separate different uses of the same technology. Newspapers often report anecdotes about phone subscribers with more than one number and their sometimes illicit motivations. For example, cases of infidelity have been discovered because of calls or text messages kept in a mobile phone memory. Email archives can be similarly revealing. Clearly, communication management becomes essential if the same techno-object roams and fulfils more than one social role.

Most such migrations occur within the home environment, as when a technology formerly used by all is given to one family member for personal use. A television set in the living room may be replaced by a larger one and moved to the bedroom of one of the children. It is now common to find more than one television in a home, whereas in the early 1950s, when the technology was first introduced, people often congregated at the house of a neighbour who was lucky enough to have a TV. Generally, these techno-objects spread as their cost drops, and their social uses change in consequence: collective television watching in a shared space becomes individual watching in separate parts of the home. This makes it possible to individualize what one watches because one has full control over the choice of content. One result is that family members may watch the same show at the same time but in different rooms. What does the privatization of watching, the new independence of media consumption, reveal? Let us look closely at a conversation with Theresa and Roger (parents in their late forties) and their children, Francis and Ève (sixteen and twenty years old).

INTERVIEWER: Do you watch TV together?

THERESA: All together?

ROGER: All four of us? Ah, um … Once in a while.

THERESA: It doesn't happen very often.

ROGER: Sometimes, not often.

FRANCIS: Often three of us, for example, or two.

EVE: Two or three.

ROGER: Unless we're watching a specific program, I don't know … When was the last time we watched?

ÈVE: Like *Columbine High*.

ROGER: Ah, maybe, yeah, maybe *Columbine High* … Maybe we were all there then … Or maybe when the Pope died or something like that.

INTERVIEWER: Major events?

ROGER: Major events.

ÈVE: Yeah, but it has to affect everyone.

INTERVIEWER: A more regular show? *Omertà*?

THERESA: Yeah, I watched it, but it's the first year.

FRANCIS: Me too, I watched it, but I was in my room.

INTERVIEWER: Do you watch TV more in your room?

FRANCIS: Yeah, or in the basement. Or if I'm alone in the house, it'll be in the living room. Otherwise it'll be in my room or in the basement.

INTERVIEWER: Rarely with your father, mother, or sister?

FRANCIS: Rarely. It's true that it's rare.

In an era when techno-objects are developing very quickly, their obsolescence is part of the manufacturer's marketing strategy. The frequency of their replacement, and of their migrations in the home, is therefore increasing. Already in the 1970s the old television migrated to a space reserved for children and became the platform for the first video games, such as Pong.

Today a more powerful computer replaces the old one, which is often sent down to the basement where it is relegated to a specific function, such as word-processing or games. We are now seeing not only migrations of techno-objects but also of their content. For example, we now watch some television shows and listen to radio programs on the Internet. By observing such migrations, we can see that the paths followed by techno-objects sometimes deviate from anticipated uses, particularly when such uses were specialized and limited.

Moreover, these geographical migrations produce changes in the way the technologies are used, thereby redefining experiences of family spaces (Iori 1996, Gumpert and Drucker 1998). It is legitimate to speak of a dialectic relationship among objects and spaces because technologies define spaces, but are also defined and redefined by their location. When we look at everyday techno-objects, we see that individuals determine their strategic locations. We have already mentioned[4] the example of a family that insisted on putting the computer in the kitchen rather than in the basement, where their son would have been unsupervised. Using the computer in the kitchen met the family's need to set up a shared location for the activity. Migrations or non-migrations as in this latter case tend to redraw, among other things, the boundaries among activities that can (and must be) shared by parents and children, and those that can remain on a personal level.

The strategic location for the computer is a little like that of the first land-line telephone, which used to be located in a shared room in the home so as to make it accessible to all. Obviously, the kitchen-panoptikon also made it possible for parents to exercise some control, since they knew who called their children, and vice versa, at what time, and for how long. Indeed, it was once again owing to the migration of a techno-object that this family dynamic had to be reinvented and carried out in new ways.[5]

Telephone technology has gone through various stages since its beginning: from a single land-line telephone located in a shared room in the home, to several telephones scattered throughout the home environment. Later, the cordless phone appeared, though it was still limited to the home. Then came the mobile phone, its defining feature the fact that it is nomadic, which has clearly changed telephone uses and functions.

Yesterday's teenagers who talked on phones connected to a line in the main hall of the house certainly did not have the same freedom of expression as a girl today who has a phone in her room and a private line or a mobile phone. Young people have always sought privacy when talking with their peers. The phenomenon of secret conversations is not new, but it takes a different form every time technological innovation opens new possibilities for privacy. Whether they use codes that are incomprehensible to other family members, go on a chat line without their parents' knowledge, stretch the extension cords of family phones into a closet or bathroom, take a cordless phone up to a bedroom, or, best of all, use a mobile to send text messages at 2:00 A.M., teenagers will always invent creative and original strategies. When communication technologies migrate and proliferate, the dynamics of collective use and implicit control inevitably change. Communication technologies, as they finally emerge from the uses we invent for them, can thus have unpredictable effects on our perceptions of the private and public spheres.

3.4 Unexpected Uses: When New Technologies Perform Old Functions

Owing to their technological features, communication objects lead to habits, and inversely, our manners of using them redefine their meanings. They are not restricted to rigidly predetermined paths. We mentioned the case of the refrigerator and its peripheral functions, but the family computer can also be used for unexpected purposes. For example, a parent may stick a reminder note on the computer screen to ask a child to take the dog for a walk. The parent knows that as soon as the child gets home from school, he generally rushes to the computer to see whether he has any important emails. The computer's physical form, a box with a screen that is always checked when the machine is in use, makes it possible to stick a message on it. It is the computer's basic function, design, and location that enable it to play this unexpected communication role, one that is ancient and distant from its digital design.

A mobile kept beside the bed as an alarm clock, a pager carried in a pocket and used as a watch: these are other examples of older peripheral functions that have been assigned to so-called new communication objects. However, such functions are not entirely unforeseen by designers, who usually combine them into the design, thereby nodding to users by suggesting possibilities of use that are different from the object's main advertised functions. Thus, manufacturers aim to broaden the scope of the various functionalities offered by a given technology so as to increase the number of reasons for buying it. For at least a decade the marketing of computers, televisions, radios, home cinemas, and telephones has increasingly been based on exploring other possible uses, connotations, and symbolism. The mobile phone is probably the best example of the present trend towards multifunctional convergence, combining verbal communication, text messaging, Internet access, photographs, and videos. However, it is interesting to note that "the more digital convergence of media seems inevitable, the more we rediscover the specificity of each media and the social uses that differentiate them" (Fisher 2001, 197). Thus, the convergence proposed by the industry is not inevitable, since real uses resulting from everyday choices by individuals are proof of users' ability to resist and be creative.

In addition to affecting the spatial environment of the home, technologies incorporate the spatial and temporal aspects of the family's social organization, thereby making new, sometimes unexpected dynamics possible with respect to use. We should note that such unexpected developments result from reciprocal changes of family habits and the technology itself.

Television is an excellent example of the way that technologies intervene in the temporal organization of family life. Comments made by families on their television use show that it strongly influences the rhythm of their daily life. Here is how ten-year-old Charlotte describes her daily schedule: "I get up, get dressed, go have breakfast ... Then if I still have a little time, I go watch TV, but most of the time I don't watch it in the morning. Then we go to school. At lunch, we watch TV while we're eating ...

Charlotte refers to the television as a marker structuring her day and ritually determining the beginning and end of other activities. In this sense, use of this technology regulates time. However, we have to see that watching it is not so much a routine in itself as an activity that produces a routine (Caron and Caronia 2000). It makes it possible to segment the day into periods for specific activities. The medium becomes an organizer of time in a way that goes far beyond the inflexibility of its programming. Until recently, if a serial drama was shown at a specific time and on a specific day, a degree of discipline was required to watch it, which could have created a routine related to content. Today, through services such as TiVo (which automatically records all programs digitally), we can watch content that we have missed whenever we want. We should also not forget the traditional VCR, which has made it possible for years to shift the time that we watch our favourite programs. Yet research has shown that it is rather rare for individuals to really use these possibilities in the course of their routine activities, and that most recordings not watched within twenty-four hours are never watched. Thus, the television remains a means of accessing a continuous flow of shows, which once again strongly indicates that our time is not dictated by the specific content offered by the technology. Indeed, more channels are re-broadcasting the news several times a day, whereas news and feature show scheduling used to be relatively inflexible.

The functions of communication technologies might seem to play less of a role in structuring our lives. Email can be checked and phone calls made at any time of the day or night, thanks to e-mailboxes and answering machines. Yet these technologies increasingly share the same time regulation phenomenon as television. Even though it is possible to read one's email at any time, most users establish routines.

In the following short autobiographical narrative, Danielle (twenty years old) describes what she usually does when she gets home from work, punctuating her account with references to how she habitually uses technology.

DANIELLE: The first thing I do when I get home is turn on the computer, if it's not already on. Sometimes I don't turn it off in the morning. I turn the Internet off so the line won't be in use all day, and then I leave the computer on.

INTERVIEWER: All day?

DANIELLE: Yes. Otherwise, if it's off when I get home at night, I don't even take my dog out, I put my bags down and then I turn on the computer and after that I come back.

INTERVIEWER: What do you do? What do you check exactly?

DANIELLE: Well, I wait for it to turn on again, then after that I go log onto the Internet, then the first thing I do, I go and see who's on the chat line [...]

DANIELLE: That's the first thing I do. Then if I see no one's there, well, I go get the email or I leave it on and I go away. Then Pat will come by, he'll change users and go see who's logged onto the chat line on his side.

Very few of us are even conscious of these hidden routines. It is only by keeping a daily record, in a logbook, for example, over a certain period, or by cutting oneself off entirely from the media and technological markers that we become really aware of their weight in our daily lives. In order to get a better idea of the impact of technologies on everyday routines, we asked young adults to participate in an experiment that proved quite revealing.[6] We asked them not to use NICTs for a complete week. No communication by computer (email, chat line, forum, etc.), mobile phone, or pager was permitted. Reactions were strong. For example, Josée was upset by the experiment, which forced her to become aware of her own habits:

"It seemed to me like a kind of unconscious routine had been set up in my media consumption. Some recurring actions seemed automatic, especially with respect to the TV and computer. The first thing I do every day is turn on the computer and the TV."

Two types of reaction in particular were identified through this exercise. First, some people saw that new communications technologies had become an artificial necessity for them and did not really meet their communication needs but rather created them. However, other people insisted on the absolute necessity of these means of communication for their social lives to function smoothly. These contradictory reactions were, however, consistent in that they showed that use of technology structured daily routines to a huge extent and that the imposed "weaning" would have been untenable over the long term.

3.5 A Cascade of Adoptions and a Cascade of Communications

The temporal organization of relations among individuals and techno-objects changes when a new technology is introduced into a family and interrupts the usual routine. The new arrival can lead to an unexpected event, such as the adoption of another technology or the addition of new functionalities to an existing technology. For example, acquiring an Internet connection has often led to the purchase of a more powerful computer or an answering machine or service to take messages when the line is busy. The metaphor of a cascade is a good illustration of the gradual chain reaction that often characterizes the acquisition of new technologies. When home computers were initially introduced, for example, we were encouraged to update them regularly by adding memory. Today the general trend is more towards planned obsolescence pure and simple. By suggesting we replace the whole machine, the industry constantly renews its market.

Email, instant messaging, and the mobile are some of the many tools we adopt to remain in permanent contact with our social network. As this dependency expands, some of us feel the need to install filters to manage and contain the skyrocketing number of exchanges. On one hand, we use a technology that makes it possible to contact us anywhere and anytime; on the other hand, we seek to protect ourselves from the flow of messages by using a pager or call display to filter or block messages. This means using an additional communication tool to protect against an overload of communication and gives the overall impression of a paradoxical cascade.

Sometimes it is the use itself of new technologies that takes the form of a cascade, for example, when we want to keep track of communications that we have missed, voluntarily or not. Instead of the above-mentioned cascade of adoption, this is a cascade of communication as can be seen in the remarks of Bruno, a young man in his twenties:

INTERVIEWER: And when you are on the Internet, the phone line is busy, right?

BRUNO: Yeah, that makes the line busy, calls go straight to the answering machine. So it rings once, and then the answering machine goes on. While if you are on, if you're talking on the phone and you don't answer the second line, it rings four times, four or five times and then the machine comes on, the answering machine. When I'm on the Internet, sometimes I take it ... when I think about it. I don't always think about it, I have to admit, I forward the calls to the mobile.

INTERVIEWER: But you have to go get the phone.

BRUNO: That, I keep it beside me. Yeah. I've got to go get the phone in the car, so I go get it in the garage, say I was near the garage so I go through the garage. I go get the mobile, I transfer the calls, I put the phone beside me at the computer, I go on the Internet, but otherwise sometimes I have to admit I don't transfer the calls. Then I ...

INTERVIEWER: What happens then?

BRUNO: People leave messages and then we call back.

We can see another variant of communication cascade in how the choice of technology depends on the closeness of the relationship we have with someone. We might meet someone on a chat line, then move the relationship to instant messaging, then use the phone, and finally meet the person face to face. An illustration of this is given by Françoise when she reconstructs the steps by which she made a friend.

FRANÇOISE: Well, it's ... it's my friend who met him on the chat line. Then she, well, passed him to me, then uh, ... That's it.

ALLAN: She lent him to you ... [laughs] Then she took him back after!

INTERVIEWER: Then later you spoke by MSN?

FRANÇOISE: Yeah.

INTERVIEWER: Have you ever spoken on the phone?

FRANÇOISE: Yeah.

INTERVIEWER: Okay. And are you going to meet soon?

FRANÇOISE: Maybe.

Thus the physical features of the techno-objects inhabiting our daily world have real impact on the social relations in which we involve them.

Once they are adopted and domesticated, NICTs help to structure the times and spaces of our lives. They become partners, concrete actors in our human relations, but they also operate as signs. We will see this in detail in the next chapter.

3.6 From Communicating Something Urgent to the Urgency of Communicating: Reasons for Adoption and Anticipated Uses

Past studies have noted the important role of rationality in the adoption of a technology (Haddon 1992, Livingston 1996). Thus life stories often begin with the reasons for acquisition, which shows that the adoption of a new object is almost always justified by utilitarian reasons. For a number of people the introduction of a new technology into the home is not an obvious decision and needs to be justified. This involves invoking the (real or imagined) needs that the technologies could help to meet. The needs form the list of official reasons used to justify the introduction of the new object into the family environment. In recent decades, as our society has taken a technological turn, many parents wishing to ensure their children's success have felt obliged to equip their homes technologically by purchasing a computer (Caron, Giroux, and Douzou 1985). For such parents the technology dictates the present and makes it possible to get a foothold in the future (Lally 2002).

Thus we are often subject to two forms of pressure: one involving social discourse, which includes advertising arguments, and one pertaining to our real needs, which determine the meaning that we personally give the technology (Kopytoff 1986). This tension is revealing and could explain the recurrence of some typical justifying discourses. Individuals generally use a culturally accepted set of reasons to explain their actions. The flurry of coverage in the media of discussions on the dangers of microwaves from mobile phones is a good example of a collectively shared social discourse. The media place concerns that are circulating in society on the agenda, and they are then accepted, rejected, or changed by individuals. Adolescents repeat many social discourses criticizing mobile phone use to justify their refusal to purchase the technology or the fact that they limit its use.

Alice appropriates the pseudo-scientific argument about the danger of microwaves from mobile phones to justify why she has decided not to own one. She also uses another argument, which appears relatively often in the media, everyday conversations, and the political arena, about the dangers of using a mobile phone while driving. Her third argument is simply that she does not need one. "Well, first of all," she says, "we know there have been studies that say it can give you cancer. And there's also that there are more traffic accidents, and then it's not something you vitally need. There're still phone booths around, you know, and you deal with it, like when you go out, you know, you take a quarter with you" (participant in Radio-Canada's "Ados-Radio" show, 31 August 2003).

When they talk about their official reasons for adopting or not adopting technological objects, users also say how they think they will use them. The frequent discourse on using new technologies with restraint gives us a glimpse of another form of rationalization. In many families the first mobile was bought by one parent and used frugally, initially, because it was seen mainly as emergency equipment. The object's location also corresponded to this rationalization, because it was usually kept in the car. A little like the land-line telephone in the home, the mobile was the permanent telephone in the family car. Thus, this new technology was used as if it were the traditional technology – in other words, as if it were an object located in a fixed spot. We have already forgotten that the discourse on use in case of emergency was until quite recently one of the most frequent justifications for a family's adoption of a mobile. While this type of discourse has become less frequent as penetration has increased, it is still often employed, perhaps because it allows the user to claim a degree of control over the techno-objects in question. We should also remember that at first it was quite expensive to use a mobile phone, which strongly motivated new users to have persuasive justifications for the investment. At the time such monetary considerations also dictated the "proper way" to use the mobile phone: selectively and with restraint.

Max, the father of a family, spoke to us about using the mobile phone with restraint. Note the number of uses acquired as the mobile migrated in the family, compared with the first reasons given for buying it.

INTERVIEWER: But in your car, is the mobile on?
MAX: Never. Never, never on.
INTERVIEWER: So you use it, but when you're not using it, it's off ...
MAX: Absolutely.
INTERVIEWER: And here, at home, is it on?
MAX: Not here either. It's not on.

INTERVIEWER: If you go to the restaurant, to see a movie, whatever... do you ...?

MAX: More and more ... we don't really know what to do with it, but ... [*laughs*] we use it to call once in a while ... check up on this, check that ... but it's more because ... we have it and ...

INTERVIEWER: At those times, is it on?

MAX: Not then either. We just, uh ... at least, like, for example, I might tell someone to call me back specifically on the mobile ... which is still very very very rare ...

INTERVIEWER: So when you go to the restaurant, you have it with you ...

MAX: I carry it around, I carry it around because I say to myself, well ... they don't need it when we're not there ... after all, they should be able to share one line between the two of them ... uh ... and we, well if ever we need it, we'll be able to use it ... and anyway ... if we go out in the evening on the weekend, most of the time it's during the times when uh ... use is free ... so more often than not we call here to see if everything, uh ... if everything is okay or things like that. We call here to say we're coming home, we won't be home for a while ... we changed our plans and we're going to such-and-such a place.

The reduction in the cost of acquiring and using a mobile has gradually led to new use habits that correspond more closely to its mobile nature. Now the practical aspect of the technology has become a more frequently recurring theme in biographical narratives justifying purchase and use. The mobile's portability makes new forms of social micro-coordination possible (Ling and Yttri 2002). For example, users no longer have to agree on a set meeting point ahead of time; the mobile phone accompanies them physically and allows them to adjust their movements according to needs. Such logistical, functional, and instrumental use highlights the practical nature of the object. Along the same lines, its portability also allows it to be used for surveillance and control. A worried father or jealous spouse can easily keep abreast of what is happening, as Danielle (married, twenty years old) told the interviewer here:

INTERVIEWER: So, with his mobile phone he is, can we say, more reachable?

DANIELLE: Yeah, yeah, sometimes I'm waiting for him there, it seems long. So then I call him, I say, "Okay, where are you?" He tells me, "I'm still in the store." So then I relax. "Okay, how much longer?" Sometimes it takes longer than expected, you know. But otherwise I'd've had to wait, I couldn't have done anything, and then I would've said, "Oh come on, where is he?" and I

would've been even more upset. But instead I can call him, and he can tell
me what's going on. I'll say, "Okay, right, I'll wait for you, you know, and
come on!"

As we noted above, both users and non-users generally talk about techno-objects from the angle of rationality or evoke their utilitarian functions. Sophie doesn't have a mobile phone, "but my dad has one for emergencies," she says. "Like when he has to work overtime, he calls us to tell us." In this example, the mobile phone becomes a practical object useful to have to alert or inform those close to us in case of a major or even a minor incident. We are still in the register of the mobile phone enabling emergency communications, the leitmotif of which seems to be "I think it is useful for safety."

For Antoine, another teenager, "It's especially if I want to be easier to reach. Anyone can call me any time, I'm sure to … if there's something pretty important, well then, I'm sure that they'll tell me as soon as possible. And me too, it's the same thing, if I have something to say to someone, in any situation, I'll be able to do it as fast as possible. It's mainly that." What is implied here is that with a mobile, one is easier to reach than with a land-line phone specifically because a mobile is portable. However, the argumentation shifts. Antoine replaces the "emergencies" concern mentioned by Sophie with a more general justification: a feeling or impression of urgency. The mobile phone is seen more as a means of contacting an "elsewhere" and/or an "other" in a synchronous manner (in "real" time), and the feeling expressed suggests an urgent need to be in communication (to be able to reach others and be reached at all times) rather than communication of an emergency. From one adolescent to the next, the mobile phone thus changes from having the status of a simple communication tool used occasionally to deal with emergencies or unexpected circumstances to a veritable ubiquitous medium that eliminates both waiting and silences in communication. Urgency could be said to be an essential feature of real time.

We should again note young people's insistence on justifying mobile phone use rationally by citing the importance of the communications they have to establish ("if there's something pretty important"). But there is some contradiction between what young people say they do with their mobile phones and what they really do. We will show this in the following chapters by analysing young people's real-time, naturally occurring mobile phone conversations. The mobile as it was originally perceived –

as a means of contacting an outside source of help when in trouble – supposed rather solitary uses; but in the case of adolescents today, the background of their use is made up of increasingly connected social contexts.

From this angle the mobile seems remarkably consistent with the primary values of adolescents, who generally place great importance on sociability and leisure activities. They live in the present or short term, which leads them to prefer adventure, flexibility, and mobility within a relatively closed circle of social relations for which leisure activities are vital (Pronovost 1996).

The social obligation to communicate that is created by mobile use, which tends to eliminate silence or least to render it suspect, is constantly found in young people's discourse. Says Sophie, "The advantages [of having a mobile pager] are that you can be reached all the time, if you leave it on and your batteries are okay, uh … people can call you in case of emergency. Then the disadvantages are that some people get really addicted to their mobile, they can't do anything without talking or calling someone."

The feeling of becoming "addicted" to one's mobile phone thus also arises in the discourse of young people, evoking the dependency on communication technologies that has already been studied in depth with respect to television, computers, and the Internet. For some, however, the "urgent need" to communicate that is more or less created by the mobile phone does not seem to be perceived in a negative manner. Philippe does not see the mobile as something he could be addicted to, and he does not seem to consider himself "addicted" to his mobile: "It doesn't bug me, it's never bugged me … I've never had someone … well, I have some friends who have people who call them all the time, all the time … Me, that's never bugged me. I'm someone who loves talking to people, very sociable … so when people call, I'm happy to … It never bothers me."

In other words, Philippe does not see the mobile (the communication that it makes possible) as an end in itself but simply as a means of contacting and being contacted by people, friends. It is useful to him as an extension of his personality ("someone who loves to talk, very sociable"). For him, what the object could cost (in terms of time, money, silence, freedom, etc.) is nothing compared with what it provides.

Yet the dependency remains, not the addiction to the object itself but to what it makes possible: to be always in contact, always connected, constantly "connected to society." This can be seen in the minimum obligation to be always, at all times, and everywhere at least available for communication.

ANTOINE: Disadvantage? It's that ... yeah, money, but also I want to say that at some point, you want, uh, ... It's not the same, you know, life you could say has changed a bit ... I mean you're always receiving, you're always, you could say, linked with society, whereas it's sure that ... That's it, the disadvantage is that you're always in contact. At some point you want to break off the contact, but it's not all that easy ...

SOPHIE: You've got to get rid of your mobile.

ANTOINE: Or you've got to get rid of it or something ... You're not free, free, free ... Someone who doesn't have a mobile, he knows he won't have any calls, he's got peace of mind. But someone who has one, maybe you never know, "Oops, there's one," it rings, you never know, always connected like ... That's the disadvantage, I'd say, to having a mobile, it's that you don't really have ... Sure, you have freedom in the sense that you can call anywhere, but when you look at it a bit, it's that you're always busy with calls coming in ... You're always connected to society.

This availability, which results from a certain form of social pressure (or at least is felt as such) and seems to accompany acquisition of the technology, is viewed by Antoine as infringing on his freedom: "You're not free, free, free ... you're always busy with calls coming in." Apparently freedom and silence are not easy to win back once one has a taste of the potential and promises of mobile communication. As we will see in the next chapter, this is precisely what the advertising discourse targeting young people seeks to sell. We are talking about an addiction to social communication. Sometimes we become literally one with technologies and take them everywhere with us; they are part of our lives in a relatively intimate manner.

The life stories of techno-objects show that family members reflect on the possession and use of these technologies and changes in the ways they use them. They portray themselves as non-naïve social actors who know why given technologies have been introduced into their homes. Parents may be able to remember the arrival of their first television set, their first experiences with computers, their initiation to the Internet. Most young people, for whom these technologies have always been part of the home environment, remember when they acquired their MP3 player or pager, and when they exchanged the pager for a mobile.

As users' discourses develop, they echo the various social discourses that infuse the cultural and social imagination and thereby play a major role in the construction of symbolic values related to new technologies. In the next chapter we will show to what point and how advertising discourses affect the meanings of NICTs, and how such objects, by playing roles in various discursive spheres (advertising not the least of them), propose cultural interpretations of themselves as objects and also of their uses and users.

Chapter 4

Now Playing: Mobiles, Discourses, and Advertising[1]

Acquired and new knowledge, experiences, beliefs, practices, habits that spring from other technologies, and information conveyed from one individual to another are all involved in forging what has to be considered an imaginary world (Semprini 1996) linked specifically to the mobile phone. This raises a number of hypotheses about its operation, the contexts in which it is used, its technical properties, its users, and its symbolic, mythological, historical and socio-cultural features. The imaginary world is also nourished by social discourses (academic, normative, and media discourses in the broad sense) that cross social space and in turn suggest both symbolic and utilitarian relationships with the technology.

Among the various discourses, that of advertising remains one of the most powerful. Beyond the usual commercial marketing, advertising confronts us daily with sets of words and images, veritable micro-narratives that both represent and construct culture. Naturally, advertising is based on users' logic and narratives, which it helps to circulate in social space. It plays a major role in our representations of the social world in which we live and of ourselves in that world. Not only does advertising convey scenarios involving techno-objects, but also and perhaps above all, it helps to define the very identities of technology users.

In the discourses that it conveys, advertising presents the desirable object and the subjects desiring that object according to the basic grammar of any advertising communication (Landowski 1989). It targets effectiveness through the productivity of the sign. However, to achieve this, it has to do more than construct a good simulation of subjects desiring desirable techno-objects. The simulation also has to be naturalized: in other words, it must circulate like a "myth,"[2] like a discourse that hides its discursive nature by presenting itself as natural instead of cultural. Advertising discourse scenarios thus suggest lifestyles and models for action and culture, thereby contributing to the overall process of integration of mobile phone uses into our everyday lives. By simply showing a mobile in the hand of a user when the ring is heard,[3] advertising suggests a picture of *normality*: always expecting a call becomes commonplace. The mobile phone appears as a normal extension of the body, like a virtually integrated prosthesis. It is the norm. Obviously advertising discourses are rarely simple creations, for they are constantly based on references that are easy to grasp and consistent with local habits. For example, they take into account the way the mobile phone is carried, which can vary from one country to another. Westerners often carry it in hands or pockets, whereas in Asia it is more commonly in a case attached to the belt (Plant 2000).

As we know, advertising discourse tries to present objects in relation to their potential value for their buyers, and to promote that value as obvious (Landowski 1989). Mobile phone advertising is no exception; it constructs representations of potential users by creating scenarios involving hypotheses about the needs, expectations, tastes, and skills of future users (Semprini 1996). To achieve the sought-after standardizing effect, advertising strategies try to give value to the lifestyles they suggest. An analysis of some mobile phone ads published in newspapers and magazines or broadcast on television over the last fifteen years, especially in Canada but also in Europe, shows the imaginary world of mobile phones proposed by advertising. Examining the discourses from here and elsewhere, today and yesterday, makes it possible to read the state of the market, see the values injected into promoting the object, and gain a better understanding of how users are seen by telecommunications companies. Advertising discourses correspond to features of society, either because they reflect it or because they are in some way a catalyst. Today, young people are a primary market, and advertising designers examine their culture from every angle to create means of addressing them and changing their very culture so that mobile phones can fit into it.

4.1 Discourses of the Past and Simple Future

While the mobile phone advertising we see today has come largely to target adolescents, this has not always been the case. Ten years ago, advertising discourses were very different and clearly aimed at other audiences. In the mid-1990s, magazine ads focused on the values of security and convenience while referring to the mobile phone's usefulness for conducting business. Magazine articles at the time announced the growing democratization of mobile phone ownership, for the industry was increasingly courting ordinary consumers by basing its sales arguments on security and practical uses. Every car needed to be equipped with a "car phone" for emergencies and breakdowns. Thus, advertising had ceased portraying mobile phones as simple work tools, though it still targeted adults. Advertising texts were generally long and descriptive, and tried to persuade potential buyers by enumerating the mobile phone's advantages in everyday life. As we have seen, when a technological innovation appears on the market, the first purchasers often initially use rational arguments to justify the financial investment required. Unsurprisingly, advertising also used rational arguments.

At the time, the object was beginning to be promoted from the point of view of the connectivity it made possible. For example, grouped together under the general slogan "Connecting People," three Nokia ads painted the portraits of Ralf, Cathy, and Mark by first conveying their busy schedules and then introducing the mobile as a good solution:[4] "Because, you see, Ralf has a Nokia cell phone. Wherever he is, he's always in contact, and his clients can always get in touch with him." The texts were explanatory and descriptive and accompanied by photos showing the three happy mobile phone owners in various situations: at the office, fishing, golfing, at the cottage. It is understandable that at that time when the degree of penetration was relatively low, it was acquisition of the object in itself that had to be justified and promoted. The campaign attempted to demonstrate new possibilities opened up by the mobile phone. In fact, what was being suggested was an extension of the office through the ability to remain connected to one's work even during leisure. The user portrayed was a conscientious employee who always had work on his or her mind.

These examples show that long before the late 1990s, advertising generally evoked *conviction-persuasion* or *projection-identification* arguments (Riou 2002, 3). While advertising arguments are more varied today, it is clear that these older forms of advertising discourse have not totally disappeared. Indeed, in some student newspapers ads, reference is made to by-gone times to indicate a new era when mobile phones are no longer dreams. Mobile phones are accessible to all, even to young people. The goal is to establish a form of behaviour as a standard so that it will spread. This is why the object is portrayed as desirable and expected, but also made standard and banal by the demonstration that today there is no longer any reason to deprive oneself of one.

Rogers AT&T print ad, summer 2003

The drop in price is often invoked to justify the mobile phone's new accessibility. Conscious of young people's limited financial resources, telecommunications companies have adapted their services to young people's budgets. Calling a mobile communications offer a *"forfait midi et après l'école"*[5] ("noon-hour and after-school plan") leaves no doubt as to the market targeted; the company is adjusting its service offer to the adolescent lifestyle, which is structured by the school timetable.

Business uses, which are already well integrated into everyday uses, are now mentioned less frequently in advertising. In contrast, the rationality of the mobile phone's practical advantages is much more present. A recent Rogers AT&T magazine ad in Quebec shows a mobile in a purse with the text *"Qui a dit qu'il n'y a rien d'utile dans un sac à main?"* ("Who said there was nothing useful in a purse?"), followed by the list: "text messaging, answering machine, address book, voice dialling." The technical possibilities listed all refer to useful aspects of the mobile phone, promoting it for its functional convenience. The need for mobile phones is also highlighted by their classification among ordinary objects normally found in a woman's purse. A purse accompanies its owner everywhere; its contents are always within easy reach and become, by association, "essential."

The second form of classical advertising discourse noted above, namely projection-identification, associates the product with a typical image. Most often this involves linking a product with an idea, opinion, or image generally shared by the targeted social group. In this case the advertising strategy simply mobilizes the cultural references usually used to understand and structure our surroundings. However, in some cases, advertising employs stereotypes reducing people to general characteristics while exaggerating and simplifying essential features, almost to the point of creating caricatures.

Using projection-identification, some ads involve idealized "typical" young people and gamble that identification will occur. By using a number of registers, such as dress, hairstyle, gestures, ways of speaking, tastes, music, and favourite activities, advertising discourses act as mirrors. But do they reflect the right image?

4.2 Type and Stereotype

In 2003 Rogers AT&T broadcast two television ads portraying adolescents. In the first, a young man was waiting for the bus, mobile in hand, listening to music thanks to the integrated MP3 player. In the second, an adolescent ran down the stairs into the basement, jumped on the couch, grabbed a slice of pizza, and started watching television, all the while sending a text message to a friend. Obviously these scenarios were not completely disconnected from reality, but they were limited to clichés circulating about young people and their lifestyles, stereotypes that simplified the features of young people's culture.

We asked adolescents what they thought about one of these ads. Their reaction was lukewarm, though they were unable to explain exactly why. Myriam said, "There's no originality, I think it's too ... it's too ... there isn't something ... it's banal." Advertising's attempts to "look young" sometimes fail. Young people are sensitive to imposture and quick to detect caricature. Thus, it is not sufficient to design an ad around colourful expressions and a few notes of dynamic music for young people to see themselves in the representation of their culture. While not necessarily saying that the two Rogers AT&T ads entirely missed their target, we can still note the difference between this type of advertising discourse and more recent ones (discussed below). This is owing to the fact that these first involved scenarios of adolescent culture as seen mostly by adults.

Advertisers are now spending more time studying how young people define themselves. They have learned to distrust adult ideas about adolescents and no longer hesitate to leave their offices and go out into the street to gather first-hand information on these cultures. They prefer to rely on such observations in a natural environment rather than on limiting themselves solely to the traditional method of discussion groups resulting in statements that are sometimes poorly interpreted or excessively directed. Marketing has adopted many approaches used in anthropology and communication sciences; ethnographic research is now popular. Advertising agencies are developing different approaches such as lending adolescents cameras and allowing them to photograph anything they want. By examining the pictures, they hope to be able to identify features specific to young people's culture. This quest for authenticity, which is a growing concern for advertisers, involves young people in construction of the discourses that will be addressed to them.

Thus, when we asked young people which mobile phone ad they thought addressed them most specifically, they spontaneously identified a more recent Rogers AT&T television ad involving three young skateboarders. Brigitte describes it: "The one with the camera and the guy who comes out of his house and jumped on his ramp, it was like he was snowboarding, you know, it's mostly young people who do that."

These ads involve young people addressing young people. They engage in activities designed to show the virtues of the new "total phone." Each ad is organized in the same way: it begins with one of the three young people addressing the camera with a sentence like "Today we are going to show you that ..." and ends with "There's the proof, the total phone is ..." The group is called the "urban squad," as if it has been given a mission. Is it to prove that cell phones are for young people? No doubt, for, from their experiences they draw conclusions such as "it's easy to subscribe to absolute wireless," or "Now we know who the total phone is talking to," or "The total phone fits my lifestyle." The humorous, slightly cynical tone of their statements should be noted because humour is a linguistic practice highly prized by young people. We will come back to this in the next section.

Moreover, these ads are deliberately designed and executed to look amateur and thus more authentic. The camera is unstable, editing jerky, shots lopsided, sound muted, as if to suggest that the young people themselves made them. These techniques are similar to those used by television channels that directly target young people, such as Musique Plus, Much Music, and MTV. The same garage-style music is in each of the ads, clearly intended to appeal to young people's tastes. Says Marie-Pierre, "Well, I'd say it was young people who were presenting the mobile phone, who we can associate ourselves with. Then there's also the music that goes with it. Anyway, the mobile phone aspect is interesting. And the little funny side to attract us a little more."

The complicity uniting the three characters in these ads portrays friendship as a basic value, and the activities in which they engage are not unlike "hanging around," adolescents' characteristic manner of occupying public space (Danesi 1994; Ohl 2001). The scenes take place in urban environments where young people are likely to be found: an alleyway with walls covered in graffiti, a park, a corner store, a laundromat, a party in an apartment. During a viewing of one of these ads, the adolescents interviewed immediately compared it with the other Rogers AT&T ad they had been shown:

MYRIAM: I think it's more dynamic.
JEAN-MARC: Instead of the fatso who's eating on the couch ...
MYRIAM: Yeah!

Their comments show that care has to be taken when portraying the audience one is addressing. Young people found it almost offensive to be seen as "lazybones lying on a couch eating pizza." They denounced the exaggerated stereotype of laziness presented as a cultural feature distinctive of adolescents.[6]

4.3 Kitsch and Discriminatory Humour

Advertising agencies do not limit themselves to typical or stereotypical images to attract the attention of young people. They also use other layers of discourse that refer us to their specific world in a more general manner. A Bell Mobility advertising campaign in Quebec employed a caricature of a gauche, out-of-fashion, thirty-year-old disc jockey named Disco Dan. It was certainly not targeting adolescents by offering them an image of themselves. How did this ad speak to them? Beyond initial impressions, there was a strategy that involved attracting adolescents by using one of their distinctive practices: discriminatory humour.[7] By presenting a laughable character, Bell was allying itself with young people. It was playing the card of exclusion, a form of behaviour utterly characteristic of adolescent culture, as a means of bringing people together. Indeed, young people are very prone to social categorization, using it to situate themselves and structure their world. Use of such stereotypes strengthens the group's internal cohesion by opposing it to a caricature of what is different.

The advertising portrays itself as an agent sharing adolescents' codes and so must demonstrate mastery of the same form of discourse they use. In this case, stereotypes are not being constructed of young people, but a second, much more subtle level is being reached, in which the advertising uses young people's own methods of stereotyping. This strategy is one increasingly employed by advertisers. Brands now have various relations with consumers at different levels that go beyond the older advertising approaches mentioned above. Today advertising often uses collusion. According to some, media culture is replacing classical culture as a system of shared references (Riou 2002). In the Disco Dan example, the anchoring is socio-cultural. The character is constructed around signs culturally recognized as indicators of unfashionability, such as his hairstyle, choice of words, clothes, gestures, facial expressions, and taste in music. A set of codes is used to portray a laughable character. While a social position is parodied in this case, the relation of collusion can take various forms: kitsch (an unfashionable style that is considered attractive when employed at the second level), "no bullshit" (playing the frankness card), mockery (ironic quotation), and recycling (gaucherie not necessarily involving imitation) (ibid.).

Bell Mobility exploits the new advertising registers skilfully. After Disco Dan, another Bell campaign[8] used images of the "good old days" to humorous effect by contrasting a traditional lifestyle with sophisticated technology. The absurdity of such anachronism seems to particularly appeal to young people. This social group generally appreciates absurdity as well as discriminatory humour. While the young people questioned said they did not feel directly targeted by this campaign, they broke out laughing when they watched the ads, a sign that a relationship was nonetheless established. To provoke laughter is to produce an effect on the audience;

Juste
pas de limite

Obtenez
3 mois d'appels
locaux illimités
et 3 mois gratuits
d'Internet mobile.

Mobilité

Solo

Bell Canada print ad,
summer 2003

laughter is confirmation that an agreement has been established between the locutor (in this case, the telecommunications company) and the allocutor (young people). The agreement is based on the humour of the scenario.

As with Disco Dan, the locutor uses parody, this time in the form of mockery by employing an artistic genre that is especially popular in Quebec – television series set in the old days in the countryside, such as the film *Séraphin, un homme et son péché*, which was a huge success among francophones. In mockery, aspects of a style are reproduced and deformed for a humorous effect; this is exactly what was done. Using mockery, the relation between the ad and the audience is established at the level of play. Perhaps young people feel attracted by the ridiculousness of that old-fashioned world, and this results in collusion.

Bell Canada print ad, fall 2003

However, the communication strategy is even more sophisticated, for it also involves showing that the technology is no longer a prohibitively expensive luxury or so complicated that only those with know-how can use it, because even the ridiculous characters in the ads integrate it into their daily lives. In this respect, it is interesting to note that at that time Bell and Telus both had general slogans playing on the idea of simplicity: "Making it simple" and "The future is friendly." *What* is simple? Were they talking about a technological future accessible to all? This hypothesis was suggested by Nicolas, one of the adolescents to whom we showed the "good old days" ad: "It's more like an ad for adults, you know, fuddy-duddy, it's more for an old person. It says everyone can have a mobile phone, you know, like people of a certain age, an advanced age, can have a mobile phone, not just young people."

Advertisers have thus skilfully reversed the situation. Before, mobile phones were meant mainly for businesspeople and could perhaps in some circumstances be useful to young people. Now, the opposite is being suggested, for the technology is being promoted to people "of a certain age." Young people thus see mobile phones as objects designed for them. Here, we should note that current mobile phone ads in fact are targeting increasingly younger audiences. In the trade it is well known that filming fifteen- or sixteen-year olds will inevitably attract twelve- and thirteen-year olds who are impatient to be taken seriously.

4.4 Talk Young, Talk Ads

Given that advertising can add new expressions to everyday language, we must acknowledge its potential for linguistic creation. Conversely, expressions used in advertising are often drawn directly out of young people's culture. The words used to construct ads and the way they are pronounced and written also deserve special attention. For example, young people are more likely than their elders to use informal terms. Advertising that speaks to young people in the same way that they talk among themselves thus directly invades their world, and can by that very fact add to it.

Despite its relative internal uniformity with respect to other social groups, young people's language nonetheless varies from one small group to the next (Danesi 1994). It is a means in itself of establishing links and integrating into a group by sharing specific communicational codes. This can be seen in particular by observing the language used in text messages sent by mobile phone.[9] Creators of advertising campaigns immediately grasped the expressive potential of this concise new language, consistent with the speech efficiency of advertising communication.

A good illustration of the diversity of text messaging codes and their role in coding identity can be seen in an ad that posits a competition in which participants have to decipher a text message sent by one of the characters.[10] The sending of a "mystery" message that is incomprehensible to the uninitiated clearly reveals the identity-creating and exclusive function of this kind of language. Mobile phone companies even use this kind of social behaviour by claiming to "teach" it to potential users. For example, the Rogers AT&T Internet site[11] publishes a "translation" table of "TXT styles," and Bell Mobility provides a list of a number of "text to talk" codes.

Advertising images also show mobile phone screens displaying messages such as "IC" ("I see"), "CYA" ("see ya"), "CY@" (see you at"), and "BHL8" ("be home late"). By employing this special language to talk about the technology, advertising helps to make it official and to naturalize it.

4.5 And Elsewhere

Some expressions pertaining to mobile phones and their use have acquired a relative stability in social languages. The variation between the expressions used in different countries is a cultural indicator of the diversity of relationships to the object. In Canada and the United States, the terms "cell phone," mobile, and "téléphone cellulaire" are the most widespread, the first two terms referring to the device's initial technology. Other cultures use expressions referring to its portability: in France, "portable," in England, "mobile," in Spain, "el movile," and in Japan, "keitai" ("portable"). The Finnish have adopted "kanny," which comes from a brand name but also refers to an extension of the hand. In more or less the same sense, the Germans call it a "handy" and the Chinese a "sho ji" ("hand machine") (Plant 2000).

Vodafone print ads, 2002

A study of mobile phone advertising in other countries reveals how the discourse varies with the culture that inspires and conveys it. First, the state of the market is a factor that has to be taken into consideration. It is particularly interesting to compare two countries with very different levels of mobile-phone use, such as Italy (high use) and Canada (lower).[12] In both sets of discourse, we find similar statements that emerge in a trans-contextual fashion, but also dissimilar statements.

We found that discourse using typical representations was much more common in Italy. Many Italian mobile phone ads portray young people, whereas in Canada advertisers prefer the use of animals. In the Italian ads, young people appear in groups, having fun together. While no cell phones are visible, their presence is implicit in the scenes, which suggests that they can easily be integrated into the group dynamics specific to young people. (In a later section, we will see examples of Canadian ads that also highlight the community aspect created around mobile phone use by young people.)

The two Vodafone ads also employ typical images, but instead evoke an intimate relationship. Once again, the mobile is absent. The interpersonal relationship is either illustrated by a face-to-face situation or represented

Vodafone print ads, 2002

through another medium in some way symbolizing the connection that the mobile creates. Thus, to promote an object, the advertiser chooses not to show it but to highlight the emotional and relational involvement it makes possible. The mobile phone may thus be seen as a way for friends to trade secrets, or for a couple to maintain their relationship.

4.6 Communicating at Any Price and All Cost

Canadian advertising discourses also refer to relational aspects, but the ads we studied more often used metaphors and analogies than typical representations. A dog gazes sadly at the photo of his beloved while languid music plays *"Je m'ennuie de toi, oh ma chérie ..."*[13] By telling the story of two lovers separated by distance, but who, thanks to their long-distance plan, can finally talk, the advertising portrays the mobile phone as a link. The company is offering to maintain the link for the buyer. Given the fundamental importance to young people of group membership and communication with peers, it seems likely that highlighting the social link will be received favourably by that target group.

The well-known slogan that Telus uses in French, *"Il faut qu'on se parle"* ("We've got to talk"),[14] is a good illustration of the feeling of an urgent need to communicate among young people. The image accompanying the slogan shows two lizards, face to face. As in the Italian ads discussed above, the mobile is completely absent from the discourse. In fact, one might think the ad was for communication in itself. Note that in such cases, communication, by becoming the object of communication itself, is part of the construction of general rhetoric on communication (Semprini 1996). Social discourse constructs an "ideology of communication" understood as a value and end in itself.

In contrast, in English, the same ad showing the lizards has the slogan "Talk their ears off with four months of unlimited local calls" – an allusion to the fact that young people talk a lot.

Still in the name of this same importance of communication, ads suggest that one send a photograph instead of a message in order to communicate better: *"Tu veux ma photo? Dites-le presto avec une photo,"*[15] and "Shy? Cool camera phones say it instantly." This time the same image sends a similar message in French and English. And of course, the importance of communication becomes a promotional argument for video phones, a new innovation in mobile communications. Communication is given such a high value in advertising discourse that there seems to be no valid reason

Il faut qu'on se parle.

Obtenez jusqu'à 4 mois d'appels locaux illimités.*

Talk their ears off with 4 months of unlimited local calling.

Tu veux ma photo ?

Shy?

Cool camera phones say it·instantly.

Telus print ads, fall 2003

not to enter into a relationship. Speak, write, send a photo, communicate! Communication is portrayed as essential and, above all, easy, thanks to all the new means available. Advertising thus exploits for commercial ends the importance of communicating, which has become a socially shared value. It presents this value on the first level, knowing that the audience will associate it with the mobile phone's capacities. Acquiring the technology makes it possible to get closer to achieving an ideal in young people's worlds, especially when we know that they view the reception of a message or call as confirmation of membership in a group (Ling and Yttri 2002).

4.7 All Included, Even Friends?

Young people use new technologies in conformity with a specific technological culture, in which shared practices create a community (Caron and Caronia 2001). The mobile phone fits in perfectly. Advertising therefore bases its approach on the competencies that constitute these communities of practices. In Italy, where the market has attained a degree of maturity, mobile phone ownership is widespread, as is the sharing of general practices that regulate its use. Sub-groups based on more specific practices are now emerging. A television ad shows fashionable young Italians having fun at a party by sending photos with their mobile phones.[16] The ad ends with the slogan "*E tu?*" ("And you?"), which directly addresses the viewer by suggesting the possibility of being included in the group. How? By subscribing to the new services offered by the mobile phone company, in this case, photo messaging.

In advertising discourse, we also find references to more traditional communities such as the family and classmates. For example, free calls are offered among members of the same family[17] or among students at the same college or university.[18] Advertising may also simply evoke family mobile phone use, for the importance of this practice often emerges in user discourse, and advertising designers sometimes exploit it effectively. While even a few years ago the first mobile phones were often introduced into the family environment by a parent, who generally reserved the device for work or emergencies, today they are passed from one person to the next. When adolescents go out at night, if they don't have their own, parents may lend theirs for safety. Some companies have noticed this and offer new subscribers a second mobile for free. For example, the "FamilyShare" plan is promoted with the slogan "Imagine sharing minutes, not your phone."[19]

Companies also try to create brand-based communities of users through offers that, for example, make it possible to communicate for free with subscribers to the same phone company. In such cases, the user belongs to the Fido, Rogers, or Telus community, and his or her friends are encouraged to do likewise in order to save money. Thus, a community is created artificially, based on a marketing ploy. Could we go from this to establishing a link with faithfulness to a commercial brand as a distinctive sign of young people's culture? A Fido television ad is based on this idea, and shows a young man physically followed by his community. A French-language ad began: "Désormais les appels entre abonnés Fido sont gratuits. Y a-t-il une meilleure façon de rester près de vos proches?" ("Now calls between Fido subscribers are free. Is there any better way to stay close to your friends?").[20]

As the slogans in the following two examples show, ads draw their discourse directly from the community dynamic: "Qui se ressemble s'assemble. Voici le nouveau forfait Telus à Telus" ("Those who are alike stick together. Here's the new Telus-to-Telus plan").[21]

Telus print ad, fall 2003

Fido print ads, fall 2003

The territorial limits of the community exclude competitors' subscribers, and internal cohesion is strengthened through insistence on members' similarity and the links uniting them: the mobile and related practices. In the previous ad the mirror effect of the two people facing each other evokes and reinforces the idea of resemblance among members of a community. In the second, "The Fido to Fido package. Regrettably only from Fido,"[22] the dogs stay together while the sheep in the foreground is outside of the group. The distance is illustrated not only by the position of the subject in space but also by its characteristics, since it is alone and belongs to another species considered less noble and intelligent.

4.8 Differences in Similarity

In parallel with advertising strategies designed to give young people the impression they could be included in a community of peers, other discourses opt to promote difference. The tension between conformity and differentiation is common in adolescent practices. Indeed, there is nothing surprising in wanting to be part of a group but at the same time to stand out within it. Advertising discourses support and feed such relational dynamics. Promotional offers that make it possible to personalize one's mobile phone by downloading different rings, buying covers in different colours and patterns, and acquiring new services are all going in the same direction. To personalize one's mobile phone is to stand out in the group, to add value to basic membership. The personalized mobile is a means of expressing its owner's distinctive style in everyday life, just like jewellery or clothing.

In Europe, Siemens is already promoting "Xelibri" telephone accessories: "For us, style is essential. We make fashion accessories that are beautiful, portable, and also let you make phone calls!" Every six months, Siemens launches a new collection of four phones, in imitation of the world of fashion. In exploiting the commercial system of fashion, which creates periodic new consumer demand and thus increases sales, the company tries to go further than simply making it possible to personalize the devices using covers and different rings. The mobile has become much more than a portable communications tool. It has to be considered a ver-

Vodafone print
ad, 2003

Siemens Internet ads, fall-winter, 2003

itable extension of the body, and thus able to express its owner's individuality in a play of identity between conformity and differentiation.

The mobile's new status as an object of value, and thus as a means of increasing its user's social standing, can be seen in other advertising strategies, such as those around Christmas. At this time the mobile becomes a significant gift. Attributing the function of gift to the techno-object automatically makes it a desirable object, and consequently an object of value.

An ad that portrays the mobile as a cool gift usually targets young people, since being cool is an attitude held in esteem in adolescent culture in general, though it takes different forms depending on the group and period (Danesi 1994). With the slogan *"Dire qu'à ce prix-là vous auriez pu recevoir un télé phone cool"* in French, and "Hurry, 'Get What You Really Wanted Week' ends December 31st" in English, we see a character disappointed

Rogers AT&T print ads, fall 2003

Telus print ads, fall 2003

by a Christmas present. The ad thus addresses several types of people concerned by shopping for presents for loved ones: gift receivers and givers, in particular parent-child pairs.

In its Christmas advertising campaigns in Quebec, Rogers uses another dimension of the concept of gift and counter-gift. The ads portray the mobile as an object as pleasant to give as it is to receive. One of the ads addresses the person giving the mobile phone (*"Donnez pour ... les fêtes"*), another, the person who receives it (*"Recevez du ... Père Noël"*), and the third ties them together by encouraging the consumer to play both roles (*"Cadeau ... à moi de moi"*)!

4.9 Mobile for Every Situation

Today mobile phone advertising campaigns are at a crossroads of interdiscursivity because the discourses circulating about them are so numerous – on television and radio shows, in films, in the press, on Web sites, chats and forums, and so on. The mobile phone is becoming more and more a part of life and, consequently, it is increasingly visible in media content. As it really becomes part of our everyday habits, we even see a strong mobile phone presence in advertising that is in no way intended to promote it. For example, a supermarket chain[23] ran an ad in which a well-known comic was doing his shopping while talking to his girlfriend on his mobile phone. The mobile was shown as an object integrated into the everyday routine, allowing people to do several things at once. Other similar examples can be seen in television ads, one showing a woman going home with her arms full of bags and her mobile to her ear,[24] another showing a child using a mobile phone to call his mother from school and comment to her on the contents of his lunch.[25]

The mobile phone's increasingly frequent appearance on the screen shows its established presence in everyday life. While smoking in public is becoming marginal, using a mobile phone is becoming less and less so. Are we trading cigarette smoke pollution for noise pollution?

A beer ad[26] shows a young woman on a date displaying a series of inappropriate forms of behaviour, such as picking her teeth at the table. The punchline, according to the ad, is to see her rudely take her companion's beer. However, what is interesting to us is the woman's second inappropriate action, which is to talk on her mobile phone from the beginning to the end of the narrative, abandoning her date by putting herself in a state of "absent presence" (Gergen 2002). Thus, the mobile is portrayed as responsible for a form of behaviour considered socially unacceptable in a romantic situation.

A number of ads now use social codes of mobile phone use to evoke a person who lacks manners or respect for others. They are evidence of the prescriptive social nature acquired by the mobile phone and its uses. Young people develop their own codes in this respect in conformity with their culture. Advertising acts upon the redefinition of this way of living together with the mobile phone by suggesting some discourses that approve and others that disapprove. It standardizes some forms of behaviour and criticizes others. New technologies, because they are new, are conducive to negotiations of meaning and etiquette proposed by public discourses.

Advertising discourses intended to sell a technological object cannot be summarized as rational arguments. They also convey propositions about lifestyles, prescriptions, values, and codes of use that define the fact of "owning a mobile phone," but above all define what it is "to be young with a mobile phone." It seems there is a large degree of imagination associated with this idea and that young people's technological culture is constructed through all the social discourses that crisscross daily. Such uses also enable young people to construct specific identities and cultures. In the next chapter, we delve into the linguistic world of young people to see their discourse's role in constructing their culture.

Chapter 5

Language, Interaction, and Mobile Culture:
Field Research among Teenagers

After their creation and circulation in social spaces as topics of advertis-ing discourse, technologies come into contact with innovators and early adopters (Rogers 1983). But only when they are adopted by an early majority do they really enter into the diffusion process and *virtually* become instruments for constructing everyday culture. Yet their transfor-mation into culture-making devices can not be taken for granted or seen as totally predictable, insofar as it does not depend only on the character-istics of the innovation. It is commonly accepted that users make the dif-ference in the ways that technologies shape and are shaped by culture and social practices.

If we want to grasp how technologies enter into social life and become tools for constructing everyday culture, we need to explore in detail the process of cultural domestication of technologies by users. But who are users? "User" is an operational definition, an activity-oriented sociologi-cal category that identifies only one aspect of the individual's identity. Whatever "being a user" means, it needs to be fully articulated with other social and cultural dimensions of personal identity and with the situated nature of human action.

Those whom by convention we call "users" are in fact embodied indi-viduals, situated actors who belong to different communities and refer to various specific cultures. Rather than reflecting on the relation between "users and technologies," we should therefore rethink the process in terms of an encounter between a technology and a *community of users*. This notion underscores the fact that technologies are adopted by situated actors and enter into an already existing network of social practices and culturally shaped ways of life.

How does the adoption and use of a technology interweave with social practices, forms of interaction, and ways of life specific to a given community? How do individuals incorporate a technology into their specific culture? In order to understand the process of cultural incorporation and grasp the nuances of the everyday practical accomplishment of such a process, we need to leave the realm of general statements, large-scale descriptions, and ideal-typical categories of people. We have to focus instead on particular uses of technologies among members of a specific community.

For reasons that will become clear, we decided to explore a specific community of users, namely urban adolescents, and their special relationship with mobile phones.

5.1 New Rites of Passage: Technology Ownership as Symbolic Threshold

It has long been acknowledged that an individual's passage from one phase of life to the next, particularly into adulthood, is an eminently social phenomenon. Even those who would like to describe the growing-up process solely in terms of physiological transformations and changing biological functions acknowledge that "no longer being a child," "being an adolescent," and "becoming adult" are culturally marked stages. Literature on this issue is full of examples of the many ways different societies construct different stages in the life cycle by creating specific symbolic steps or denying any relevance to otherwise noticeable biological changes. As for any socially constructed phenomenon, life stages exist or do not exist depending on words to name them and on ways to symbolically mark their boundaries.

In contemporary industrial societies, the word "adolescence" is still part of everyday language, and the corresponding period of life is a common-sense category. Nevertheless, it is generally accepted that the symbolic thresholds delimiting its beginning and end have become vague. It has become a popular leitmotif that late modernity no longer employs rites of passage to symbolically mark the loss of child status and entry into adulthood. Yet this is not the case. Contemporary western societies have their own cultural rites of passage that mark the various stages in an individual's life. Even if these initiation rituals do not take the form of public ceremonies, they still occur as private rites. The growing-up process is segmented on the micro-order of everyday life in which a plethora of events and practices symbolically mark the time when childhood is left behind and adulthood begins. Initiation rituals no longer need to occur on the collective, public stage. Transformed into small, repeated, even predictable common events, contemporary rites accomplish the same old function of creating the stages of life in new ways.

It seems undeniable that getting a driver's licence is a rite of passage. Is not piercing various body parts a way of claiming the autonomy of what Merleau Ponty called "one's own body" (*le corps propre*, Merleau Ponty 1945) and removing it from parental control? If parental governance of the child's body is one of the defining characteristics of childhood, then claiming the right to manipulate one's body and inscribe on it signs of one's own culture are symbolic ways of stating the end of childhood.

Sociological analysis of fashion and clothing stresses the expressive value of the choice of clothing and its role in creating social identities (Davis 1992). In and through their ways of dressing, teenagers construct both their resemblance with peers and difference from adults. However, the rules governing teenagers' dress are the result of a previous and highly symbolical identity-making process. Children claiming their freedom to choose their own clothing and, conversely, parents allowing their children to wear what they want, are symbolic thresholds that mark the loss of child status and the passage into another stage of life.

In contemporary information and communication society, communication technologies too play this traditional identity-building role. Some social uses of these objects make them work as ritual markers of the end of childhood. While economic factors should not be underestimated, access to information and communication technologies marks the passage from childhood to adolescence. As soon as one obtains one's own phone or computer, something has changed. Freedom to manage information and communication tools and privatization of their use say that a child is no longer a child.

In Italy in 2005, 28 per cent of ten-year-old children had a mobile phone. By age thirteen, 68 per cent had one.[1] Besides its usefulness in mutual coordination of children and parents and its claimed use as a security/safety/control device (Rakow and Navaro 1993, Ling and Yttri 2002, Caronia and Caron 2004), the mobile phone's entrance into children's lives has a strong symbolic function. It signals the age at which Italian culture situates the beginning of adolescence. It is not by chance that the mobile enters children's life through one of the most symbolic social exchanges: the gift.[2] Typically, children receive a mobile phone from their parents as a present at a highly symbolic point in their lives: for their tenth birthday or at the end of elementary school.

In addition to the social dynamics unleashed by the gift-giving-receiving exchange,[3] giving a mobile phone as a present at these ritualized "completion points" has a strong identity-making function. Those who receive such gifts are defined as "no longer children." As a matter of fact and aside from any biological definition, psychological classification, or legal convention, in Italy children begin to define themselves and be defined as adolescents at the age of ten or eleven. At this point most of them personally own a mobile phone for the first time, and they are no longer infants.

While the personal ownership of such technologies performs the functions of a rite of passage, *uses* of such objects also work as identity-making devices. Like taste in fashion and music, ways of walking and styles of using bikes or scooters, typical ways of communicating with technologies enter the repertoire of signs through which adolescents express and construct themselves as such. Fashion, styles, possession of information and communication technologies: the consumer society offers a range of goods that can be used to accomplish this otherwise ancient symbolic function (Douglas and Isherwood 1979, Ohl 2001), but there is a substantial reason that makes communication technologies powerful identity-making objects, at least for young people. Communication technologies are, first, tools for verbal interaction, and it is a matter of fact that language, interaction, and verbal performances are the most powerful semiotic practices in and through which adolescents construct their identities, their specific culture, and the boundaries of communities of peers.

Our hypothesis is that the inherent link among contemporary communication technologies, verbal interaction, and language performances is at the core of the extraordinary and partially unexpected spread of such technologies among young people. To gain a better understanding of the many links between situated uses of technologies, language practices, and the very specific accomplishment of "becoming an adolescent," we must first delve into young people's world of language.

5.2 Linguistic Creativity and Cultural Innovation

To be an adolescent is to become one: to cross thresholds, overcome differences, and produce variations that make it possible to define oneself. Adolescence means constructing a specific social identity that distinguishes one from the age group that one is supposed to have left and enables one to integrate and gain recognition in a new group.

Language plays a decisive role in this process (Labov 1972a, Cheshire 1987, Eble 1996, Eckert 1988, Andersen 2001). In many societies adolescents have their own specific language. Often referred to as "slang," it is made up of neologisms and peculiar lexical choices and is characterized mainly by specific ways of speaking and forms of oral discourse that differ from adult registers.

What are the issues underlying the phonetic, pragmatic, and lexical variations of young people's ways of speaking? Literature on young people's language practices consistently highlights three strictly related identity-making functions: constructing a difference with respect to parents' culture and life-style; affirming young people's peer group membership; and confirming the social cohesion of such a community (Andersen 2001).

Groups of adolescents distinguish one another by referring to the way the "others" speak. For example, adolescents from downtown may denigrate those from the suburbs and vice versa. Overall, however, the differences between their language and that of adults are far greater than those between groups of the same age. Of course, level of education and social and cultural background play a role in variations among different groups of adolescents. Nevertheless, there are significant recurrent patterns in the ways they construct specific ways of speaking.[4]

On a *lexical level*, adolescents incessantly create and use slang, employ surprising onomatopoeias, and constantly expand their repertoire of swear words, insults (Labov 1972b), and curses. On a *paralinguistic level*, they often adopt non-standard pronunciation and show great talent in using language expressively to strongly convey personal stances towards what they say, to express value judgments and enthusiasm, and to endorse ideas ("high-involvement style," Andersen 2001). In one way or another, adolescents always seem to be strongly committed to what they say. Style – *how* one talks – is more significant than *what* is being talked about.

The *social organization* of their verbal interactions is also striking. Adolescents' conversations seem to be governed by a principle of urgency, ensuring the survival of the fittest (ibid.), which entails success in taking or maintaining a turn in a conversation. Speed is a basic rule of their verbal interactions and oral performances: young people speak considerably faster than adults, and their statements are generally shorter.

Storytelling, gossip, and parody are among the most significant verbal performances in adolescents' language world. Adolescents' conversations are often characterized by enthusiastic narrations of stories. Anecdotes in their conversational storytelling are structured through reported speech giving rise to script-format narratives. Nothing is more striking than how young people embed past verbal exchanges in their actual ongoing conversation, as shown by this extract from a mobile phone conversation: "Then I said to him like 'Well, if you want,' then he says 'You want me to ask him tomorrow?' and then he says, 'Well, if you want,' then I say, 'You want to?' then he asks it again, he asks the same thing four times."

This narrative construction, based on a succession of interlocking parts of the sort "I said to him, then he said – I said," is also at the core of one the most typical of young people's language games: *gossip*. Besides its role in creating social structure in teenagers' groups (Goodwin 1990),[5] this narrative format is a distinctive form of adolescents' talk. Another typical verbal performance among teenagers is parody, particularly *parody of other people's ways of speaking*. By caricaturing teachers, parents, girls, boys, teenagers from the suburbs, teenagers from downtown, and so on, adolescents order their social world, construct social groups and categories, define differences, similarities and social membership. Parody reveals adolescents' deep commitment on language issues: ways of speaking are not only used but also perceived as strong *membership categorization devices* (Sacks 1972).

Linguistic manipulation of other people's language is a cue signalling that adolescents are quite aware of the meanings of the variations they introduce and often play with very skilfully (Andersen 2001, Cheshire 1987). Contrary to the common rhetoric used to describe young people's linguistic carelessness, their linguistic variations do not reveal laziness or indifference towards language at all. Rather, they show teenagers' metalinguistic competence and the enormous importance they place on linguistic practices. Adolescents' *strategic carelessness* towards standard language is a meaningful verbal performance in which the stakes are primary social. By constructing linguistic differences in relation to adults and inventing specific ways of speaking through the use of slang, vulgarity, and special ways of pronouncing words, adolescents free themselves from their parents and create their own signs of social membership. Simply put, they accomplish the work of "being an adolescent."

Do these linguistic alterations play a role in the evolution of the language? The identity-creating function of such variations entails that most are temporary. They are abandoned by adolescents themselves as they get older. It is difficult to imagine adults who would start speaking like their children or who still speak as they did when they were in their teens. The ridicule that they would suffer (especially from adolescents) confirms the social meaning of such uses of language. When adults speak like teenagers, they are not using language in a degenerate way but trying to portray themselves as young through a conscious linguistic regression.

Yet though they may be tempered over time, it is clear that the lexical, phonetic, and syntactic changes specific to adolescents contribute to the evolution of the language. Some innovations are adopted by other social actors in other linguistic domains (advertising copywriters, for example) and begin to circulate outside their original contexts of use. As they cross the boundaries of young people's oral performances, they lose their identity-making function and increasingly become standardized, commonly accepted forms of talk. In this respect, groups of adolescents are undeniably linguistic innovators and play a central role in the evolution of all natural languages.

5.3 Teenagers' Mobile Culture: The Shaping Role of Everyday Discourse

Young people's linguistic practices are thus powerful tools in the construction of their identities. Let us look now at how communications technologies are related to this process of culture and identity construction. At risk of extreme simplification, we will highlight three hypothetical links:

1. Linguistic practices and uses of new communication technologies are both socio-symbolic tools. Like language styles, possession of technologies and ways of using them indicate membership in a group.
2. New communication technologies amplify and even create new forms of interaction and social participation. They broaden the range of communicative events, social encounters, and everyday verbal exchanges. Thus they provide new semiotic tools and social scenarios for constructing and displaying culture and identity through language and interaction.
3. New communications technologies are not only instruments of exchange and activity coordination but also *topics of discourse*. Young people use them to communicate with one another but they also speak *about* them. As long as technologies become topics of teenagers' everyday conversations, they are domesticated according to adolescents' specific economy of meaning.

The last point may require explanation, for the issues at stake are not obvious. As Ochs pointed out, "Language use is a major if not the major tool for conveying sociocultural knowledge and a powerful medium of socialization" (1986, 3). Indeed, it is mainly through participation in language-mediated interactions that children become culturally competent members of their social community. What we think, believe, and know, how we do things, our representations of ourselves and the world around us – cultural meanings and values, local theories of world – are first and foremost products of everyday linguistic interactions. It is through the banal fact that we *speak* about the world, people, activities, and events that we construct and share cultural versions of them (Bruner 1986).

Socialization through language concerns not only children and early learning: it is in fact a life-long process (Ochs 1988) and concerns almost all aspects of everyday life that become objects of discursive reference.

According to such an approach, teenagers' mobile culture is embedded in everyday activities and practices, and it is a result of the social interactions and discourses that surround and accompany the use of communication technologies themselves. Adolescents' mobile culture is more then a matter of ownership, access, and use. It is also a system of shared ideas, knowledge, and local theories about these tools as well as ways of using them, which teenagers construct through their discourses about the technologies.

By talking *about* new communication technologies, teenagers give them relevance inside their specific culture, legitimate patterns of use, and cultural versions of their functions. Thus they establish and share ways of thinking about what technologies are, what they are not, what they should or should not to be, and why. In short, adolescents' everyday technology-mediated language practices *and* discourses about technologies are sociocultural means for both integrating those technologies into their own culture and constructing their culture as a "mobile" one.

5.4 Making the Familiar Strange: A Chronology of Field Research

The astonishing number of studies on youth and mobile communication appearing in the last few years[6] is a major indication of a growing social phenomenon: the pervasive use of mobile communication devices among young people and the naturalization of technology-mediated communication as an everyday, quasi-natural practice. Aside from the academic interest in such an issue, we need only observe what happens in the street, cafés, buses, and subways to see how mobile communication devices are integrated into young people's lives. Hooked up to their computers almost anywhere, pushing buttons on mobile phones in the strangest spots, always attentive to the little window on the screen that says "Neva has come on line," adolescents appear to be comfortable and nonchalant in the contemporary changing media environment. How does this happen? How do mobile technologies so naturally shape and how are they shaped by teenagers' already existing culture and social organization? It is this apparently familiar world that we decided to investigate through an ethnographic field study and ethnography-based analysis of teenagers' mobile conversations.

The phenomenological tradition in social studies has stressed the importance of performing a cognitive epoké to bracket off the obvious, taken-for-granted aspects of everyday practices (Garfinkel 1967, Schutz 1962, 1967). It is only through such cognitive distancing that we can gain access to implicit meanings and tacit conventions that constitute the invisible dimension of everyday culture. This system of cultural beliefs, local theories, definitions of the world, and meanings given to practices partially escapes us because we are immersed in it and share it (at least in part) with people we are interested in. Especially when we are faced with what we see as normal behaviour or ordinary actions, we need to bracket off all obvious interpretation and natural meaning, and break with the appearance of normality through the golden question of all ethnographic-oriented research: *Why this now?* As Sacks has pointed out, the very question facing research in ordinary life is not what is normal but how such normality is constructed. Rather than investigating what people do or who they are, we need to empirically explore how they make what they are (Sacks 1984).

Yet when we adopt such a phenomenological perspective in order to go beyond an impressionistic observation of what happens and achieve an understanding of *how what happens happens*, apparently obvious facts become problematic. To begin with, who are adolescents?

Researchers who want to enter the fascinating world of adolescents' technological culture immediately encounter a major problem: they have to define the people involved. What does it mean to be an adolescent? Does it suffice to fall into a certain age group, or does one have to be part of a community that shares a lifestyle, language, and culture?

An age-based definition may be conventional, set, and thus safe. As it is for most "etic" categories,[7] it relies upon and refers to the researcher's theoretical frameworks. Extrinsic with respect to the informant's point of view, "etic" categories are meaningful dimensions and make meaningful distinctions *for* the analyst. Identifying our informants as "adolescents" by relying only upon their age would have been a common sociological way to solve the problem,[8] but it would not have taken into account the process of identity designation used by the people concerned.

Moreover, such a definition fixes people in social identities as if they were prior ontological characteristics – in other words, essential features independent of an individual's actions in context. Yet social identities are *made* constantly; they are ongoing, situated practical accomplishments strategically activated and deactivated, displayed and abandoned by individuals, depending on the time, situation, and scenario. As Garfinkel pointed out, the characteristics of social life, dimensions constituting a shared culture and relevant features of identities, are regularly constructed at specific times through situated practices (Zimmerman and Boden 1991). Do adolescents use technologies in a certain way because they are adolescents, or are they adolescents because they use technologies in a certain way? It quickly became clear to us that we could not categorize adolescents according to age alone.

While more attractive, the culturally based definition posed just as many problems. What does it mean to be a member of a community? Does it mean identifying oneself as such or being identified as such by others? Which others would be in question? Is self-identification sufficient to define membership, or it is also necessary, and perhaps crucial, to act in a certain way and share lifestyles, practices, and interpretative frameworks? If this is the case, what has to be shared and up to what point in order to be a member of a given community? Indeed, basing our approach on the idea that adolescents form a cultural community created problems, because it took for granted and assumed as a given exactly what needed to be analysed.

Despite these difficulties, common to all fieldwork, we had to start somewhere. The traditional "etic" perspective of the researcher, ready to slot individuals into predefined categories, was the only point of departure that could have enabled us to perform an initial identification of the people concerned. Age thus became our first indicator of identity. Relying on a grounded theory framework (Glaser and Strauss 1967), we assumed, however, that this initial identification would remain provisory.

Basically, a grounded theory approach takes a bottom-up perspective in creating both the research hypothesis and the interpretive analytical categories. When researchers are interested in how people define themselves through actions and discourse, or in how they interpret and make sense of their life-world, their analytical categories should be "emic" – that is, oriented to the participants' point of view. Emic categories are intrinsic cultural distinctions that are meaningful for the informants themselves. Adopting an emic analytical perspective thus means using categories that are oriented towards and mapped upon those used by people to account for and interpret their own practices.

Of course data-driven categories and analysis are never pure, and a researcher's inductive or grounded approach is always a theoretically oriented activity. The final interpretive scheme is a result of a back-and-forth process in which researchers' theoretical frameworks orient their interpretation of research data and data reorient their theoretical frames of references. Our challenge was then to see whether and how belonging to an age group was a relevant and meaningful identity-making device for our informants, and whether and how they related it to their technology-mediated communicative practices.

For our study we had first to find a person who belonged to the age group in question and would accept the presence of a researcher in his daily life for a few months. We encountered Assoum, a seventeen-year-old boy, who agreed to participate in the study and let us, and our recording devices, enter his everyday life and that of his friends.

However, our categorization of Assoum as an adolescent became more a hypothesis to be explored than a foundation on which we could base satisfactory descriptions or explanations of uses of technology and language. Notwithstanding his age, would he have defined himself as an adolescent? Would he have made the connection between this definition of himself and his friends, and specific ways of using technology? Would he have considered it important to mark his difference in identity with respect to other age groups? When and how? Did we have a right to suppose there was something like a particular culture specific to him?

During one of the first meetings held to identify the range of his everyday practices and share some interpretive categories, Assoum told us:[9]

You know, adolescents, like us, we have like clans. There're people who skateboard, there're people who are hip-hoppers – that's what we call people who listen to rap, who dress like rappers, who walk around like rappers. Skaters, often, are like, human rights, sometimes anarchy, communism, anti-globalization. Very ecologist, like, pro-nature. And then you've got geeks, nerds. Nerds are like, students who study, who do their homework, sometimes they go like, "Oh, I can't go out, I have a test tomorrow." Then everyone goes and they can't understand why the person doesn't want to go out, because he has an exam the next day? it doesn't make sense! Then there are geeks, they're crazy about technology, it's like they've got cell phones, laptops, MP3s, CD players, they've got everything electronic, and then when you see them in the hall it's often: "Hey did you see my new Web page? I reprogrammed it in HTML, then in Java, and I changed the PHP protocol." Then there are musicians, musicians are weird, often they dress in black and listen to Metallica. Like Chan, he's a gamer. Gamers are another group; they're people who only play video games, spend their time playing video games.

Assoum's words were reassuring. Finally we had found what we were looking for: traces of the identity-definition process. At least in this context – in other words, when speaking to adults – "being an adolescent" was a relevant identity for our informant, a meaningful distinction to account for certain everyday practices from his point of view. However, there was more than this.

Being an adolescent was not just a question of age. It was also (if not mainly) a matter of sharing certain ways of acting, engaging in certain activities, and identifying oneself in relation to that behaviour: skateboarding or listening to rap music, dressing and walking according to a specific code, ritually rescheduling schoolwork in relation to outings with friends, being part of a group with its own operational culture but also being able to leave it at the right time.

Possession and use of technologies were among the lifestyle features that were supposed to make a difference. In addition to the practices of those who were designated as *geeks*, there were some other technology-related skills and practices that adolescents themselves considered necessary for acting as adolescents and being part of the community of peers. Talking with Assoum about his daily life and that of his friends, analysing their mobile conversations, and jointly interpreting notes in the log book, we discovered that adolescents do not listen to music on just any medium: they listen to it on the computer, "because that's what's cool." And it was cool because "it's more practical and also visual."

Based on these kinds of data, our hypotheses took clearer form. Rather than considering age as an explanatory or descriptive feature in relation to certain uses of technology, we found it much more interesting to reverse the hypothesis: how were such uses employed to construct identity and membership in a cultural community? How did Assoum and his friends, through manners of speaking and everyday practices related to technologies, do the job of "being an adolescent?"

5.5 Culture in Action: Adolescents as Cultural Translators

Once our field of inquiry was defined, research began, and it was not without a few surprises. As we took a closer look at the everyday life of adolescents, in particular with respect to practices supposed to be familiar to us, such as sending emails, calling others on the mobile phone, sending text messages, and visiting Web sites, we quickly realized that there were hidden aspects, specific uses, and meanings that escaped us. The naturally occurring mobile conversations among Assoum and his friends, the intimate everyday telephone dialogues between Sophie and Antoine, and the SMS conversations among Matilde and her friends were often unfamiliar, incomprehensible, if not foreign linguistic events, at least in our eyes. Every time this happened, every time someone did or said things the meanings of which were unclear to us, we used our lack of understanding as a cue signalling an underlying invisible but operating cultural dimension.

It was not so much a question of noticing that adolescents made different uses of technologies or engaged in different technology-mediated communication: most of the time it was a matter of understanding what the hidden dimensions were at stake in practices that were known to and shared by the researchers themselves. In meaning-oriented field research, one of the most difficult problems in trying to understand somebody else's social practices and ways of speaking is radically epistemological. Knowledge and interpretations of social phenomena are situated practices, always embodied in and dependent on the interpreter's subjective stances. Yet who is the best interpreter? The (partially) outside researcher whose "gaze from afar" enables him or her to see what escapes the awareness of the involved actor? Or the insider whose understanding of what is said and done may be more accurate precisely because he or she is the author of those actions?

Contemporary ethnography endorses an interactive theory of meaning. The meaning of social practices and issues of communicative events are located at the intersection of two often different orders of description: the outsider's and the insider's. This is what Geertz long ago called "thick description" (1973), in which representations of events are inextricably linked to polyphonic interpretations of their meaning.[10] The voices of the actor and the researcher interplay to create a multi-layered account of the events and produce situated, distributed knowledge of them. Oriented towards the actors' own explanations and sensitive to their meaning, this jointly constructed interpretation is supposed to go beyond what the members of the community grasp. Involved in their everyday practices and engaged in everyday understanding of ordinary life, actors do not always need to produce reflexive knowledge of the ways they live. The research interaction is thus a means for co-constructing such knowledge and integrates what Schutz called "multiple realities."

Creating an interface between the researchers' regard and that of the actor is more than an epistemological concern. Sometimes it is necessary in the field. One day we were looking at notes in the journal of one of the adolescents in our study. In one of the spaces provided for a short description of what he was doing when he received a phone call, he had written "vegging." In other spaces he had written, "I wasn't doing anything, I was watching TV." It was not clear how to understand these notes. What did "vegging" mean? How could he write that he was doing nothing when he was watching television?

Unless we were to treat the informer as a *cultural idiot*, we had to suppose that "vegging" and "doing nothing" were folk categories for specific everyday activities. Were they specific to that adolescent, or were they shared by the larger peer community?

Sometimes we suffered the same kind of frustration when analysing mobile phone conversations among young people.

ANTOINE: Y'a fini, ça fait une demi-heure qu'y'est fini.[11] (It's over, it's been over for half an hour.)

SOPHIE: He:in!? (Huh!?!)

ANTOINE: Sauf que on **a jasé** un peu dans la classe là. Sérieux, y'a donné une demi-heure ⌈de [???] (Except we chatted a bit in the classroom there. Seriously, he gave half an hour of)

SOPHIE: ⌊[???]

ANTOINE: He:in? (Huh!?)

SOPHIE: Ayoye, **y'a genre** duré une heure ton cours, même pas? (Oh, wow, it like lasted one hour, your course, not even?)

ANTOINE: Ah, y'a duré une demi-heure. (Yeah, it lasted half an hour)

SOPHIE: Seigneur. (My god.)

ANTOINE: Oui. (Yes.)

SOPHIE: [???]

ANTOINE: C'est vraiment **le fun, faque là, j'ai niaisé** un peu, on a parlé de médecine et toute **le kit**. (It was really fun, so then I fooled around a little, we talked about medicine and all that.)

SOPHIE: Avec qui? (Who with?)

ANTOINE: Ben avec Martine la bollée. Et là en tous cas. (Well, with Martine the brain. And then anyway.)

What was going on? What were the issues involved in these uses of communication technology in the lives of these young people? For example, how could we know that it was a conversation between a boyfriend and girlfriend? When and how did they portray themselves as adolescents? Even though we could easily understand some highly recognizable expressions, there were many words and expressions that were completely unknown to us, and they were perhaps precisely the ones we needed to focus on in order to understand what the speakers were doing by saying what they did.

This typical problem in analysing field data became an interpretive resource. We could hypothesize that data we did not understand were precisely those that referred to shared implicit meanings and to an unnoticed but operating common cultural background. The incomprehensibility of such exchanges signalled that we were outsiders with respect to a *cultural and linguistic* community whose shared dimensions enabled participants to coordinate their conversations, mutually understand one another, and construct their daily lives out of the threads of wireless exchanges. We thus had to focus particularly on the data with cultural dimensions that prevented us from understanding them.

First, there was a lexical problem. When the young people spoke with us, it was not in the same way as among themselves or when they were taking notes for themselves. They used different linguistic registers and situated ways of speaking: some excluded us, at least in part. Analysing their conversations required several levels of understanding. There were words that some of the team's researchers, who were adults and came from the same linguistic and cultural background as the informants, could understand and easily recognize as adolescents' jargon. However, other expressions were completely unknown, even to those of us who spoke the same mother tongues as the adolescents in the network.

This clearly revealed that there was another level of language that was shared by the adolescents in question. When we encountered expressions such as, in French, "*la bollée*" (the brain) or "geek" and "*vedger*" (to veg, vegetate), we had to ask one of the young people, Alex, to translate them and confirm that they were indeed typical expressions in the language of his peers. We also had to learn totally unknown terms and understand telephone exchanges such as:

ASSOUM: Yeah, still can't ping. Ping m-s-n dot com send okay thirty two bites of data pinging msn dot com, request timed out hu:h?
CHAN: What could that mean?
ASSOUM: Request timed out?
CHAN: What could that ⌈be?
ASSOUM:　　　　　　⌊please-work-please-work-please-work-please-work request timed out. Okay, that means we are very slow.
CHAN: Possibly.
ASSOUM: Package sent four lost hundred per cent.
CHAN: Ouch.
ASSOUM: Okay. w-w-w-dot ping w-w-w dot videotron dot c-a tron dot c-a and send reply from videotron dot c-a tome seven milliseconds eight-eight-seven lost, zero per cent four package received four maximum seven millisecond average issss ...[12]

However, learning vocabulary was not sufficient. We had to understand not only the meaning of the words but also and above all the meaning of certain practices and local categories. For that we had to question the actors themselves. Assoum became the interpreter of the social practices that characterized his community. He could explain to us that for adolescents "doing nothing" did not mean nothing was being done, that using a mobile phone to call from home did not necessarily have something to do with a busy land-line but also indicated a desire to enter a secret area of communication, and that a geek friend was always online and that when one spoke to him on the phone, there was always also another party involved: the computer.

By trying to understand what was meant by "the land-line phone is in the other room,"[13] we discovered that most new communications technologies were consistent with a *cultural laziness* that young people were ready to acknowledge as a specific feature of their lifestyle.[14] Little by little, young people become our cultural translators. Their interpretation was indispensable to understanding the meaning of and issues involved in their practices, for the cultural background in which they had to be situated and the frameworks of reference needed to understand them partially escaped us. The gap between the researchers and the adolescents clearly delimited their membership in a cultural community with respect to which we were outsiders.

However, this gap told us more than that. We were facing a specific culture, different from our own, but we had also discovered a powerful tool for studying the day-to-day creation of that culture. Indeed, ways of speaking not only reflect given contexts and identities but also help create those same contexts and identities. The various ways that young people spoke among themselves and with us were means for them to define themselves and be defined as young people, experts in technology, and members of a specific cultural community, and to constantly identify which activities were their community's. Their discourse provided clues to a specific culture that at the same time were tools for constructing and maintaining it. Thus it was in the details of their discursive practices linked to new communication technologies that we could observe the process by which their specific young people's culture was constructed.

Yet which language practices specific to the everyday life of young people were the most important?

5.6 Naturally Occurring Mobile Conversations: Social and Cultural Microcosms

After almost four decades of studies in conversation analysis, it is now commonly accepted that ordinary everyday conversations work as a veritable "architecture of intersubjectivity" (Heritage 1984, 255). The first generation of studies focused mostly on describing the inherent syntactic machinery of conversation and the structures of its interactive organization;[15] contemporary scholars now highlight the role of everyday conversation in constructing and displaying the crucial dimensions of participants' life-world. According to this perspective, conversation is a context-creating/context-sensitive linguistic activity, for it creates culture and social organization moment by moment, *and* it is shaped by members' background knowledge and social world (Cicourel 1992).

Conversation is among the powerful linguistic interactions through which people both construct and exhibit a common world of locally shared meanings, their identities and mutual relationship, a sense of the social context, and their stances towards the topics at hand. Even in short conversations, participants take and construct their turns to talk in ways that are oriented towards who they are, what their definition of the ongoing situation is, what the relevant context is, and what local culture members refer to in producing and mutually understanding their actions (Wilson 1991).

Everyday conversation enables coordinated, shared construction of mutual understanding of the topic (e.g., a Web site that doesn't work), the identity of the actors involved (e.g., friends, parents and children, boyfriend-girlfriend), the activity in which participants are engaged (e.g., storytelling, exchanging gossip, planning a Saturday-night outing), and the local conceptions about what participants are talking about (e.g., friendship, school, family life). However, participants' mutual understanding is not a mysterious magical accomplishment. It results from conversational strategies that in turn become tools of understanding for researchers, who listen, analyse, and try to interpret the exchange (Heritage 1884, 259). The basic principle of conversation analysis is that the sociocultural dimensions of an exchange are encoded in conversations in ways that are available and intelligible both for participants and, at least partially, for the analyst.

The dual nature of everyday conversations (in both creating *and* displaying culture and social organization) make them useful for understanding how members of a community construct an identity and culture through everyday activities. However, among naturally occurring conversations, telephone conversations appeared to be even more valuable, at least for the purposes of our study. Everyday telephone conversations are among the linguistic activities in which language's power as a tool for constructing and displaying culture, identity, and social organization is the most visible.

Telephone conversations have a unique advantage for researchers: their semiotic limits. The impossibility of using non-verbal signs and the lack of common deictic focus forces participants to use language alone to carry all the nuances they wish to convey. On the telephone one has only words, vocal components, silences, and the speakers' turn–taking interaction. In short, speaking on the telephone is strongly dependent on the technological features of the medium (Bercelli and Pallotti 2002).

Take the case of identity. On the telephone it is impossible to rely on visual information to communicate and acknowledge who is speaking. Speakers have to identify themselves. Whether this is done using words, the sound of the voice, or identification formulae, participants have to project their identities and the (supposed) identity of the addressee on the surface of their discourse. The various ways of expressing identity are also means of saying what kind of relationship links the speakers.

When Assoum begins one of his calls with "Hey, man" (rather than "Hi, this is Assoum," or "Hi, Chan"), he is identifying himself as a friend of the addressee and identifying the addressee as one of his friends. He is also defining the action as a call to a friend of the gang and identifying a cultural reference of this community: the African-American street culture.

Antoine begins a phone conversation with Sophie by saying "Hi, Sophie, it's me," and Sophie answers "Hi, so ..." A number of things are happening, and both we and the participants can grasp them: the words Antoine did not say indicate "my voice is sufficient for you to know who I am" and Sophie's acceptance of this indicates that "your voice is enough for me to recognize you." In short, the boyfriend and girlfriend are expressing and strengthening their relationship.

On the telephone, identities, relationships, and shared references are discursive and cannot be otherwise. In order to understand the identity-related, social, and cultural issues involved, the analyst therefore has to look at the verbal means used by the participants themselves. When we consider these characteristics of telephone conversations and the methodological advantages of analysing conversations in general, it becomes clear that telephone conversations are a prime resource for studying the interactions among technology, language, social structure, and cultural issues (Hopper 1991).

Yet there is another aspect of telephone conversations that makes them very valuable. Each is an event that has its own boundaries. The beginning and end of the conversation are defined by the participants. This enables the researcher to single out the event in a non-arbitrary manner and analyse it as a microcosm reflecting and even constituting the crucial dimensions of the social and cultural macrocosm of which it is a part. Many researchers have studied in detail and even dissected the specific modalities of telephone conversations,[16] but there is still a lack of analysis of naturally occurring mobile phone conversations.[17]

If we want to understand how technology-mediated communication shapes and is shaped by the culture and the social organization of a given community, we have to analyse how users speak *about* and *through* communication technologies. This was the main reason for analysing young people's mobile phone conversations and plunging into this new area of communications. In the next chapters we take a detailed look at the microcosm of young people's verbal and written mobile phone conversations. Their verbal performances provide us with special insight into the world of teenagers' mobile culture and permit us to see its construction in action by following the process in everyday life.

Displaying Identities in Urban Space: How Do Young People Talk on Mobile Phones?

6.1 Telephone Conversations as Linguistic Patchworks

Like any other form of communication, technologically mediated conversation is a tool for constructing culture, identity, and social organization. Beyond the topics, stories, and purposes, participants in this type of communicative event construct their social life in and through their *ways of speaking.* Given that communicating through mobile phones has become a typical communicative practice in young people's everyday lives, it is worth exploring the social and cultural issues associated with this phenomenon. Teenagers' ways of talking on mobile phones both produce and are produced by the crucial dimensions of their specific culture. By observing and analysing these speech modes, we can gain access to the social world of the participants and to the process whereby their social world is constructed moment-by-moment. Specifically, we will examine how young people talk on mobile phones and the ways in which discourse patterns serve as identity-making, membership-defining, and culture-building devices.

One of the most striking phenomena that we noted in our research on teenagers' mobile phone conversations was the blending of different languages. Adolescents' verbal exchanges resemble incredibly complex linguistic patchworks. They were punctuated with regional expressions that were completely incomprehensible to people who knew only the standard language, jargon that only the youngest members of our team could understand easily, and technical expressions belonging to a specific language that was absolutely unknown to most of us. As expected, all of the conversations also contained expressions and manners of speaking that were intelligible only to the parties involved in the conversation. In addition, we identified various linguistic codes shared by insiders, used not only for communicating but also to mark the membership of the speakers in a particular group.

6.2 Speaking "Teenager"

When listening to young people's mobile telephone conversations, we distinctly perceived that we were entering a separate world from which we, as adults, were excluded. The first noticeable obstacle was language.

Here are Antoine and Sophie[1] are speaking on their mobile phones about mobile phones and their everyday life at school:

SOPHIE: Tu disais **c'était toute fucké** là à cause du message là sur la boîte vocale.[2] (You said it was all fucked up because of the message there on the voice mail.)

ANTOINE: Non, non, non, non ça je vais m'arranger avec ça parce que là il faut que **mettons si** je réponds pas ou mon téléphone est fermé, là je vais voir mon message ça va dire: "Oui, oui, vous avez rejoint la boîte de," tu vas entendre: "Antoine Boileau-Paquin, veuillez laisser un message." Mettons là je vais savoir comment aller les chercher, pis tout là. (No, no, no, no, that I can deal with that, because I have to − like if I don't answer or my phone is off, I'm going to see my message, it's going to say "Yeah, yeah, you have reached the voice mail of ..." you're going to hear, "Antoine Boileau-Paquin, please leave a message." Like then I'll know how to get in touch with them and everything.)

SOPHIE: Okay. Tu devrais trouver quelque chose de plus original que "Antoine Boileau-Paquin," **ça fait téteux.** (Okay. You should find something more original than "Antoine Boileau-Paquin," it sounds sucky.)

ANTOINE: En tous cas, peut-être, c'est pas grave là, **fuck eille Sophie!** (Anyway, maybe it doesn't matter, fuck, hey Sophie!)

SOPHIE: Oui mon examen est fini. (Yeah, my test is over.)

ANTOINE: Oui, chanceuse. (Ah, lucky.)

Assoum and Sharif are talking on their mobiles. At one point Assoum starts talking about a film he is thinking about making. Sharif shows a lot of interest.

SHARIF: Mais c'est quoi vraiment le film? (But what is it really, the movie?)

ASSOUM: Okay, vite vite vite là. (Okay, very quickly.)

SHARIF: Ouè, ouè. (Yeah, yeah.)

ASSOUM: C'est comme une fille qui est **comme spéciale** et là tsé, elle est pas comme les autres filles [???], en tout cas, elle tombe amoureuse d'un gars **ben ben ben** ordinaire. (It's like, a girl who is like special and then ... you know, she's not like the other girls [???], anyway, she falls in love with a really really ordinary guy.)

SHARIF: Okay.

ASSOUM: Tsé comme un gars **super gentil tsé comme** [???], là elle essaie de devenir ordinaire parce que elle l'aime. (You know, like a super nice guy, you know like, [???], so she tries to become ordinary because she likes him)

SHARIF: Okay.

ASSOUM: Pis là ben elle essaie **plein de trucs**, ça marche pas. (Then she tries all sorts of things, it doesn't work.)

SHARIF: Huh, huh.

ASSOUM: Pis là après elle va lui dire, pis lui se suicide **genre**. Il laisse une lettre pis lui dit de pas changer. Mais là je le dis vite, pis y'a pas beaucoup de péripéties là mais ça s'en vient. (Then after she goes and tells him, then he like commits suicide. He leaves her a letter saying not to change. But now I'm telling it fast, and there's not many ups and downs there but they're coming.)

SHARIF: Ah, okay, c'est toi qui l'a écrit? (Ah, okay, you wrote it?)

ASSOUM: Oui, c'est le synopsis là, on n'a pas encore écrit l'histoire. (Yeah, it's the synopsis, the story's not written yet.)

SHARIF: Ah, okay.

ASSOUM: Pis y'aura là comme plein d'affaires là pis **ça va être cool**. (And there'll be lots a stuff and it'll be cool.)

Even if the adult researchers of the team did not understand everything that was going on in these conversations, they quickly and easily identified the rapid and very involved style of Antoine and Sophie as teenager talk, similar to the jargon of Assoum and his friends. "All fucked up," "sounds sucky," "it's really cool," "it'll be cool," "super nice guy" – the list of expressions identified as teen jargon is certainly much longer. This code is truly a language with its own lexicon, recurring pragmatic markers, and specific ways of talking. The use of hyperbole is one of the most striking examples.[3] Most of the time the younger members of the team did not even notice anything special about the language. This difference in categorizing data was a clear cue that the expressions analysed were occurrences of a language specific to an age group:[4] our informants spoke "teenager" on the telephone. They understood one another, shared a code of communication that identified them as different in the eyes of adults and as similar in the eyes of those in the same age bracket. Speaking "teenager" is thus a membership categorization device. Over and above what they were talking about and what they did with their mobiles, Antoine, Sophie, Assoum, and Sharif were constantly identifying and constructing themselves as adolescents, members of a specific cultural community that shared, above all, a language.

Of course, this role of language in creating and maintaining identity and membership is not a product of the telephone or its contemporary avatar, the mobile phone. Young people have always created and used languages to construct identity and create social cohesion. Nonetheless, new technologies have increased the repertoire and the number of encounters and social situations in which adolescents construct themselves through speech patterns. In particular, the mobile phone has transformed spaces (e.g., the street and bus) and times (e.g., before class or after school) into unprecedented opportunities to talk on the phone, and thus increased the number of communicative events available for displays of identity. As the number of routine exchanges increases, new scenarios arise in which everyday language takes on crucial roles such as constructing identity and membership in a cultural community.

6.3 Bad Language and New Technologies: An Identity-Producing Synergy

The use of swear words and insults is one of the verbal strategies young people use to project their identities on the social scene. Mobile-phone use is part of this process. It provides the participants with another, more or less public forum to define and assert themselves as teenagers.

SOPHIE: Okay, ben tu disais tantôt que ça marchait pas. (Okay, well before you said it didn't work.)
ANTOINE: Comment ça marchait pas tantôt? (What do you mean, it didn't work?)
SOPHIE: Tu disais c'était **tout fucké** à cause du message là sur la boîte vocale. (You said it was all fucked up because of the voice mail.)
ANTOINE: Eille c'est ça, je t'ai pas dis ça hein? (Hey, that's it, didn't I tell you that, eh?)
SOPHIE: Quoi, quoi donc? (What, what is it?)
ANTOINE: Une petite proposition. (Just an idea.)

SOPHIE: Okay.

ANTOINE: Y'a un voyage qui s'organise là heu, à Miami à Noël. (There's a trip there, planned for Christmastime to Miami.)

SOPHIE: Okay.

ANTOINE: J'sais pas, en tous cas, r'garde, on ... on regardera ça mais j'ai capoté là. (I dunno, anyway, look, we ... we'll think about it, but I really freaked out.)

SOPHIE: Avec l'école? (Over school?)

ANTOINE: Sérieux, oui, oui, avec. (Seriously, yeah, yeah, over it.)

SOPHIE: Eille ça coupe hein? (Hey, it's cutting off, eh?)

ANTOINE: Oui, **ça fait chier**. Eille, c'est de la matière malade, c'est vraiment poussé, là. Faque en tout cas, je te raconterai tout ça tantôt hein, pour pas, pour pas trop parler, Sophie? (Yeah, it's a real pain. Hey, it's sick stuff, it's really hard. So, anyway I'll tell you everything later, to not – not talk too much, Sophie?)

SOPHIE: [???]

ANTOINE: Hein? (Hey?)

SOPHIE: Oui.

ANTOINE: Voyons ostie [???] crissement bogué. (Okay, shit, fucking full of bugs.)

In the most ordinary exchanges, in which they are unlikely to be pertinent, swear words are part of young people's lexicon, another verbal strategy through which adolescents express and acknowledge themselves as adolescents. They go hand in hand with jargon (*"capoter"* ["freaking out"] neologisms created out of computer terms (*"bogué"* ["buggy"]), and conventional oral expressions (*"eille"* ["hey"], *"faque"* ["so ..."]), whose meaning is strongly related to identity and membership construction. The most striking use of bad language is perhaps the use of insults (Labov 1972b, Goodwin 1990). Here is an excerpt of a conversation between Karim and Assoum:

ASSOUM: Elle m'a appelé samedi, c'est correct avec elle. J'vais l'appeler demain, on va voir c'qu'on va faire là. (She called me Saturday, that's okay with her. I'll call her tomorrow; we'll see what we'll do.)

KARIM: Yé:::::! No.

ASSOUM: Why yé?[5]

KARI: C'est beau, on ira samedi, c'est cool. (That's fine, we'll go Saturday, that's cool.)

ASSOUM: T'es correct avec ça là? (Are you okay with that?)
KARIM: Ben oué. (Yeah, of course.)
ASSOUM: You're happy I called for you?
KARIM: What? No::! [???] [*laughing*]
ASSOUM: [*laughing*] You're busted.
KARIM: [???] **Don't fuck with me, okay?**
ASSOUM: [???]
KARIM: [[???]
ASSOUM: [[???] Après y vont m'croire. (After that, they'll believe me.)
KARIM: [You don't know me] man **Fuck you [???] je sais que vous écoutez la conversation!** [*yelling*] Non, qu'est-ce que j'dis là, man? ([You don't know me] man! **Fuck you [???]** I know you're listening in on the call! Oh no! What am I saying, man?)
ASSOUM: [*laughs*] T'es fou ... [*laughing*] (You're crazy.)
KARIM: What? **Fuck, I have a bomb! [???]**

The conversation above occurred while Karim was at home playing a video game on the computer,[6] which became not only one of the topics of conversation but was also the third "partner" in the exchange. The whole scene typifies an increasingly common scenario: the mobile phone and Internet allow joint simultaneous performance of action and mutual coordination at a distance. The social situation was nonetheless wider: the exchange occurred in a room where other people were, perhaps unintentionally, playing the role of an overhearing audience (Goffman 1981) and witnessing the performance. Moreover, Assoum and Karim were well aware that the conversation was being recorded. The social participation structure inherent in the research context introduced another character on the stage: the researcher who would be listening to the conversations as a legitimate eavesdropper.[7]

Anglicisms, code switching between French and English, non-standard pronunciation of certain words: this excerpt of conversation contained occurrences of almost the full range of traits defining teenage language, including swear words and insults. It is also clear from Assoum's reaction to his friend's insults that these utterances are not provocations per se, nor do they represent a lack of manners or verbal aggressiveness. Irrespective of the encoded meaning, the use of such a lexicon affirms the certainty that the addressee will not be upset. The reception continually confirms this shared belief. Adolescents' use of insults and swear words implies that participants share the same linguistic conventions. It indeed both expresses and reinforces a relationship of friendship, solidarity, and membership in a community.

The whole scenario is a good example of the synergy among new technologies, language, and forms of interaction in the process of constructing a specific identity and a common culture. Faced with two audiences witnessing their exchanges, Assoum and Karim mutually acknowledge one another as friends and teenagers, and vigorously display these identities in public. They are well equipped, using computers, jointly playing video games and inverting the usual meaning of insults and swear words, all signs of teenagers' identity. They also wield mobile phones, which allow joint activity and provide a social stage for their performance. Through all of these technologically mediated practices, Assoum and Karim vigorously define themselves as adolescents in front of the overhearing audience. The specific context created by the recording devices amplified the social dimension of their verbal performance ("Fuck you, I know you're listening to the conversation!"), and provided us with a special point of view from which we could grasp this strategic use of the public nature of mobile phone conversations.

6.4 Crossing Linguistic Boundaries: Cultural Identity on the Mobile

A kind of socio-cultural microcosm, the communication via mobile phones that characterizes these adolescents also reveals certain broader aspects of their cultural milieu. In a North American city the culture and language specific to teenagers also reflect the cultures and languages of the various ethno-linguistic communities to which they belong. Assoum, Karim, and their friends use, borrow, and disseminate ethnic expressions that they strip of their initial social meaning, namely, membership in a specific ethnic group. Detached from their original linguistic context, such expressions enrich the special language of these adolescents and support their claim of belonging to an intercultural community.

This cross-ethnic language (Rampton 1995, Andersen 2001) is a kind of interlinguistic patchwork or pidgin constructed by young people as they interact with one another. Surprisingly, this language is de-ethnicized in the way it is used by adolescents, in that the expressions lose the systematic ties with the speakers' ethnic origin.

The two dominant languages, French and English, are not necessarily used to indicate or reflect membership in different communities. On the contrary, they are treated as two expressive repertoires used differently depending on the circumstances and topic. Regardless of their mother tongue, the young people demonstrated the ability to switch from one language to the other.

Here is Assoum, who is fluent in Arabic as well as French and English, speaking with Chan, an English-speaker of Chinese origin.

ASSOUM: **Yes.**

CHAN: Yeah?

ASSOUM: **Ouais, ça va?** (Yeah, how's it going?)

CHAN: **Yeah.**

ASSOUM: **So what you doing?**

CHAN: Trying not to say anything incriminating.

ASSOUM: [*laughs*] [???] **Yes, this conversation is being recorded.** [???] T'en fais pas là, y'a pas de noms, anonyme ... Allo? ([*laughs*] [???] Yes this conversation is being recorded. [???] Don't worry, there's no name, anonymous ... hello?)

CHAN: Yeah.

ASSOUM: Ouah.

CHAN: Well, tomorrow, we have to meet this guy.

ASSOUM: Ah, ouais, c'est vrai, c'est demain le: le: "J'veux pas vous entendre parler en même temps que lui." [*deep voice*] (Oh, yeah, that's true, it's tomorrow the: the: "I don't want to hear you speaking at the same time as him.")

CHAN: [*laughs*]

ASSOUM: [???] Ouais, "okay, mais si j'ai une question?" Là y dit '[???] des questions inutiles, moins cinque" [*deep voice*]. Comme "Wha:t?" (Yeah, "Okay, but if I had a question?" so here he says "['???] Silly questions, minus five." Like "Wha:t?")

CHAN: [*laughs*]

ASSOUM: C'est tout l'temps comme ça man ses cours, c'est terrible. On est allés voir la directrice aujourd'hui han? (It's always the same, his classes, man, are awful. Today we went to see the principal.)

CHAN: Hanhan, what d'she say?

ASSOUM: She said – elle a pris genre <u>plein</u> de notes, après elle a dit, "I'll see what I can do," pis là on était comme, "What the hell? What kind of answer is that?" (She said – she took tons of notes, then she said, "I'll see what I can do," then we were like, you know, "What the hell? What kind of answer is that?")

Assoum, fluent in both English and French, could switch from one language to the other and carry on the conversation without the code switching's affecting the flow of the discourse and its mutual intelligibility. Chan, an English-speaker, follows and participates appropriately. Aside from their mother tongue, both teenagers have a pragmatic competence that allows them to participate in verbal exchanges that characterize their multilinguistic community.

In conversations among young French speakers, code switching to English is often associated with gossip and related reported speech. For example, Annie and Assoum were organizing an outing, which led them to talk about Karim and to engage in an exchange in the typical format, "I'm telling you that he said ... and I said to him ..."

ANNIE: Qu'est-ce tu penses d'eux autres? moi [???] (What do you think about them, me [???].)

ASSOUM: Ouais, c'est **bad** [*laughs*] euh, hah, pour samedi? (Yeah: that's bad [*laughs*], uh, ah, what about Saturday?

ANNIE: Ouais, j'travaille pas le jour. (Yeah, I'm not working during the day.)

ASSOUM: Ah, ouais, c'est génial ça. Karim y'arrête pas de [*deep voice*] **"Call her, call her, call her"** (Oh yeah, that's great. Karim doesn't stop going "call her, call her, call her.")

ANNIE: Fuck, pourquoi [[???] (Fuck, why?)

ASSOUM: [**"Yo, come on**, calme toi," "Call her." "Karim, calme-toi." ("Hey, come on, calm down." "Call her." "Karim, calm down.")

In such an exchange, and especially in reported speech, the languages are mixed together. These adolescents often use English, which seems to provide them with a concise, expressive technique for characterizing people. For example, Assoum was telling Chan what had happened at school:

ASSOUM: What the hell? Après elle dit "est comme toute **bitch**, pis toi t'es toute smart, je veux pas que tu deviennes ami avec elle." Je suis comme, euh, **"I'm the guy that everyone likes, so I'll do what I have to,"** là elle dit, **"Okay, we don't want to lose you as a friend,"** comme [???] **"You won't, you won't."** Là je suis parti et elle a fait, **"oh my God, <u>oh my God!</u>"** [*parodying a girl voice*] (What the hell? Then she goes "she is like, bitch, you are so smart. I don't want you to be his friend." I'm like, uhh, "I'm the guy that everyone likes, so I'll do what I have to," so then she said, "Okay, I don't want to lose you as a friend," like, "You won't, you won't," then I left and she said "oh my God, <u>oh my God!</u>")

CHAN: What?

ASSOUM: Someone searched you on Google and found a picture of a Chinese guy.

The storytelling is mostly in French, but when Assoum gives voice to the characters gossiping, the language used for the reported speech is often English. However, when the adolescents discuss music, the use of English terms or code switching to English becomes almost the rule. Annie told Assoum that she was going to go to a concert by a singer who was very popular among adolescents. As a result, she would not be available to go out that Friday. Music, leisure activities, weekend plans, homework, the concert: their conversation covered almost the whole range of the typical topics of calls among adolescents. The use of mixed languages also confirmed the teen identity:

ASSOUM: Qu'est-ce tu fais vendredi? (What you doing Friday?)

ANNIE: J'm'en vais voir Avril Lavigne, hahi [*little giggle*]. (I'm going to see Avril Lavigne.)

ASSOUM: Hen! Moi j'voulais y'aller. (Ha! Me, I wanted to go too.)

ANNIE: Ah, c'est vraiment **cool**! [???] j't'allée sur Internet. (It's really cool, [???] I went on the Net.)

ASSOUM: Ah, ouais.

ANNIE: Pis là ... tsé j'pensais qu'le **show** était comme en été là. (And then, you know, I thought the **show** was like in the summer.

ASSOUM: C'est l'dix, non? (It's the tenth, isn't it?)

ANNIE: C'est vendredi, c'est l'onze. (It's on Friday, it's the eleventh.)

ASSOUM: C'est ça, le eleventh? (Is it? The **eleventh?**)

ANNIE: Oui! Pis là j'm'en vas **checker**, j'suis comme ça s'peut pas ... (Yeah, then I'm gonna go check it, I'm, like it's impossible.)

Going to a pop concert is a crucial event in young people's culture. Assoum and Annie talk about this again in a subsequent mobile conversation.

ANNIE: J'vais être comme, "**We::ll** t'as vu le bonhomme qu'ai j'ai vu sur scène, ça doit être Avril" (I'll be like, "We'll, did you see the guy I've seen on the stage, he might be Avril.")

ASSOUM: Ah t'es genre loin? (So are you, like, far?)

ANNIE: Je pense que oui, ben oui. (I think so, yeah.)

ASSOUM: Parce d'habitude les **concerts** [*English pronounciation*] tu peux aller où tu veux ('Cause usually at concerts, you can go wherever you want.)

ANNIE: Be::n tsè, euh ... (We::ll you know, uhh ...)

ASSOUM: Ben dans le fond là, Our Lady Peace on pouvait aller jusque: [dans le fond là] **too bad**. (Well, at the end there, Our Lady Peace we could get to: [at the end, well,] **too bad**.)

ANNIE: Ah, ouè. (Oh, yeah.)

ASSOUM: Ouais c'ètait l'**fun** ça, **good times, good times**. (Yeah, it was fun, good times, good times.)

In keeping with the cultural rule that requires members of the network to share information on events concerning other members, the next day Assoum told Karim about Annie's decision to go to the concert. In the conversation they talk about music, and English appears again.

ASSOUM: Devine quoi? (Guess what?)

KARIM: Quoi?

ASSOUM: [???]

KARIM: Quoi?

ASSOUM: [???] Elle va voir Avril Lavigne, man. (She's going to see Avril Lavigne, man.)

KARIM: Okay?

ASSOUM: Pis moi j'suis encore ici man, j'aurais pu aller avec elle, **but no:::::** (And I'm still here, man, I coulda gone with her, but no:::)

KARIM: Aller voir Avril Lavigne? (Go see Avril Lavigne?)

ASSOUM: Oui.

KARIM: [Comme vendredi?] (Like on Friday?)

ASSOUM: Oui. Elle est chanceuse la fille, man [*laughs*]. (Yes, she's a lucky girl, man.)

KARIM: C'est pas juste [*laughing*] [???]. (Not quite.)

ASSOUM: Han? (What?)

KARIM: **[You're gay,] fuck!**

ASSOUM: **No, I'm an artist.**

KARIM: [???] C'est pas d'la musique ça, Avril Lavigne. (It's not music, that, Avril Lavigne)

ASSOUM: De quoi tu parles? **You can't judge anything** ... (What are you talking about? You can't judge anything)

KARIM: [Ça s'appelle] **a product**. ([That's what they call] a product.)

ASSOUM: Ha, ha, ha. [???]

Some implicit conventions seem to guide verbal interactions among the members of the group. When allophones speak among themselves, the conversation can be in French, but if they are talking about music or gossiping and reporting the speech of other people, they frequently adopt English terms or switch to English. When an English speaker is taking part in the conversation, those who speak the language tend to use English, though this does not prevent them from switching to French if necessary. This nonchalance shows that linguistic mixing is highly acceptable in this group's everyday life.

Technology is also a subject of conversation that triggers a switch to English, no matter what the mother tongue of the young people speaking. Assoum and Chan were talking on the phone while using their computers, each in his own home. The Internet and mobile phone allow them to jointly carry out the same task simultaneously, in different places. Since their ongoing activities concerned technologies, gradual code switching to English became almost inevitable. As soon as the conversation focuses on doing something with technology, Assoum adopts his friend's language and switches to English for a while.

CHAN: Arthur?

ASSOUM: Y t'a pas envoyé genre un truc [???] sur les e-mails ... [???]. net dot mp3 ... Limp Bizkit – oh, non pas encore! [*referring to what happens on his screen*] Parce tsé quoi, il m'a envoyé une version, tsé dans le ref name là? (He didn't send you like something [???] about an e-mail [???] net dot mp3, Limp Bizkit – oh, no, not again! [*referring to what happens on his screen*], 'cause you know, he sent me a version, you know, in the ref name,)

CHAN: [???]

ASSOUM: Ouais [???] ouais ce qui s'est passé avec le [??] tk? (Yeah, yeah, what happened with the [??] tk?)

CHAN: I don't know. [???]

ASSOUM: Ouin, c'est ça, y'a pris le ref link [???]. (Yeah, that's it, he took the ref link.)

CHAN: Ouais non. <u>Ah</u>, there, finally ... (Yeah, no. Ah, there, finally.)

ASSOUM: **What?**

CHAN: [*Yawning*] The web page is loading.

ASSOUM: **What?**

CHAN: The web page is loading [*yawning*].

ASSOUM: **Ours?**

CHAN: No, another one. I'm looking for design here.

ASSOUM: **Well, it doesn't do anything with our pages down.**

CHAN: I yeah uh [???] y'a genre un p'tit vidéo. (I yeah uh [???] there's like a little video.)

ASSOUM: Ah euh [???] va être avec nous full time bientôt. (Ah eh [???] gonna be with us full time soon.)

CHAN: Oh yeah? [???]

ASSOUM: Pour le ... le, le [???] du théâtre. (For the: the, the [???] of theatre.)

CHAN: Oh, when's that? May?

ASSOUM: **May,** ben fin avril-mai. [...] Tu te rappelles quand je t'ai dit qu'on allait voir un film? Qu'il y avait un film qui l'a traumatisé là? (May, by the end of April-May. Remember when I told you that we saw a movie? that the movie traumatized him?)

CHAN: Oh, yeah!

ASSOUM: Après il capotait, c'était drôle, hein, là y m'a envoyé une chanson de Limp Bizkit pour aucune raison. (And then he freaked out, it was funny, I mean ... and now he sent a Limp Bizkit song for no reason.)

CHAN: **It's not good** [*referring to what is happening on-screen*].

ASSOUM: Huh?

CHAN: It's not good. Don't take it

ASSOUM: **I have no choice.** [???]

CHAN: [???]

ASSOUM: Can't.

CHAN: Yes ⌈[???]

ASSOUM: ⌊[???] **Then again, then again, then again** −

CHAN: Welcome.

ASSOUM: Arête, tout le monde fait ça [c'est pas gentil.] (Stop it, everybody does that [it's not nice].)

CHAN: (Laughs)

ASSOUM: Sèrieux, tout le monde est comme **"I want to block you and [you've lost]."** (Seriously, everybody is like "I want to block you and [you've lost].")

CHAN: Va sur Google, écrit chan hong, va dans image. (Go on Google, type chan hong, click on image.)

Code switching is not the only phenomenon that characterizes the conversations in this peer group. As we have seen in most of the previous extracts, there is also syncretism: French words pronounced English style, extremely gallicized English words, linguistic tics, and morphological features of the other language that fit smoothly into the language chosen for the conversation. This linguistic mixture is so well crafted that no breaks are perceived.

In their nomadic calls to their family members, allophones also switch from the official national languages to the one spoken in the family. Walking down Lajoie Street on his way to the subway station, Assoum calls his sister Nayla to check his messages at home.

NAYLA: Ouais. (Yeah.)

ASSOUM: Y'en a-tu quelqu'un ...? (Are there any ...?)

NAYLA: [???] Karim.

ASSOUM: Oh.

NAYLA: Mais, euh, oh, Corinne [[???] l'université. (But, uh, Corinne [???] the university].)

ASSOUM: ⌊Okay. Pis qu'est-ce qu'a veut, Corinne? (What's she want, Corinne?)

NAYLA: [*speaks in Arabic*]

ASSOUM: [*speaks in Arabic*]

NAYLA: Hen?

ASSOUM: Okay, c'est beau. (Okay, that's good.)

NAYLA: Bye.

ASSOUM: Bye.

In their everyday mobile conversations, these young people constantly cross linguistic boundaries, code-switch between the two dominant languages, create pidgins, and use the language of their community of origin when appropriate. In so doing, they construct and display their radically inter-ethnic social identity.

These phenomena are neither unusual nor unexpected. Indeed, they are perhaps the foremost distinguishing features of language use in North American multi-ethnic societies.[8] However, we want to stress the role of the mobile in creating a new context for these phenomena. Turning virtually each urban space and almost every time of the day into a context for particular communicative events, it provides new social arenas for public displays of language games. Spread over urban spaces and available for an expanded, overhearing audience, adolescents' verbal interactions become more of a public performance. Given the virtually public nature of mobile conversations, urban adolescents' multi-linguistic competence and their ability to belong to and cross between different communities are increasingly visible everyday phenomena. The mobile phone is thus a tool for the moment-by-moment everyday construction and expression of North American urban adolescents' inter-ethnic identity.

6.5 Cultural References in Teenagers' Mobile Conversations

In addition to the linguistic traces of inter-ethnic identity, the nomadic conversations of these young people are punctuated by terms from other cultural domains that transect the ethno-linguistic communities concerned. Sometimes they are consistent with the topic of conversation, sometimes not. In the following conversation between Assoum and Sharif, there are traces of almost every mark of "teenage" language: swearing, parodies of other people's ways of speaking, reported speech, enthusiastic storytelling based on everyday events, and insertion and gallicization of English terms. The conversation also contains discursive markers signalling a shared reference to a specific culture, the African-American street culture.

SHARIF: Y'a une fille dans mon cours d'anglais là. (There's a girl in my English class.)

ASSOUM: Ouais. (Yeah.)

SHARIF: Oublie ça, **man**. (Forget it, man.)

ASSOUM: [*laughs*]

SHARIF: Elle est toujours [???] pis j'suis-j'ai vraiment aucune idée [???] Qu'est-ce que j'peux faire, **man**? (She's always [???], and I'm – I really got no idea [???], what can I do, man?)

ASSOUM: C'est qui? (Who is she?)

SHARIF: Elle est tout l'temps avec une amie, **man**. (She is always with a friend, man.)

[...]

SHARIF: [???] **For fuckin' like.**

ASSOUM: Ouais.

SHARIF: D'un autre côté, je: (.) Yo, un jour j'te dis j'vais en avoir marre, j'vais dire "yo [???] laisse-moi parler!" (On the other hand, I ... hey, one day I'm telling you, I will have had it, I'm gonna say "Yo, let me speak.")

ASSOUM: Non, pas comme ça, mais tu dis **ge:nre** (.) attends comme nous on fait? Sinon c'est une improvisation que j'fais tout l'temps tout l'temps tout l'temps. (No, not this way, but you say li:ke (...) wait like how da we do it? Otherwise it is a performance, I do it every time, every time, every time.)

SHARIF: [???]

ASSOUM: Han?

SHARIF: Je vais lui dire, **man**, "Vous, allez allez allez jouer ailleurs," mais je veux parler tête-à-tête, **man**. (I'm gonna say, man, "you, go go go away," but I want to speak one-on-one, man.)

ASSOUM: Nonon, tu dis euh "J'aimerais ça te parler **one-on-one** là." (No no, you say, uh, "I'd like to speak with you one-on-one.")

SHARIF: [???]

ASSOUM: Pis là a va dire [minououiou] [*makes a sound to imitate the girl*]. (Then she will say [minououiou].)

SHARIF: Mais sais-tu c'est quoi l'affaire? (You know what's the problem?)

ASSOUM: Quoi? (What?)

SHARIF: [???] **Man**, dès que une fille est dans un groupe de fille là ... (Man, once a girl is in a group of girls ...)

ASSOUM: C'est ça, c'est pas rap y vont tout se dire entre eux. (That's it, it makes no sense, they will talk together about everything.)

SHARIF: Tsé tu viens, tu dis, "Est-ce que j'peux parler **one-on-one**." Qu'est-ce que tu penses que les autres vont commencer à dire: "**Oh, check** ce gars-là, qu'est-ce qu'y veut," tsé. (You know, you say, "Can I speak to you one-on-one?" what do you think the other girls would say? "Oh, check, this guy, what he wants," you know.)

ASSOUM: Ah oui, j'sais les p'tites rumeurs, **ça fait chier**. (Yeah, I know, all the little rumours, it really pisses me off.)

The systematic use of the vocative "man" punctuates the conversation and adds to teenagers' language a reference echoing African-American street culture. By indirectly referring to this cultural universe, the speakers signal it as a frame of reference and as a relevant component of their multilayered cultural background. As we have seen, this mixture of different voices, languages, terms, registers, and cultural references may be truly rich. It sometimes also incorporates terms belonging to expert domains, such as new information and communication technologies.

6.6 Belonging to a Community of Practices: Geek Language and Culture

Adolescents' competence in new information and communication technologies may extend far beyond their practical use. The mastery of technology-specific knowledge, a set of practices, and related linguistic code is a way in which adolescents define themselves as belonging to a specific community of practices (Lave and Wenger 1991).

In order to grasp this *knowledge in action*, we will now follow two friends talking together on their mobile phones, each in front of his computer, reading to each other what appears on their screen. While decontextualized understanding of any highly situated conversation is always difficult, in this case it becomes almost impossible.

CHAN: Wait, I'll go check. No, damn tk is down.

ASSOUM: Why is it down? Is it like server problem, did they remove it completely? Euh ...

CHAN: Oh, it doesn't seem to be working ... Wait, I'll use [Opera].

ASSOUM: <u>Ha</u> ha.

CHAN: ⌈Okay.

ASSOUM: ⌊I only have ⌈Explorer.

CHAN: ⌊It's very strange.

ASSOUM: What?

CHAN: [???] **Prompt euh ping www dot tk.**

ASSOUM: **Run cmd ping www dot tk send ping response ping** ⌈**response.**

CHAN: ⌊No response.

That sucks.

ASSOUM: Moi non plus (Not even me) ... Tanatananana [*sings the music from Jaws*].

CHAN: **Ping request cannot find the host dot tk hum.**

ASSOUM: Oh my God! It's been completely eradicated!

CHAN: Cannot ⌈locate

ASSOUM: ⌊**Ping request could not find host www dot tk.** Please check the name and try again.

CHAN: Only people like us would be able to do this.

ASSOUM: **I know – www dot msn dot com ping huenh? www dot msn is not recognized as an internal.**

When Assoum, Chan, and Karim discuss technologies or engage in related activities by combining mobile and computer use, they show another facet of their cultural identity. They are insiders in the community of techno-adolescents. Here Assoum and Chan are talking on their mobiles about what was happening on the Web, their Web pages, changes that one of them had made, and the quality of service. They also are jointly performing a simultaneous technological task. However, in order to understand the details of this conversation, knowledge of the deictic context alone is not sufficient. One has to share the same expertise, be familiar with the same practices, and know the linguistic code that participants are using in this activity. It is exactly this obfuscation that signals that Assoum and Chan are engaged in an activity for experts that share knowledge, skills, techniques, and, above all, a language. In short, they share a specific *operating culture* (Goodwin 1990,9).[9] Participants' mutual understanding and joint engagement in a technological task reveal their belonging to a community of practices, defined by an expertise, an (almost esoteric) knowledge and a language shared only by its members, which sets them apart from non-members. As Chan himself says, "Only people like us would be able to do this." Adolescents have already given this activity-defined community a name: *the world of geeks.*

CHAN: Did I send you that **geek joke**?

ASSOUM: Non, laquelle? (No, which one?)

CHAN: Attends, wait, I'm looking for it ... Today, no not today.

ASSOUM: T'as écouté la chanson? J'ai pas écouté la chanson. C'est une search chan hong lol [*reads Arthur's message to Chan*]. C'est pas drôle pis. Tu cliques sur le pique du gars pis ça devient une fille lol. [reads Arthur's message] Encore pas drôle. C'est Arthur, man, boring jokes (Did ya listen to the song? I didn't listen to the song. It's a search chan hong lol [*reads Arthur's message to Chan*]. It's not funny. You click on the dick of the guy, and it becomes a girl lol [*reads Arthur's message*]. Not funny again. That's Arthur, man, boring jokes.)

CHAN: Okay, I'll send you the joke. That's health.com.

ASSOUM: There's no place hahahuh. [*laughs*]

CHAN: Yeah, **only a geek would get it.**

ASSOUM: **Geek power. What a geek I am.**

Assoum and Chan are in their own homes on their computers, talking on the phone and jointly trading jokes, music, and messages over the Net. Here again the activity is defined as an activity for experts: geeks who master advanced knowledge, practices, and codes. Being a geek is something to be proud of: "Only a geek would get it," "Geek power. What a geek I am." Modelled on "black power," "geek power" is clearly used to express pride in membership.

Like a shortcut, this linguistic allusion to black pride also brings two cultural worlds closer together: those of black urban culture and geeks. By creating a local discursive link between these two worlds, participants signal some of the multiple frames of references that compose their identity and culture.

6.7 Crossing Words and Cultures by Mobile Phone

Systematic use of words belonging to different cultures and their creative appropriation, integration, and fusion in discourse create a specific language strongly characterized by heteroglossia. The interpenetration of different voices speaking "other languages" weaves together different cultural frames of reference and reflects the multiple, heterogenic nature of these teenagers' cultural belonging.

Radically inter-ethnic, their language is also trans-cultural. It crosses not only the borders of ethno-linguistic communities but also those of different communities of practices. Adolescents seem to move easily in and out of the worlds their words refer to, cross the boundaries of local cultures, and create a totally unprecedented fusion of languages and encoded cultural perspectives. Yet their linguistic syncretism also evinces the cultural histories hidden behind words and evokes the worlds from where their ways of speaking originate. The coexistence of various ethnic communities, the history of power relationships between linguistic minorities and majorities, the symbolic value of types of music and sports, the identity-making role of expertise in the technological domain, the urban culture of African-Americans: all these historical and cultural references are encoded in adolescents' language and define their specific culture.

However, adolescents do not constitute a closed community. Their linguistic syncretism and innovations are more than auto-referential identity making-devices, and their social consequences go beyond the construction of a specific "age culture." By borrowing words from different cultural domains, extracting them from the original context of use and reinserting them into circulation through their everyday verbal interactions, adolescents both display and help create the cultural mosaic of the city they live in.

The widespread use of mobile phones contributes to this dual process of displaying membership in a polyphonic culture and constructing the social milieu as a heterogeneous cultural mosaic. Mobile phone use dominates teenagers' everyday life; they use it to talk to each other everywhere and at all times. The everywhere location of communicating with peers virtually transforms every time and every place into an open context for peer culture, peer language construction, and public displays. As mentioned above, as the mobile increases the number of conversations among young people, it also adds a public dimension to the traditionally private world of telephone conversations. In so doing, the mobile phone acts as a completely new sounding-board for adolescents' linguistic syncretism; it increasingly stretches the boundaries of their community and integrates their language in a broader context. In this sense, its use is more than a window on the everyday lives of young people or an amplifier of the cultural issues at stake. It is a tool for the constant construction of self and communities through language use in daily life.

Chapter 7

Mobile Culture in Everyday Life: Teenagers Talking on Their Mobiles

Everyday life can be conceived as a never-ending cultural work through which individuals constantly produce the meanings, structures, and social organization of their world, as well as their social identities and those of the people they interact with or talk about. Teenagers' mobile communication practices are an extremely significant example of this process. In the previous chapter we have analysed their *forms of talk* on mobile phones and showed how and to what extent mobile ways of speaking are social tools used to construct identities and culture. To further explore these fascinating processes of culture construction, we now analyse the contexts and topics of teenagers' mobile communication.

7.1 Making Sense of Space: Where Do Young People Talk on Their Mobile Phone?

Tracking mobile phone use in everyday life basically entails knowing when, where, for what purposes, why, with respect to whom, and in what social circumstances young people use the technology. As ethnographers, however, we wanted to go beyond compiling a descriptive list of activities and related contexts. What we were really interested in understanding were the ways that our informants interpreted and gave meaning to their own mobile phone-related practices. To gain access to this world of meanings and actions and to be able to produce a *thick description*[1] of them, we employed an effective methodological tool: the logbook, compiled by our teenage informants as they made and received calls. They were asked to record where they spoke, when, why, with whom, and about what. Their notes and, moreover, their explanations provided an extraordinary insight into how they domesticate mobile phones in their everyday practices and culture. As well as revealing everyday use of the technology, they also defined and clarified the uses from the point of view of the teenagers themselves.

Assoum made half his calls from his family home.[2] But why did he prefer to use his mobile to call his friends when he was alone in his room? At home, the technology let him create a private space, a bubble of intimacy that defines his home as a "public" space, by opposition and symbolically. The mobile phone thus works as a sense-making device: it reverses the usual meaning of the family home, making it no longer the private space par excellence.

Christine told us that her sister talked on her mobile in her room at night. This seemed a little strange to her. As she sought a possible reason, she focused first on the rules of family life: "In fact," she told us, "we are not allowed to talk on the phone at night." But while the parental prohibition could have been sufficient to explain the nocturnal mobile phone calls, it did not explain other home uses of the device. If it was the only reason, Christine wondered, why didn't her sister use the normal phone on weekends during the daytime? Here too there was an official reason: her sister claimed that she did not want to monopolize the line that was shared by everyone. However, once again Christine was not convinced. She concluded that her sister wanted to enclose herself in a personal space where no one could bother her. The bubble, its boundaries symbolically marked by the mobile phone, gave the other members of the family the status of strangers. Like outsiders who did not have access to a private club, her brothers, sisters, and parents were excluded from the circle created in the house by mobile communication technology.[3] Simultaneously meeting several developmental needs that characterize this stage of their life cycle, the mobile phone seems to allow adolescents to achieve their constant quest for a personal oasis away from the eyes (and ears) of other family members.

This process of meaning-creation is not confined to the home. It also extends to the school, one of the most meaningful environments of teenagers' social world. Assoum's mobile was always turned on during extracurricular activities, breaks, and the two main ritual moments of school life: coming to and leaving school. He received and made calls at those times. What we found most surprising was that 70 per cent of the calls took place in front of someone else, such as friends and classmates. At home, things were different: he was more likely to be alone when he talked on the mobile phone. Moreover, when he was at school, the number of calls skyrocketed: he used his mobile at school much more often than during his free time.

This overuse of the mobile phone, always on and always in front of someone else, defines school as a *social space*, where the point is not to enclose oneself in a private bubble but to allow one's private life to be public. At school Assoum could have withdrawn from his friends to make or receive calls, but he did not. By strategically using his mobile, he constructed himself as the crucial centre of a social network. Calling and being called in the presence of friends and acquaintances is thus a powerful means of creating one's social identity and those of others, and a tool for constructing and maintaining the social organization of the peer group.

While using a mobile phone at home reverses home's meaning as a private space and defines family members as outsiders, mobile phone use at school strengthens the shared signification of school as a public space and defines the users and the audience as members of a community of peers.

The way in which mobile phones redefine social spaces was one of our most striking discoveries. Not only do they reformulate the social meaning of *no-when times* and *nowhere spaces,*[4] but they overturn and break down the categories of public and private. The logbooks of our informants and the explanations they gave us about some uses of their mobiles shed light on the ways these phones impart meaning to places and people; moreover, they also educed the fluid nature of the categories people routinely use to organize reality. Far from being established notions, common-sense shared definitions such as home as a private place and school as a public one are deconstructed and reconstructed in and through everyday interactions. Mobile phones become tools for this process of everyday creation of meaning. They are powerful means for social actors to rebel against labels assigned by the dominant culture and against the normative nature of everyday knowledge. Tools for creating different meanings for social times, places, and identities, mobile phones participate in the process of (re)constructing a shared culture.

7.2 Repertoire of Cultural Reasons: Technologies and Teenage Laziness

In his logbook Assoum did more than just note locations; he was also asked to note *why* he chose to call or answer. The most frequent answer to this question was "It's easier." Sometimes he simply wrote "available." Often he didn't write anything in the box of the logbook. He seemed to have no explanation at all for why he had used his mobile instead of the traditional phone at home, Messenger on his computer, a public telephone in the street, or SMS.

Given his commitment to the research, these answers and even the missed answers raised questions. Beyond the obvious, what did "It's easier" mean? Why didn't he write anything in other cases? Asking him directly about the missing records seemed to be the best way to gain a cultural understanding of the simple, routine action of making a call on a mobile phone.

In the street, the mobile phone is obviously closer than any public telephone. As explained, "I've got my mobile in my hand, and the public phone is like over there, and anyway I'm lazy, I don't want to go over there." So it's not a question of money? one of us asked. "No, it's just closer," he replied.

We couldn't help asking, "When you say that it's because there was no public phone nearby, if there had been one – ?" He replied, "I probably wouldn't have used it either."

Trying to account for his use of the mobile phone on the street, he acknowledged that his actions could be interpreted as an individual attitude, but that was not at all the case. "If you've done research on teenagers," he went on, "you know that we're like that, we're lazy. If the remote control is over there, we won't get up and get it. We'll try to find a way to get it over!"

Thus it was our interpreter himself who established a link between the technology and a specific feature of young people's culture. He did not choose the mobile phone because there was an emergency or because he had no spare change but out of laziness. And he assumed that laziness, not as an individual trait but rather as a radically cultural reason, explained his uses of the mobile phone.

While choosing to use a mobile in the street was now understandable to us, why choose it when he was at the school office with a friend? Because there too "it was more accessible. I could have gone to the phone but it was far away." Then, seeing that he had to translate his conception of distance for us, Assoum spelled it out: "Well, it wasn't far away, it was at the end of the hall, but I didn't feel like walking. I could have gone over to it, but then I decided I wasn't going to walk all the way to the end of the hall."

Even the explanations for uses in school were fairly consistent with this logic: "Yeah, that day I was in drama and it's downstairs, and the phones are upstairs, and I don't know, sometimes they lock the doors, and I didn't feel like going up and then waiting fifteen minutes for them to open the door for me ... I just used my phone." Climbing stairs, running the risk of having to wait for someone to open the door: the mobile phone makes it possible to avoid all that.

And at home? In his notes about his home use of the mobile phone, Assoum did not limit himself to allusions to his quest for privacy. There too the mobile was chosen over the regular phone or other communications technologies because it was "more accessible," "easier," and "more available." When we asked him whether there were other phones in his bedroom, he said: "I had one, but the wire broke and I don't have time to go get a new wire and fiddle around with it." The broken wire seemed to be a good explanation of why he used the mobile phone in his room, until we learned that there was also a wireless phone in the house. Why not use that? Assoum's explanation left no doubt: "Then I'd have to go looking for the phone for three minutes because it's hidden somewhere, then I'd have to page it, and then it'd ring and make noise. So I just take my [mobile] phone and push the buttons and call the person."

During our dialogues in the field, we gradually discovered the underlying logic of Assoum's preference for the mobile phone: it let him *save* a significant amount of effort.

Assoum did not have a paper address book. Writing addresses or telephone numbers on paper seemed too old-fashioned to him. He kept phone numbers on his Palm Pilot and mobile phone. Usually, however, "instead of going and getting the other phone and then trying to find the number in that [the Palm Pilot] or in the other, I just look here [the mobile phone]. Then I've already got the number, and I just press the buttons and speak to the person." Once again the mobile phone revealed that it fits perfectly into teenagers' culture: not only was it an up-to-date, cool way to store addresses but it was a shortcut.

Unless the wireless phone was really available right next to him or he was seized by economic scruples (he was well aware that he spent money when he used his mobile phone), he used the mobile. All he had to do was press two or three buttons, and he was connected.

This was not an isolated case, nor an individual pattern of meaning. His friends also called him more often on his mobile phone for reasons related to this economy of actions: "Everyone calls me on my mobile because they don't want to waste time and call me at home just to find out that I'm not there and then have to call me on my mobile."

But what about other communications technologies? Messenger and SMS have all the features required to be included among the technologies culturally defined as "cool."[5] These items mark the difference between young people and adults, and their use is a strong identity-making device by which adolescents define themselves. Yet in this community of peers, mobile calls are often more popular. Why? In one of his notes in the log-book referring to the reasons he was using his mobile at that moment, Assoum wrote: "Easier than writing." His interpretation of his own words clearly shows how and to what extent teenagers domesticate technologies according to the cultural frames of references of their specific culture: "Oh yeah, I was on Messenger. Then sometimes when we're chatting, you know, you've got to understand I'm lazy, I don't feel like figuring out how to explain it in words, I just call the person, and talk to him, it's easier. For example, he probably asked me a question [the friend with whom he was talking on Messenger], then instead of writing because I found it <u>long</u>, I didn't feel like typing for two hours to make him understand. So I did the little phone sign and called him. I do the telephone [icon], or else I say 'pick up now.'"

Thus the two communications technologies are not interchangeable but complementary, in keeping with criteria that are cultural rather than tech-nological. This was clearly exemplified by the use of hyperbole[6] ("typing for two hours") to underline the effort that would be required if he did not use the mobile phone. The logic of laziness determines whether there will be a switch to another technology.

Talking is easier than writing. This cultural perception of the difference between oral and written communication partly explains the total absence of sms exchanges between these teenagers. At least this is the reason Assoum gave to account for it. Among the people he knew who were his age, "practically no one uses it. They'd say why? 'Why write the message? I'm just going to talk to him directly, then tell him in words, out loud.' If you look at the technology, it's really three letters per number, it takes like ten minutes to write 'hello.' I'm not going to bother."

This hyperbolic reference to the technology's mechanical limitations ("it's really three letters per number, it takes like ten minutes to write 'hello'") is slightly suspicious, coming from a teenager for whom there is no possible faster action than to type on a keyboard. The absence of sms seems to lie in the *writing* itself and in its perceived difficulty relative to talking.

In contrast with the European context,[7] the limited use of text messag-ing among the mobile communications practices of these North American teenagers is striking. The mobile cultures in the two areas where we did fieldwork – despite some strong analogies – differ considerably in the use of sms. Almost absent at the time among Canadians teenagers, sms was the first and often only choice of young Italians. Our field data confirm the general trends in the two countries and may be explained in terms of the strong differences in price policies and certain marketing decisions made by telephone companies.

However, these explanations are not the only ones, nor the most relevant, at least from our informants' viewpoints. Setting the economic explanation aside, we advance an *ethnographic interpretation*, that is, an interpretation oriented to the way our informants explain their own choices. As we have seen, they invoke not economic but cultural reasons for mobile phone use. The logic of laziness associated with their perception of writing suffices to explain why their mobile culture is mainly oral. Faced with the two forms of communication offered by mobile phones, this group of North American urban adolescents chooses what seems to fit best with their claims to laziness – namely, oral conversation.

This cultural interpretation that the preference given to mobile phones over systems that require writing is grounded in laziness applies as well to the use of other technologies. The preference highlighted by Assoum for listening to music on the computer again shows that the real strength of some technologies lies in the way they allow for an economy of actions: "It's like music on a CD, every time you've got to get u::p,[8] o::pen the thing, find ano::ther CD, pu::t it in, pre::ss play, then go:: to track. On the computer you just take the song you want, put it in a list, then hit play, and then they follow. You don't have to change the CD every time. On top of it, I've got a remote control for my computer. I can be far away, then do NEXT, STOP, raise the volume."

From our informants' viewpoint, the preference for the computer over CD players has nothing to do with quality of sound or additional functions such as the ability to compare or combine versions of the same song. Once again Assoum invokes laziness[9] to explain why adolescents prefer listening to music on the computer.

The more we learned about this cultural world of adolescents, the more it became clear that we would have to take this feature of their culture into account in order to understand their use of technologies.

7.3 Domesticating Technologies: Vegging, Doing Nothing, and Talking on the Mobile

In the course of our fieldwork we gradually discovered that teenagers' everyday life consists of a set of cultural practices that are accomplished and, more significantly, accounted for by "laziness."

In the logbook where Assoum was supposed to note what he was doing while using the mobile phone, he sometimes wrote only: "doing nothing" or "vegging." What did that mean? Even Assoum found it difficult to explain the meaning of such a routine: "Well, 'doing nothing' isn't really doing nothing, it's just like, how to explain 'doing nothing,' it's just that I'm sitting at home talking on the computer, doing nothing also means sitting on my bed staring, not thinking about anything at all, or just staring at a point on the wall." Thus "doing nothing" includes quite a few activities, including using a mobile phone.

While difficult to define even for our informant, "doing nothing" is a very specific activity, and a characteristic way of being for Assoum and his friends. The same for "vegging." Trying to translate this "experience near concept" (Geertz 1977), Assoum said:

"Vegging," it's like you're with someone and you're talking about something useless, often after drinking, we call that "vegging." You can veg at school too, like when you're sitting in the auditorium or when you're sitting and talking about really useless things, like the worst films you ever saw or new ones, or the new game system that's coming out next year. Stuff like that, really useless, or about how to save guitar and drum samples in my computer, things like that, it's vegging, it's conversation about completely useless things. But you can also veg when you're watching TV. It's like if I call Chan I say, "What are you doing," he's going to say "Vegging," I say, What?" and then he's going to say, "Watching TV."

To elaborate on the importance and legitimacy of laziness, Assoum went into detail about his cultural universe. Laziness is a category of action, a relevant frame for certain forms of behaviour and attitudes that have been labelled "doing nothing" and "vegging." Reference to the emptiness and (apparent) uselessness of what one is doing or saying and to the (apparent) waste of time seems to be the common feature of these ways of acting and being: "It's that you're at a point where you go home and don't want to do anything, so you think about nothing ... You know, it's like at some point you're really vegged out, so you just sit and don't move for like an hour, then you look at something, stare at the wall, talk about things that make no sense ... Often me and my friends, we veg together, we talk about something, watch TV or a film, but we don't move, physically we do nothing."

Yet "vegging" and "doing nothing" are in no way meaningless activities. Through useless conversations about "unrelated things," by saying that they are vegging, through hours spent slumped together somewhere watching TV, young people in fact weave social ties and reinforce the cohesiveness of the group. In the end, you do not veg with just anyone!

How does the use of communication technologies fit into this lazy world? Communicating with friends via mobile phone is an activity perfectly consistent with the display of cultural laziness, with this "doing nothing" that is not "not doing anything," with the waste of time that is not time wasted, and with the predilection for oral exchanges that are apparently easier than writing on a screen. Mobile phone use thus naturally acquires a place in the practices of adolescents' everyday life that are associated with nothing and emptiness. Why?

As usual, the answer was there from the beginning. The mobile is "easy," "available," "on me." It is not even necessary to move – you can communicate "without wasting time" in writing or looking for an address or phone number. The facility of the mobile phone, its accessibility, its mobility, and the fact that it can become an appendage are technological and material characteristics that make it a perfect match for laziness and allow it to integrate easily into adolescents' universe.[10]

Is this why companies increasingly target young people in marketing campaigns?[11] Perhaps young people are the best interpreters of the logic embodied in this technological communication object, even better than businesspeople?

7.4 Breaking the Rules: The Implicit Logic of Mobile Phone Use

Assoum's reasons for using his mobile provided extraordinary insight into the interpretive repertoire through which teenagers domesticate this technology in the terms of their specific culture. Assoum was supposed to note in his logbook not only why he called but also why he *answered* the mobile phone every time he did. Often he wrote nothing. The box reserved for "Why you answer" was empty. When he explained his reasons for not filling out the box,[12] Assoum revealed the realm of self-evidence in telephone communications: "I didn't write anything because I didn't know what to say, I found it really useless. Why did I answer? Because it rang. I don't know, to me, to me, you answer. In my head that's how it worked, if it rings, I answer. I don't need to justify why I answer."

The only reason to answer a mobile is because it rings. As we have noted, the telephone is a technology that *makes us do things* because its first action (ringing) is understood as involving a duty to answer.[13] This applies to both mobile and traditional telephones. We do not even know why we do it, and when we think about it, the only reason we can give is because it rings. The reaction is an automatism, and the vast majority of people answer their phones because they accept this kind of manipulation. However, it should be noted that in the case of mobile phones, unlike many traditional telephones, the phone *could* not ring. Mobile phones are designed as communication tools that can be turned off and on again by the user when needed. Yet most adolescents do not seem to consider that a mobile can be turned off.

Their logic[14] can be summarized as follows: If you have a mobile phone then you keep it on. Since it is on, it rings. Since it rings, you answer.

When asked to choose between answering and not answering, the adolescents in our study did not seem to consider the possibility of turning off their mobile phones. They had therefore decided that there would not be a choice. This is a clear example of a human actor's power over technology. The technology can manipulate only if one chooses to be manipulated – except that in the case of adolescents, this is no longer a choice but an automatic habit, and they simply have no idea why they answer. For Assoum, as for the other adolescents we met,[15] owning a mobile entails that it always be on and that he answer all calls that come in. This kind of use is consistent with a broader approach that governs this specific culture, namely that of being reachable at all times, being constantly connected. As our data show, this quality is what has led teenagers to adopt mobile phones.

Besides confirming the cultural reasons for teenagers' adoption of the mobile, the entries – or rather, non-entries – in the logbook revealed other aspects of the implicit logic underlying the everyday use of the technology. Since the calls received and made had been recorded, we knew that they had occurred. Given Assoum's willingness to participate in the research, the empty spaces intrigued us. What had happened? Assoum explained: "I found it a little … let's just say that our brains are a little – very – lazy, so sometimes it was a bit boring. You call someone to say 'I'm at your street corner, where are you?' I didn't feel like filling out a thing and then wasting five minutes writing that I'd got to his house … you know, it's because you're outside, it's cold, and I'm like in the street, and there's not really anywhere I can lean against to write, and there's like wind and water … And on top of that people in the bus looked at me like I was weird."

Thus the commitment to record everything in the logbook contradicted both the logic of laziness and that of mobile phone use. For researchers, this is not a methodological failure but an opportunity to gain understanding. Breaking implicit everyday rules is sometimes the most powerful way of bringing them to light.

As from the point of view of adolescents, a primary virtue of the mobile phone is that it allows for economy of action, filling out the logbook entailed precisely the opposite degree of effort, in that it required a certain amount of work. Whereas "using the mobile" meshes perfectly with teenagers' cultural laziness, recording notes in a logbook does not. Another revealing difference between the two activities concerns the simultaneity of behaviours: mobile phones let people accomplish several things at once, such as walking while talking on the phone or using a computer while talking to a friend. In contrast, taking notes in a logbook required interrupting co-occurring activities, which was one of the reasons why Assoum sometimes neglected this task. By breaking the logic of overlapping, the logbook revealed this logic in action.

The examples Assoum gave to illustrate why he had not filled out the logbook provided an excellent glimpse into the underlying rules governing mobile phone use. However, these examples revealed more than that, confirming our hypothesis on teenagers' prototypical use of mobile phones.[16] Young people's canonical use of mobile phones (not necessarily the most frequent) occurs in the street or on the bus when they are going somewhere, in everyday no-when times and nowhere places.[17] This ideal-typical use covers only 20 per cent of the real uses that we observed. Nevertheless, it is the scenario that young people refer to when they speak of mobile phone use.[18]

If the paradigmatic background is "the street," what is the typical conversation on a mobile phone? The examples Assoum gave also revealed the teenagers' cultural model of this communicative practice: "I'm at the street corner, where are you?" and "I've arrived in front of his house."

Again, this is only an ideal typical model of a mobile phone conversation. Most calls between the young people studied were much longer and more detailed. They were often reports about everyday events, storytelling activities where conversational narrative took place and the latest gossip was exchanged. Yet despite the real uses, the typical example of a mobile phone conversation was "I'm here, I'm almost there, where are you, join me here." If we combine this model of a mobile phone conversation with teenagers' cultural rule that "requires" one always to keep the mobile on, we obtain an extremely consistent thick description: mobile phones let adolescents know moment by moment who is where, doing what, with whom. This "ideal" use of the mobile is precisely what differentiates this technology from traditional telephones.

As soon as mobile phones became part of teenagers' routines, the fancy metaphorical formulas "social network" and "social link" became literal. Mobile phones do more than allow users to enter networks of friends or establish links between two people who are a couple. They create those networks and links. "Always being in touch" lies at the core of the repertoire of cultural reasons why the mobile has been so quickly integrated by adolescents into their everyday social practices.

7.5 "Being a Couple": Maps of Everyday Life and Simulacra of Proximity

To educe the role of mobile phones in constructing social links, we will look at the exchanges between two other adolescents.[19] It is mainly in the way that the partners begin and end phone calls that they establish and confirm the type of relationship they are in.

(*Opening*)
ANTOINE (caller): [Ring]
SOPHIE (called): Hey, Antoine.
ANTOINE: So.
SOPHIE: Okay?
ANTOINE: Yeah.
[...]
(*Closing*)
ANTOINE: Ah::m, Sophie, I can't wait for you to be here.
SOPHIE: Hei, yeah [*laughs*].

(*Opening*)
ANTOINE (caller): [Ring]
SOPHIE (called): Yes.
ANTOINE: Well, Sophie?
SOPHIE: Yeah.
ANTOINE: So.
[...]
(*Closing*)
ANTOINE: I'll call you back, okay?
SOPHIE: Okay, okay, darling, I love you.
ANTOINE: Bye.

Antoine and Sophie do not need to start with the canonical sequence for introducing a telephone conversation ("Hi, how are you doing?" "Okay, and you?" "Okay"). Their relationship lets them start a conversation on a communication channel that is already established and permanently open. The economy of words presupposes and also confirms and displays a high degree of intimacy. Yet this strategy is not enough, in that close friends too may bypass the introductory sequence. To demonstrate the kind of relationship they have, they compensate for the brevity of the beginning of their conversation by expending more conversational effort in concluding it. When they end the call, the two partners tell one another (as well as the imaginary audience that is always there when one uses a mobile) that they are in love.

We have only to compare the above conversations with how Antoine talks to other girls to see that mobile phone calls are communication devices young people use to maintain and create social ties.

(*Opening*)
AMÉLIE (caller): [Ring]
ANTOINE (called): Hi, Amélie.
AMÉLIE: Hi, how are you doing? Are you busy?
ANTOINE: No, no, no, I just finished dinner
[...]
(*Closing*)
AMÉLIE: Okay, I'll call you back.
ANTOINE: That's fine, Amélie. Okay, bye.
AMÉLIE: Bye.

(*Opening*)
CÉLINE (caller): [Ring]
ANTOINE (called): Hi, Céline.
CÉLINE: Hi.
ANTOINE: So.
CÉLINE: You're doing okay?
ANTOINE: Yeah. And you?
CÉLINE: Yeah. Are you busy?
ANTOINE: No, I'm reading my *Don Juan* for the second time.
[...]
(*Closing*)
CÉLINE: Okay, great. Bye bye.
ANTOINE: Bye.

The difference between the opening and closing formulas used by the couple and by the friends is striking. The technology solves the problem of identifying who is calling, and friends may also be close enough to recognize one another's voices, but they still have to establish the platform of courtesy ("How are you?" "Fine and you?") that authorizes them to enter into the subject of conversation. The closings are also different: friends use the conventional formula. These differences show us how young people use telephone calls to establish each other's relative positions in the network and create a social order.

Their conversational strategies form a recurrent pattern of telephone calls as such. But where does the mobile phone make the difference, and when is it a preferred social tool? The portability and delocalization specific to it provide new means of and new stages for establishing and confirming the kinds of social relations among young people.

Traditional telephones make it possible to anticipate the range of actions in which the person being called could be engaged. Depending on the time of day and on the location (which can always be known), traditional telephones allow us to calculate a call's degree of social appropriateness. Members of a cultural community share typical scripts of activities-in-context that enable them to know who can call who, where, and at what time. The mobile phone has broken the anticipatory mechanism that regulated the appropriateness of telephone calls and limited the technology's intrusiveness into other people's lives.

Mobile phones allow, even if unnecessary, "perpetual contact" (Katz and Aakhus 2002) with someone who could be anywhere and doing anything. This intrusive feature becomes a symbolic threshold that makes it possible to distinguish those who have access to perpetual contact from those who cannot take it for granted. It is not by chance that the mobile phone has introduced a virtually obligatory new opening for telephone conversations: "Are you busy?" Typically situated at the beginning of the call, it is the necessary requirement for the conversation to continue. Like knocking on a half-open door, the question is not asked by everyone. Sophie could take it for granted that she can "disturb" Antoine, but Antoine's other friends had to negotiate the appropriateness of their intrusion.

In exchanges using mobile phones, the various members of a social network constantly create and confirm the kind of the relationship they are in. They define themselves as friends or lovers through the words they use and those they do not, and depending on the interactive strategies that they use to enter the lives of others.

Let's follow this couple during another of their mobile conversations:

ANTOINE: So.

SOPHIE: Hey!

ANTOINE: Yeah, so tha:t I just got back from my workout.

SOPHIE: Oh, yeah?

ANTOINE: Then, uhhh, then −

SOPHIE: [???]

ANTOINE: Oh, aw fuck, [*English in the original*] shit, I lost one of my fuckin' gloves.

SOPHIE: Not your nice blue ones.

ANTOINE: Yeah, well, I lost one, bu:t maybe at gym or in French class, so tomorrow I'm going to check [*English in the original*].

SOPHIE: Nothing to say, me too. I lost my mittens. [*laughing*]

ANTOINE: Yeah, I know.

SOPHIE: I could call you an airhead, but you might call me one too.

ANTOINE: Yeah ... shit, shit, shit, what's that?

SOPHIE: What's happening?

ANTOINE: That's okay look ⌈Sophie:

SOPHIE: ⌊No:: !

ANTOINE: I'm going home now. I'll call you back, okay?

SOPHIE: No::... [*laughing*]

ANTOINE: Co::me on! That's okay? [*laughing*]

SOPHIE: Yeah.

ANTOINE: Okay? So in a few in a few seconds, um.

SOPHIE: But you're going to have dinner!

ANTOINE: Huh?!

SOPHIE: Your sister just told me that you're going to have dinner.

ANTOINE: Ah, fuck. But, um, but look, I'll call you right after dinner.

SOPHIE: Okay.

ANTOINE: Okay, right away, right away after.

SOPHIE: Okay, dear.

ANTOINE: I love you.

SOPHIE: Me too, a lot. [*laughs*]

ANTOINE: Okay, see you soon.

SOPHIE: Bye. [*English in the original*]

Note first that this conversation gives us a glimpse of the linguistic patchwork that characterizes exchanges among North American urban youth.[20] Swearing, certain terms typical of teenagers' ways of speaking, and regional variations[21] identify the partners as young French-speaking Canadians. However, note also the conventional formulas of intimate language ("darling," "I love you"), the lexicon, and some language games specific to this couple ("Nothing to say, me too," "You can call me a airhead"). By listening to this conversation, we can see their relationship in action. When, upon learning of the loss of Antoine's glove, Sophie answers, "Not your nice blue ones," she is showing how much she knows about him and that she has acquired the right to express regret and get involved in Antoine's clothing concerns. The language game set off by notification of the imminent end of the conversation ("I'm going home now, I'll call you back okay? – No::... – co::me on! okay? So in a few in a few seconds, um. – (…) – Look, I'll call you right after dinner – Okay – Okay, right away, right away after"), simply confirms the kind of relationship between the two adolescents. They speak like this because they are young, French-speaking Canadians and in love, but the opposite is also true: they construct their identities of young Canadians in love by using this way of speaking.

The mobile phone has given people more opportunities and new stages for language games and verbal performances through which they construct their identities and relationships. They can do it at times and in places that were until recently meaningless: in the street, on the way out of the gym, just before arriving at home.

7.6 Live Narrating of Everyday Life: Storytelling on the Mobile Phone

Besides creating new stages for representing oneself in everyday life, there is at least another way in which the mobile phone makes social relationships: *in the living narratives of daily events.*[22]

While everyday life events and routines have always been topics specific to (telephone) conversations between intimates, the mobile phone has changed the nature of this discourse activity. The storytelling of daily life events no longer occurs after the fact: it is now possible to engage in live narration. Let us look at another "mobile dialogue":

SOPHIE: How come you're talking on the mobile?
ANTOINE: Um, because, look, I'm at Val des Arbres School.
SOPHIE: Huh!?
ANTOINE: I'm at Val des Arbres School.
SOPHIE: How come?
ANTOINE: Because, no, I:: um, I drove to go get my sister. She's finishing her

kinball game right now.

SOPHIE: Okay, you went to her kinball game?

ANTOINE: Yeah, well, um, I arrived right now. Look, I left home ten minutes ago and at the same time I'm practising. I have to drive a bit.

SOPHIE: Okay, well, are you going to stay there for the whole game?

ANTOINE: No, no, it's finished, she's finished now. Everyone's coming out and then we're going home.

SOPHIE: Ah! okay.

[...]

ANTOINE: Uh, so, um, that's it, so aside from that [???] um look, we're giving a lift to her friends. They are getting in now and then we go drive them home and then I'm coming home. So it's just to say I'll call you, like when I get there.

Much has been written on the micro- and hyper-coordination that characterizes mobile phone use among adolescents (Ling and Yttri 2002). Indeed, the social construction of coordinated activities for a common goal (such as to meet in a café) is really one of the most striking examples of creative use of this technology by young people.[23] Live narration is another one. It is neither a question of mutual coordination to attain a common goal nor of constructing a joint action (i.e., meeting). It involves real-time, step-by-step mapping of the actions performed and places visited by the user: "I left 10 minutes ago," "I'm at the school," "Everybody's coming out," "Her friends are getting in now," "it's just to say I'll call you." The present tense now governs storytelling on the phone. Narratives no longer inform others about what one did during the day but let them participate in what is going on while it is happening. The mobile phone lets Antoine and Sophie live each other's lives in real time, which means creating a simulacrum of proximity despite geographical separation. Through live narration of the events of their everyday life, Antoine and Sophie can build one of the crucial dimensions of "being a couple": they can merge their lives.

Their case is not exceptional. The mobile phone has clearly become a part of the everyday lives of couples and has introduced a new repertoire of actions that make it possible to talk about and build a life together. Let us look at what is said by Patrick and Danielle, a couple in their twenties:

DANIELLE: But especially when he's at the store, I never use the store line anymore, I call on the mobile. Because I know that if I call on the mobile, I'm not going to block the store line. I can call ten times a day! I have a question, sometimes there are lots of people who ask me questions because they know that he works in that, and they want some information, I dial the number, I say "Do you have that, blahblahblah," I hang up. Some days I talk more than others, like there are days when I don't call at all. It really depends on how the day is going. If I'm not in a good mood, I call him, I go "grrr!!!," I grump, I hang up. Then he does the same thing!

RESEARCHER: He doesn't say anything?

DANIELLE: He just listens.

PATRICK: Me, I'm the big passive type!

RESEARCHER: So, with the mobile he's, how to say, easier to reach?

DANIELLE: Yeah, yeah, sometimes I'm waiting for him there, it seems long. So then I call him, I say, "Okay, where are you?" He tells me, "I'm still in the store." So then I relax, "Okay, how much longer?" Sometimes it takes longer than expected, you know. But otherwise I'd've had to wait, I couldn't have done anything, and then I would've said, "Oh come on, where is he?" and I would've been even more upset. But instead I can call him, and he can tell me what's going on. I'll say, "Okay, right, I'll wait for you, you know, and come on!"

Calling one another ten times a day, the fact that one has the right to do so, calling one another to say where one is and what one is doing, and having the privilege of not having to wait one's turn for the traditional phone – the mobile phone has opened a truly new range of means to construct, maintain, and express a couple's relationship.

Obviously this does not mean that the mobile phone itself creates social links that would not exist otherwise, or that it imposes a specific way of expressing such links. Antoine and Sophie, Patrick and Danielle are not victims of technological determinism; rather, they choose to let technology enter their lives and transform their ways of "being a couple." Providing users with a grammar of action, mobile phones invent a new language. Who calls whom, when, from where and about what are a new alphabet that allows people to express and fine-tune their relationships. As a technological social actor, the mobile phone cooperates with humans in the subtle, delicate construction of relationships.

7.7 Mobile Phone Use as a Friendship-Building Activity

Friendship is one of the most meaningful aspects of teenagers' specific culture. Friends and their mutual relationships, their shared activities and their organization, are a priority if not *the* priority of the daily life of adolescents (Galland 1996). How do they integrate mobile phone use into this crucial dimension of their lives? Does the mobile add something new to the friendship-building activity in which they invest so much time and cultural effort?

Aside from the ways of speaking through which they express and maintain their friendships, young people continually talk on their phones *about* friendship. Below is an example of this recurring topic.

Assoum is at home doing "nothing special." He calls Sharif. A conversation begins concerning a film on which Assoum is working. It is about young people, and Assoum needs to find someone willing to play the role of the boy. One thing leads to another, and Sharif tells his friend this story:

SHARIF: Me, then there was another, you know, there was that Chinese guy there?

ASSOUM: Yeah, oh yeah, him, Billy.

SHARIF: Billy. He failed French three times.

ASSOUM: Damn ... I don't know, I can't understand, but you know sometimes in math, bing! you understand, and then sometimes later you don't get it. That's really frustrating. [*laughs*]

SHARIF: Yeah, but with Billy it's something else.

ASSOUM: [???] At lunch, it's because he doesn't understand French really well.

SHARIF: [???] It's because he doesn't understand. [???]

ASSOUM: That's it [???] They said "Ah, he went to China and forgot his French, and now he's back."

SHARIF: [???] But you know [???], you know, it's like, first step, okay?

ASSOUM: Uum.

SHARIF: He told me, you know, the first year when he failed?

ASSOUM: Yeah.

SHARIF: In 436, he said "Help me." You know in the second year.

ASSOUM: Yeah.

SHARIF: So I helped him in the first step, ⌈okay?

ASSOUM: ⌊Then after he didn't come back?

SHARIF: He was serious, he had eighty-four in the first.

[...]

SHARIF: Second step, I asked him, "Why aren't you asking me any questions anymore?" He told me, "Ah, it's over, I don't care."

ASSOUM: Ah, so that's why ⌈there

SHARIF: ⌊[???] Still ...

ASSOUM: So like an idiot, he could have like saved tons of points, eh.

SHARIF: That's it, eh, I had the time man, anyway I don't care, I wasn't doing any- thing anyway.

ASSOUM: Yeah and on top of it you were in the same school as him.

SHARIF: That's it, you know.

ASSOUM: You could help him every lunchhour.

SHARIF: You know, we talked all the time, every lunch hour we were together, ⌈in the morning

ASSOUM: ⌊he, he talked about cars. [*laughs*]

SHARIF: [???] Yeah, he talked about cars.

[...]

SHARIF: Yeah. So since then, eh.

ASSOUM: Yeah.

SHARIF: [???] he called once, man, that's all.

ASSOUM: [Billy]? Fuck. It's been a long time too. Before you were together all the time, you and him.

SHARIF: Yeah, but it's over.

ASSOUM: It was fun before. Every time I saw you two, you were together, you came over together.

SHARIF: Now he wants ... It's him, eh, who doesn't want to talk anymore. I don't know why.

ASSOUM: Didn't he say he had a girlfriend in China or something. I dunno? [???]

SHARIF: Yeah, yeah, he has a girlfriend in China, eh.

ASSOUM: Oh.

SHARIF: [???] So he said, "Now I'm serious, I'm studying at Marianne."

ASSOUM: Maybe, maybe, because he wants uh::: I don't know, maybe he's concen- trating on that because he thinks that ...

SHARIF: Yeah, he's concentrating on school, but I dunno, I dunno what he's doing besides being ...

ASSOUM: I don't know. When he's ready, he'll call you, eh.

SHARIF: Well, I hope [???]

ASSOUM: Otherwise you've always got me, you've always got Mike, you've always got the others.

SHARIF: Yeah, but I don't care, he doesn't want, doesn't want ...

This long story about school problems[24] is really a long discussion about friendship. Being a friend means helping someone in trouble (the "Chinese guy" who had trouble learning French), trying to understand why he has problems (the friend did not really understand French), justi- fying his actions, taking his side (the others said that in the end it was almost Billy's fault because he went back to China), giving one's time, and offering to help for free.

However, the offer of friendship entails something in return: the person who receives help is expected to assume reciprocal friendship duties and not suddenly disappear. Sharif's friend disappeared and did not honour the contract implicit in Sharif's behaviour. Moreover, he was not grateful for Sharif's offer to help him a second time. Billy refused the offer ("It's over, I don't care"), and instead of taking advantage of Sharif's offer, he seemed interested only in cars. Yet with Sharif's help he had got his average up to 84 per cent!

In the first part of the story, Assoum and Sharif are establishing and renewing their definition of friendship, and they highlight its components. Friendship is a social pact that prescribes specific behaviour for both parties. Sharif's disappointment – while repeatedly denied ("I didn't care anyway," "I don't care, he doesn't want, doesn't want") – is still strong. He does not seem to be able to accept that Billy turned his back on him once he no longer needed his help in French. When they were together all the time, always seen together and going to Assoum's together, others would have said they were friends. What happened is thus experienced as a betrayal of the contract of friendship.

In response to this story about a broken friendship, Assoum decides to assuage his friend's disappointment and acts as a friend. He tries to find reasons in Billy's life (maybe he had a girlfriend in China, and maybe he was concentrating on his schoolwork) that could explain why he disappeared from Sharif's life. By doing so, he tries to heal his friend's wounded pride: Sharif has not been exploited or betrayed, and what has happened parallels what might happen everyday to everyone. The conclusion of the story is a reaffirmation of what it means to be a friend and of the friendship contract that links Assoum and Sharif: "When he's ready, he'll call you, otherwise you've always got me, you've always got Mike, you've always got the others." Sharif has real friends and they are faithful because they are always there. For those who are not really part of the group, it is ultimately pointless to worry about them.

In the dialogue the two friends do many things: they re-establish their friendship, confirm the terms of that kind of social contract, and establish the borders between those who are part of the group and those who are not. The group is thus the social cell in which the contract is really binding, and it is among the members of the group that one should expect it to be respected.

This long mobile conversation about friendship is one example of a recurrent pattern: real or presumed friends, their behaviours, reflecting the constraining rules of friendship, have always been relevant topics of teenagers' conversations. They recur in mobile dialogues as well. The mobile phone, especially designed for communicating in emergency situations, is totally integrated into pre-existing discursive practices such as telling stories about friends.

This "nothing new" quality of mobile conversations among young people is a sign of the global process whereby new technologies are domesticated into the economy of meanings of a given community. As soft media, they may be integrated into shared and yet established social practices and manipulated by users to attain their own specific aims. In the background of this "nothing new" quality of the mobile phone in teenagers' everyday cultural practices, there are nevertheless some uses that highlight how the encounter between technologies and cultural practices creates new ways of constructing social links.

7.8 Guess Where I Am: Delocalization as a Social Game

As we have seen, user delocalization has created new, specific subjects of conversation. For example, "Where are you?" and "Are you busy" have become typical introductions for mobile phone conversations. The presence or absence of these formulas marks the partners' degree of intimacy and the legitimate level of intrusion into the other's space and activities, which the mobile has now made unpredictable. This specific dimension of mobile communication has been grasped by teenagers and used to confirm their friendship in new ways.

ASSOUM: Yeah, what's up?
CHAN: Uh, playing [???] you know.
ASSOUM: Uh huh. [All game], no life.
CHAN: Yeah, no.
ASSOUM: [*laughs*] Guess where I am?
CHAN: Uh, Outremont?
ASSOUM: Yeah, dude, you're goo::d. How did you know?
CHAN: Oh, man ... you're always there.

The user's delocalization makes it possible to trigger a social game designed to confirm the relationship: "How did you know?" "You're always there." Being a friend means many things, including knowing where the other usually is. This exchange, which the mobile phone makes possible, thus becomes a test of how well two friends know each other. Passing the test is a way of confirming and identifying the degree of friendship, renewing the contract, and saying "we're friends." Mobile use, or perhaps this specific use of the mobile, thus makes it possible to display *the kind* of friendship among members of the group: the "merging friendship" entails a high degree of reciprocal revealing of detailed knowledge of the routine habits of the other and the possibility of anticipating his or her movements because both know the other's routine.

7.8 Borrowed Calls and Co-Conversations

By following the daily phone calls of this network of adolescents, we were able to identify two other phenomena that were consistent with our interpretation of the use of the mobile phone as a friendship-building activity. Some of the calls on Assoum's mobile were made by friends. Under what circumstances? And what were the reasons for these "lent" and "borrowed" phone calls?

Asked to describe the context of one of these borrowed calls, Assoum gave us a few details: "That time it was Hugo, well, he was waiting for his father who was supposed to come and get him, but he wasn't coming. Then he called his mother and then his father [...] we were at school hanging out.[25] Yeah, he was waiting for his parents. His father was supposed to come and get him."

As Assoum described other occurrences of this specific use of the mobile, we saw that the scenario is more or less always the same. At school or in other social places such as a café, one of his friends asks to borrow his mobile to make a call. The people called are either parents or another member of the group. The conversation is rather brief and always takes place in front of Assoum. As we learned more about the borrowed phone calls, we started to see certain implicit rules applying to borrowers and lenders. For the owner, it was clear that he could not refuse to lend his mobile phone to a friend who asked. For the friend, it was clear that he could not ask for the phone to call whoever, anywhere, and any way he wanted. He could call his parents or common friends, but he could not engage in a long conversation or go away from the owner to talk privately. This set of unspoken rules showed the profoundly social nature of this use of the mobile phone.

It is only by situating these practices in the broader context of teen-agers' specific culture that we can better discern the issues at stake. Call-ing your parents to get them to come and pick you up or to let them know that you are going to be late is an acknowledged and shared necessity. Helping a friend discharge this obligation is part of the friendship con-tract. Calling common friends is a different case of lending, because the owner shares the goal and is concerned by the call in the same way as the user. In both cases the sharing leads to an expectation of something in return. The owner has the right to witness the calls, which gives him a position of control and confirms the deeply social nature of the phone lending. Whereas within the family the mobile enters the dynamic of "gift/counter-gift exchange" (Mauss 1950)[26] as an object, within friendship re-lations the gift exchange concerns *the use* of the mobile (Weilenmann and Larsson 2001). In this case as in the others, the offer of the gift creates a system of debits and credits. A friend's request obliges the owner to satis-fy it, which, in return, puts the friend in debt to the owner. The elemen-tary structure of the social link is thus established. Obviously the exchange triggered by the borrowed call is totally symbolic. Assoum, as the owner of a good that he could lend to his friends, confirms his leadership in the group, and the friends receive his gift, thereby confirming their member-ship as affiliates.

Nonetheless, this exchange achieves more than confirming reciprocal social positions among peers. It also confirms the friendship between the owner and the users (because it costs money, you do not lend it to just anybody, and you do not ask just anybody for it) and the membership link between caller and called, because you do not call just anyone with a friend's mobile phone.

Once it enters the gift exchange, the use of a mobile becomes a power-ful tool for constructing culture and social organization among peers: it establishes social positions within the group and confirms the weight of certain aspects of young people's culture, such as constraints due to rela-tionships with parents, the obligations that go with the status of friend, and maintenance of contact among members of the network.

The extremely complex nature of this social phenomenon has additional consequences. Calls on borrowed mobile phones produce social relation-ships and exchanges not only between owners and borrowers, between those who call and those who are called, but also among those who use a friend's mobile and those who witness the conversation. Borrowed calls entail another phenomenon: *co-conversations*.

In co-conversations, the traditional model of a telephone conversation disappears. The mobile is passed from one person to the next, and the conversation is thus distributed among a number of co-speakers. Karim called Assoum, who was going to see a movie with Annie and Chan. They were speaking when Annie yelled something.

KARIM: What did she say?
ASSOUM [to Annie]: I think I'm not going to tell him that either.
KARIM: What?
Assoum: She says that there's a little dog that's walking all alone and then jumping. [???]
KARIM: We can cook it at my house.
ASSOUM: Tell Manouche we'll take it to your place, your place. Annie! Annie, don't [???]
[...]
KARIM: Okay, pass me Chan.
ASSOUM: Why?
KARIM: Pass me that Chinaman!
CHAN: Hello?
KARIM: Hey, man.
CHAN: Yeah, yo, how're you doing?

Far from isolating two people and engaging them in a one-on-one inter-action, the mobile phone here constructs a social cell out of three or four friends who participate in a joint action at the same time but who are not all in the same place. As we saw in the case of borrowed calls, the user does not have the right to retreat to speak on the mobile phone of a friend. He or she has to involve the owner, not as an additional person *overhear-ing* the conversation but as a *co-speaker* – in other words, as a player on the stage. All borrowed calls to common friends in the network become in fact co-conversations.

Here is another case. Assoum and Chan are at Starbucks. Chan asks Assoum for his mobile so he can reach Yves. Assoum dials Yves's number, starts the conversation, and only then passes the mobile to Chan.

ASSOUM: Yeah.
YVES: Huh.
ASSOUM: So what's up?
YVES: Nothing. I'm vegging.
ASSOUM: Huh? Ah, okay, Chan wants to talk to you.

CHAN: Yo, what's up? So, man.

YVES: Okay. [???]

CHAN: Yeah, so you doing nothing after?

YVES: Well, I didn't get any news from Hugo. Did he call you?

CHAN: No. I got [???], who said that they weren't doing nothing special at Hugo's because like his mother is still sick, something like that.

YVES: So where is he now?

CHAN: Uh, he was at [???]

YVES: [???]

CHAN: Huh?

YVES: [Did you see Antoine?]

CHAN: The Forum.

YVES: With who? All alone?

CHAN: No, with Karim and the usual. He joined us, the usual gang that live there.

YVES: [???] Are you at home?

CHAN: No, I'm at Starbucks.

Borrowed calls, like the co-conversations they trigger, are an excellent example of the process of reciprocal construction of social links and uses of technology. While the friendship contract "requires" partners to engage in certain mobile phone uses (share it if necessary and comply with certain rules when borrowing it), these uses display the bonds of friendship and strengthen social cohesion among members of the network. In other words, adolescents domesticate the technology according to the rules of their own cultural grammar. But the opposite is also true. By turning it into a social tool, they construct their own culture and social organization in and through the use of this technology.

7.9 Saturday Night: Telephone Organization or Social Control?

Organization of Saturday-night activities and parties (Danesi 1994, Green 2002) is a prime occasion for adolescents to confirm their membership in a network. Below is a typical Saturday-night joint organization discussion.

Beginning Wednesday, the telephone starts ringing to create links and establish who belongs to the group. Assoum has just called Karim and Annie to start the round of phone calls that will result in organization of a Saturday night. The next call is for Chan.

ASSOUM: I called Karim and Annie.

CHAN: Karim, okay, yeah. Okay, Karim.

ASSOUM: So, uh, Saturday, we're doing something.

CHAN: Uh, okay, what?

ASSOUM: You wanna come?

CHAN: Uh, what are we doin'?

ASSOUM: We don't know yet. Oh, I'll tell you, okay?

CHAN: That's fun.

[...]

ASSOUM: Are you trying to get me angry?

CHAN: Yes.

ASSOUM: Okay, fine, uh, you wanna come along?

CHAN: Depends. Where are we going?

ASSOUM: Saturday afternoon, I don't know yet.

CHAN: [???]

ASSOUM: What do you wanna do?

CHAN: I don't know, man, you tell me.

ASSOUM: I'm not gonna tell you anything.

CHAN: [???]

ASSOUM: I'll tell you tomorrow, 'cause I'll talk to [???] tomorrow.

CHAN: Okay, okay, we'll see then. What day is tomorrow?

Chan is breaking the social norms that regulate Saturday night planning. He dares to ask "What are we doing?" before confirming that he will be available. Assoum simply does not yet know, because what is really at stake in the event is not "what are we doing" but "being there." Assoum's replies clearly express the extent that this behaviour is inappropriate: first, he simply avoids answering Chan's "wrong" question and then expresses a social sanction: "Are you trying to make me angry?"

Assoum continues taking Chan's presence for granted by asking if he is going to come along. Chan keep putting conditions on his participation: "What are we doin'?" and "Depends. Where are we going?" These are inappropriate questions. They are talking about Saturday, and it is out of the question that they know in advance what they are going to do and where they are going to go! By saying "I'm not gonna tell you anything," Assoum reasserts the basic rule: Participation in Saturday night is unconditional.

The next day, the telephone organization continues. After having called Annie and Daniel, Assoum calls Chan again.

ASSOUM: [*Laughing*] Well, uh, ummm, so you're up for Saturday?

CHAN: Depends.

ASSOUM: What do you mean, "depends"? [???] Daniel might come too and Sylvie's coming [???]

CHAN: Ha ha ha [??? ho:me].

ASSOUM: What the hell? You got ho:me?

[...]

ASSOUM: No, it isn't. Oh man, anyway [???] for Saturday?

CHAN: Uh, yeah, depends where we're going.

ASSOUM: Yeah, I don't know yet, I'm gonna call tonight.

CHAN: Good man. [*silence*]

ASSOUM: Because I need to know how many we are to define where we're going.

CHAN: Uh.

ASSOUM: Besides, you don't usually do anything on Saturdays except get drunk and uh [???].

[...]

ASSOUM: Okay, well, call me ba:ck for Saturday.

CHAN: Yeah, yeah, okay.

ASSOUM: All right, don't forget. Bye.

CHAN: Bye-bye.

Once again what counts is "being there," in other words, confirming one's presence in an unconditional manner. When Chan states his reservations again ("Depends"), Assoum is rather surprised (if not irritated) and reproaches him for breaking one of the group's rules: "What do you mean, 'depends'?" The others are coming (they did not set any conditions on their participation), and that is what counts. Avoiding Saturday night means avoiding the group and giving priority to the activity rather than to being together. This would be to reverse the cultural order that structures the event. Moreover, Chan does not usually do anything on Saturday night aside from get drunk. At the end of the conversation, his position is criticized as nonsense and unacceptable.

By following how Saturday night is organized by mobile, we learn what it means to "be friends."

ASSOUM: Well, I wanted to know if you were still up for Saturday?

KARIM: Of course!, besides because – [*someone calls*]

ASSOUM: I called Chan to find out what we're doing [*silence*] huh?

KARIM: Hello?

ASSOUM: Yeah, I called Chan.

KARIM: Yeah.

ASSOUM: Yeah, I called Chan, then he wants to know what we're doing before he comes, then Daniel said because he talked with Sylvie yesterday, eh.

KARIM: Yeah.

ASSOUM: And she might want to come, is that okay with you?

KARIM: Of co::urse [*little laugh*]

ASSOUM: I told him to bring Sylvie if he came.

KARIM: Okay.

ASSOUM: All right?

KARIM: Yeah, yeah.

ASSOUM: Okay. But uh ... okay, uh, if [???] Chan as you tell me, he wants to know what we're doing.

KARIM: What we're doing ahead?!

ASSOUM: Yeah, so what are we doing there, where we're going to go and everything.

KARIM: But – okay, we're gonna go, don't know, to a café, wherever you want.

ASSOUM: Okay.

KARIM: [???] Normal.

The call to make sure Karim was coming becomes a confirmation of what it means to be friends: "Of course!," "Of co::urse." The kind of answer Karim gives and especially the intonation of his words situate his presence at "Saturday night" in the category of "goes without saying." Assoum cannot help himself from telling Karim that for Chan once again things are different: their mutual friend wants to know what they are doing before agreeing to come. This little bit of gossip creates surprise that constitutes a real social sanction. Assoum says that Chan wants to know what they are planning to do, which causes Karim to exclaim, "What we're doing ahead?" thereby underlining the meaninglessness of the behaviour. The response, "But – okay, we're gonna go, I don't know, to a café," shows that Assoum and Karim share the same order of priorities and the same logic. It doesn't matter where they go or what they do, and no one knows ahead of time, because that was not the real purpose of Saturday night. Being friends means being together for only one real purpose: being together.

Building friendship by phone calls means using the devices as a system for controlling members of the group, identifying their willingness to confirm their membership, and (re)constructing the specific aspects of this community's culture, which is based primarily on friendship and the rules of friendship.

7.10 Who Is Where Tonight: Mobile Phone as Panoptikon[27]

On the Friday before the Saturday that is the subject of the above calls, the members of this peer group engage in an interaction providing another example of how adolescents use mobile phones to create ties among members of the group. Daniel calls Assoum, who is going to see a movie with Karim. The call becomes a co-conversation.

ASSOUM: Dan?

DANIEL: Yes?

ASSOUM: Yeah, what's up? Uh, look, me and Karim are going to see a film, you coming?

DANIEL: Well, what time does it start?

ASSOUM: With Dino.

DANIEL: What time does it start?

ASSOUM: It says like ten around. It's okay, okay, his dad's going to drive us home.

DANIEL: What?

ASSOUM: His dad's going to drive us home.

DANIEL: Yeah, but me, I'm in Lachine, it's far.

ASSOUM: I know. [*speaks to Karim*] He lives in Lachine, it's kinda far.

KARIM [*to Assoum*]: Where's Lachine?

DANIEL: We'll see each other tomorrow.

KARIM [*to Assoum*]: He doesn't live in Lachine!?

ASSOUM [*to Daniel*]: Karim doesn't know where it is.

KARIM: I don't live there, not me.

ASSOUM [*to Daniel*]: You may go sleep at Sylvie's, go sleep at Sylvie's.

DANIEL: Uu:h.

[...]

DANIEL: [*Noise*] Uh, no I'd rather see you tomorrow. I'm tired anyway.

ASSOUM: You sure?

DANIEL: I already saw the film, so [[???]

ASSOUM: [[???] Me too, but I don't know, Karim says like "Come on, man." [???]

DANIEL: [???]

ASSOUM: Huh?

DANIEL: [???]

ASSOUM: Ah, okay, well, I'll call you tomorrow. Perfect.

DANIEL: Okay, good. [???]

ASSOUM: Okay, ciao.

Mobile phones make it possible to contact people and coordinate activities almost to the minute. This is how Assoum could suggest that Daniel meet them at the theatre. The first problem pointed out by Daniel, namely the time, is immediately eliminated by Assoum because Karim's father was ready to drive them home. However, Daniel points out another obstacle: his home is far away. According to Assoum, this problem could also be solved because he could go and sleep at a friend's house. Assoum puts pressure on Daniel, who gives another reason to avoid the "obligation:" he is tired. This kind of tiredness excludes friends and has nothing to do with "cultural laziness," which, on the contrary, includes members of the group. Personal fatigue therefore cannot be accepted as a good excuse. Daniel adds a final reason: he had already seen the film. This is when the three friends reach the highest definition of what it means to be friends. Assoum has also already seen the film, but Karim has said, "Come on, man." He is going just because his friend had asked him to. It is not the film that gives meaning to "going to see a film," but the bond of friendship. Daniel, like Chan earlier, seems to slip out of this logic, and the mobile phone is what makes his resistance and the weak ties to the group visible, even too visible.

For adolescents, the mobile has become an instrument of social control, a panoptikon that makes it possible to know who is where, what each member is doing, who is avoiding social obligations, and who accepts the constraints of friendship. In other words, the mobile phone makes it possible to create one of the foundations of the universe specific to adolescents: social cohesion in a community of friends and the control it entails.

Despite what one might imagine, parents are not the only ones who use mobile phones to control young people,[28] and mobile phones concern more than just the dynamics of the relationship of a couple. Friendship networks also employ "mobile control" as a way to construct and maintain reciprocal links among members. Foucault wrote of surveillance and punishment. Could the mobile be a new tool for ancient social practices?

7.11 The Ritual Meeting: Micro-Organization through Mobile Calls

Even though it is not necessarily the most frequent kind of conversation, the formula "I'll be there in five minutes, where are you?" represents nonetheless a specific use that teenagers make of the mobile phone: "hypercoordination" (Ling and Yttri 2002). This notion refers to the meticulous process by which young people gradually get closer to one another by coordinating their movements using short, frequent phone calls. This continues right up to the end: more and more frequently, when teenagers arrive at the door of a person who is waiting for them, they no longer ring the doorbell but call on the mobile phone.

On Saturday afternoon Assoum, who is near the Metro station, calls Chan:

ASSOUM: Yes:
CHAN: Yeah.
ASSOUM: Um:: meet me on, well, outside the subway, like on Van Horne.
CHAN: Okay.
ASSOUM: Are you taking the bus?
CHAN: Me?
ASSOUM: Yeah?
CHAN: Uh, we'll see.
ASSOUM: Okay, so there, at least I'll find you there, that way I won't – cause the others, I don't know where they gonna be so ...
CHAN: They're not there yet?
ASSOUM: Well, it's [twelve] forty-four dude, I'm gonna go downstairs and see.

Right after, at 12:45, he calls Daniel.

ASSOUM: Hi.
DANIEL: Yeah?
[...]
ASSOUM: Anyway, I just found Annie and Sylvie.
DANIEL: Okay.
ASSOUM: We're in front of the subway, we're like a bit late.
DANIEL: Okay, no problem.
ASSOUM: Okay, Chan is coming, he's going to be here like, right away, so that's it.
DANIEL: Well, I'm going to meet you [???] wherever you are.
ASSOUM: Okay, call me and I'll tell you where.

At 1:00 P.M. he receives a call from Marc:

ASSOUM: So?
MARC: Hey.
ASSOUM: Where are you?
MARC: I'm in the car, I wanna know where you are.

ASSOUM: We':::re in Beaubien Park.
MARC: Beaubien Park?
ASSOUM: You know, at Outremont School there? Yeah.
MARC: Outremont School.
ASSOUM: Yeah.
MARC: Okay, are you staying there for like another half hour? Twenty minutes, something like that?
ASSOUM: If you wa:nt.
MARC: Okay, I'll be there in like twenty minutes in Outremont.
ASSOUM: All right, we're on the soccer field.

Scattered across the city, adolescents set up meeting places as they go along. With mobile phones always turned on, meetings are no longer set in advance once and for all, at specific locations and times. They become a practical achievement, a process of gradual adjustment. The place and time can remain vague because the mobile phone guarantees that coordination will be successful.

The scenario is fascinating. The mobile allows young people to gradually approach one another and converge on a location, each according to his or her own trajectory. However, the location as such does not exist because it is not established ahead of time. It is constructed little by little as the "meeting place" through movements coordinated using mobile phones. The meeting time has also lost its original meaning, because it is no longer a constraint but is established gradually, and is in fact created and constructed through mobile phone coordination.

Adolescents' rituals that turn a gathering into a social meeting are changing. Traditionally, certain typical locations in urban space were defined as meeting places and attracted young people as destinations of their nomadic wanderings. With mobile phones, it is now the process of mutual coordination, the gradual adjustment of the movements of members of a group, that defines a place as a ritual meeting point. Geographical location and spatial boundary markers have lost their original symbolic function because mobile coordination can instantly turn almost any location into a place where the group can converge.

The ritual function of time boundaries has also changed radically. Young people are now neither late nor early with respect to a meeting with peers. "Being on time" has become a gradual construction that is erected jointly by the members of the group. One no longer adjusts one's activities according to a time set in advance. The schedule is constantly adjusted in accordance with the members of the group.

However, there is another consequence of using the mobile to construct ritual encounters, and it is perhaps the most relevant. Given the gradual determination of the meeting location and time, the meeting itself no longer works as a means of exclusion. Traditionally, people who could not be reached at the time a rendezvous was set, for whatever reason, might not "be there," and "being there" is fundamental, because such ritual events define and confirm membership in a community of peers.

The new ways of constructing meetings, created by the emergence of mobile phones in adolescents' daily life, have eliminated this dramatic consequence of this ritual. Mobile phones have become tools for systematic inclusion, means of social gathering that allow all members to get together by phone, to "be there" at a given time, to construct a feeling of belonging and to define themselves as members of a group. Is this why owning a mobile is increasingly becoming a social necessity for teenagers?

ASSOUM: You don't have a mobile phone yet?
SHARIF: What?
ASSOUM: You don't have a mobile yet?
SHARIF: No, man, not yet. I haven't ordered one yet.
ASSOUM: Ah, okay. You're gonna get one, eh?
SHARIF: Well, I dunno, I wanted one, but on the other hand ...

It is clear that we are moving towards a situation in which not having a mobile phone is a failing that causes problems. Its use is increasingly a social necessity, at least for adolescents. Indeed, owning a mobile, always having it at hand and always turned on, the co-conversations it allows, the way adolescents can use it to exert pressure on others, the possibility of coordinating daily life and participating in shared rituals – all these benefits are means to create the social bonds that make adolescents a community.

7.12 Technology Domestication and Cultural Changes

If we look carefully at the ways young people use mobile phones, what they say on and about mobile phones, we see that their mobile practices are deeply rooted in the most salient characteristics of their adolescent cultural universe. By following the conversations on mobile phones, we discover that teenagers talk about almost everything: Saturday night, friendship, school, the degree of "required" carelessness in their attitude towards schoolwork, where to get the best bargains, how to get to know a girl, where they are in a video game, and the inevitable differences between boys and girls. Their conversations concern all of the worlds of meaning that characterize their culture and are interspersed with all the forms of talk specific to adolescents: from the use of an almost secret language to storytelling and gossip, from parody to "bad language."

Their mobile conversations are effectively powerful social glue. They make it possible to share crucial events and stories that belong to the group, they create the identities of the members by fixing personality traits, they create opportunities for theorizing about the rules of the adolescent world, and they are also the means by which the rules are shared. In short, through their mobile conversations adolescents use discourse to create their everyday shared and controlled social world.

Of course, this process is not new. It has not been created specifically by the mobile phone; it has already been seen in traditional telephone communication practices.

This lack of originality with respect to technological innovation suggests a fundamental observation: young people have totally integrated the mobile phone into their cultural universe. Domesticated and used in a way consistent with their well-established cultural systems such as "laziness," it has taken over the functions of the traditional, "sedentary" telephone. Adolescents have translated the technology into the terms specific to their culture and submitted it to the social norms typical of people their age.

Introduced on the market as an emergency device[29] to be used for exceptional communication in difficult circumstances, the mobile is now, thanks to adolescents, no longer extraordinary. It has become the rule, now used to construct the everyday world. After studying adolescent routines in the field and trying to understand their relationship with this new communications technology through their behaviour and conversations, we must conclude that for them, the mobile phone is certainly no longer a new technology.

Distance is required to understand young people's virtually complete domestication of this technology, because every cultural process is always more contradictory than it first appears. We therefore need to be attentive to signs of the opposite process and see whether the technology has changed the world in which it has so naturally found a place. A few elements that we noticed in routine mobile phone use indicated that there has been significant innovation. For example, there are co-conversation; the public–private opposition has been eliminated; the meanings of places and times have been redefined; the myth of "merged contact" has become a reality; and social ties have been *objectivized*, or even materialized. However, in order to grasp the truly new phenomenon that is most specifically linked to the technological features of the mobile in adolescents' lives, we have to take into account their *representation* of typical mobile phone use, namely that of being in the street and saying "I'll be there in two minutes, where are you?" Much more than the uses that are statistically the most frequent, this representation indicates how, from the point of view of contemporary youth, this communications technology has transformed everyday life.

While young people have completely integrated the mobile phone into their habits and made it comply with prior cultural systems, the mobile has nonetheless created new forms of behaviour. Members of a group are now "visible" to one another, events are narrated blow by blow, others' movements are systematically shadowed in order to allow gatherings, and real-time mapping makes it possible to know who is where and doing what minute by minute. These are all new forms of behaviour made possible by the mobile phone.

In the following chapter we will explore the cultural and social issues of another kind of mobile communication: text messaging.

Chapter 8

SMS in Everyday Life: Ethnography
of a Secret Language

8.1 Text Messaging in Peer Culture: A Field Study

It is perhaps in their uses of SMS that adolescents truly reveal their creative appropriation of the mobile phone, the multiple ways in which they mould it to fit their lifestyles and transform its technological opportunities into new language games. In Europe, use of text messages has become the typical way young people use their mobile phones.[1] In exploring its social uses, it quickly becomes evident that among European teens or even children as young as ten, text messaging is the main, if not the only way they use mobile phones to communicate with one another in their everyday life.[2] The astonishing adoption by teens of what can be considered an otherwise secondary function of mobile phones explains contemporary academic interest in this phenomenon (Cosenza 2002, Grinter and Eldridge 2001, Rivière 2002, Grinter and Palen 2002). Indeed, the mobile phone is an extraordinary example of the creative role of early adopters in shaping the functions of a technological object, creating its relevance and granting it a social life.

Certainly economic factors are at work here: the significant difference between the cost of an SMS and that of a voice call has surely been decisive in the widespread adoption of text messaging among teens. Yet many analysts claim that this factor does not entirely explain the astonishing diffusion of this system: the number of exchanges among adolescents reached the point that companies had to upgrade their systems to accommodate the volume.

Designed for communicating information in a telegraphic, asynchronous manner, short text messages quickly became adolescents' primary tools for relational, synchronous, detailed communication. How did this transformation come about? To understand the social and cultural reasons for this phenomenon, we carried out an ethnographic field study among a small group of Italian teens.[3] Our observations confirm those noted by other studies: the exchange of mini-messages was integrated to a very large extent into the everyday routine of the members of this peer group.[4] Messages were sent and received at home, in the street, before basketball workouts, on the bus, at the end of the school day and even in class. SMS use was so omnipresent that it would be hard to single out any time or place when it was most likely to occur. Texting in this peer group appeared to be a radically cross-context and cross-activity practice. The young people always had their mobiles in hand, veritable embodied appendages. Beyond doubt, their most frequent action was not to answer the phone or make a call but to type with their thumbs on the tiny keyboard at an astonishing speed.

Drawing upon our field notes we sketched a typical and recurrent scenario: Matilde[5] is stretched out on the couch while commercials are on the television or is sitting at the table between the main course and dessert. She unfolds her mobile. She types, waits, reads the screen, smiles, types some more, waits, reads the screen.

This kind of sequence could be repeated four or more times until the dominant activity took over again, and Matilde went back to watching a film or eating her meal. All her waiting time was immediately filled by this kind of mobile phone interaction, which supposed that on the other end there was always someone who was involved in the same dynamic. But what did they have to say that was so urgent?

8.2 The Secret Language of SMS

We asked Matilde to transcribe the SMSes sent and received by her and her closest friends during one month.[6] When we met with her to look at the exchanges she had recorded in her logbook, she began reading them to us in case we were unable to decipher her handwriting – which was likely since she had filled the pages in a wide range of places, such as school, the park waiting for friends, or outside the gym after a basketball workout. As she read the entries out loud for us, she noted that in most cases she stopped not because of her handwriting but because of what she had written. At one point, she asked us if we would like her to make a dictionary:

"Otherwise you're not going to understand anything." Indeed, owing to the number of unknown abbreviations, alphabetical and numerical symbols, and spelling and grammatical short cuts, the messages were almost incomprehensible to us.

With the help of a friend, Chiara, who let her use her archive of text messages, Matilde produced the following ad hoc glossary for us:

Dizionario [a glossary]

---

xkè = perché (why/because)
tt/ttt = tutto/tutti (all)
bn = bene (good)
xò = però (but/however)
cm= come (how)
ke = che (that)
m = mi (to me)
kiedi = chiedi (you ask)
kiesto = chiesto (asked)
tnt = tanto (a lot)
x = per (for, the sound "per")
cn = con (with)
cs = cosa (thing)
1cs = una cosa (one thing)
doma = domani (tomorrow)
qnd = quando (when)
1po' = un po' (a little)
nn = non (no)
sn = sono (I am)
d = di (of, and the sound "di")
t = ti (to you, and the sound "ti")
skerzo = scherzo (joke, I'm joking)
+ o - = more or less
+ = più (more)
- = meno (less)
anke = anche (also)

ankio = anch'io (me too)
6 = sei (you are)
inca = incazzata (angry)
siam = siamo (we are)
cmq = comunque (anyway)
tvtb = ti voglio tanto bene
  (I love you a lot)
tvb = ti voglio bene (I love you)
tv1kdb = ti voglio un casino di bene
  (I love you a ton)
tvtrb = ti voglio troppo bene
  (I love you really a lot)
tv1mdb = ti voglio un mondo di bene
  (I adore you)
qlcs = qualcosa (something)
qlcl = qualcuno (someone)
qualke = qualque (a few)
qll = quello (him)
dll = delle (some)
al- = almeno (at least)
risp = rispondi (answer me)
rx = rispondi (answer me)
stv = si tu veux (if you want – in
  messages exchanged with French
  friends
biz = baci (kisses)

Before describing this new code in detail, it is worth analysing the interaction that gave rise to the production of such a document. First, when dealing with adult researchers, Matilde recognized the need for a glossary.[7] This was in itself somewhat strange, since the adults in question were Italian SMS users. Yet Matilde treated us like foreigners or speakers of a different language who needed to learn a basic vocabulary. Long before broaching the analysis of the corpus of text-messages, she provided us with a frame of reference in which the discourse was to be situated. Our informant was effectively instructing us in a separate language, a code of communication shared by peers and considered to be beyond adult comprehension.

The ethnographic approach showed us the "natives'" point of view on their own indigenous communications practices. According to them, they were using a secret language,[8] a code that they had constructed, that they shared and, above all, that marked the boundaries between their social world and that of adults.

While it was "secret," the language was not hidden. On the contrary, it was displayed with a certain pride and obvious pleasure. Matilde and Chiara seemed to enjoy this linguistic code, which enabled them to not only transgress the strict rules of language but also and especially to keep adults out of their symbolic space. Use of SMS language thus seems to fulfil the same symbolic function as a typical practice of young adolescents, namely, that of posting signs on their bedroom doors indicating that the space is off limits to those without authorization to enter. The two main reasons behind the construction and use of the secret language of text messages appeared to be the exclusion of adults and the construction of complicity among peers.

8.3 Inventing a Code: Mini-Messages as Secret Handshakes

Every language and system of notation has rules. The language created for texting is no exception. How is its alphabet constructed? What kind of logic underlies this secret writing? The dictionary compiled by Matilde and Chiara had no classificatory system; its function was purely pragmatic, designed to help non-native speakers read texts requiring translation (at least in the informants' view). Nonetheless, through the analysis of their vocabulary, we can derive the basic rules for generating this language, along with the metalinguistic processes underlying this writing system. While the words and formulas created by Italian adolescents are evidently related to their language, the operations performed on the morphology of the language are the same as those found in the text messages of English- and French-speaking adolescents (Grinter and Eldrige 2001,

Kasesniemi and Rautiainen 2002, Rivière 2002):[9]

1. *Abbreviation*: One of the features of verbal communication among adolescents, it is the foremost rule of SMS writing. Words are simply cut (*doma* stands for "*domani*," that is, "tomorrow"). The context and especially the language's inner redundancy enable the receiver to understand the word implied.
2. *Consonant writing*: This involves eliminating vowels for the most frequently used short words, prepositions, and demonstratives (*nn, bn, qll, cs*).
3. *Phonetic writing*: Obviously, adolescents do not use the phonetic writing of linguists, though the same principle applies. The point is to create ad hoc symbols to convey the pronunciation of words or components of words (*k* for *qu*).
4. *Use of mathematical symbols* (*1, x, 6*): mathematical symbols are used to write quantitative adjectives or because of their pronunciation; for example, in Italian, the numeral "6" is pronounced "sei," which sounds like "you are" in that language.
5. *Use of acrostics*: A complete sentence becomes a single word composed of the initials of the words in the original sentence. Acrostics are used mainly for formulas such as greetings: *tvtrb* = ti voglio troppo bene (I love you really a lot).

These basic rules can also be combined and used to create original, complex forms, such as *tv1kdbn*, an acrostic for "ti voglio un casino di bene" ("I love you a ton"), which combines phonetic and consonant writing, and mathematical symbols.

Through abbreviations, phonetic writing, grammatical and spelling short cuts, use of mathematical symbols, and some completely local graphic solutions, adolescents have constructed a conventional system of writing that has effectively achieved the level of encryption of an insiders' language. Messages are like linguistic winks or secret handshakes. In addition to their content, their form defines those who are outsiders and those who belong to the same community of practices.

As we noted above, our first field evidence of the secret nature of such a language was our teen informants' belief that adults would need a glossary to decode their messages. The way such a glossary was compiled by Matilde and Chiara was evidence of how this secret language was shared by members. They put together the short basic vocabulary very quickly, agreeing on most of the symbols immediately and concentrating only on not forgetting any. The degree of intersubjective agreement was high and signalled the extent to which the code was shared. However, at one point, Chiara said to Matilde, "You have to add that one too – otherwise she won't be able to understand any of mine."

This microinteraction shows that the symbols of this writing are not all codified at the same level. Some are standardized and shared widely while others belong to sub-codes specific to certain members. Even the use of more conventional signs allows a degree of individual variation. The frequency of certain abbreviations and even the tendency to use some abbreviations rather than others are signs of individual styles. While it is true that competency in this form of writing marks the boundaries of a community of users, the code nonetheless remains under construction. There is still room for creativity, and writing can be individualized. Personal marks of identity can be included in messages so that speakers can be distinguished from one another.

Like a real language, sms writing is highly standardized but also makes variation possible. It is constructed on basic rules such as the abbreviation principle, using certain symbols, although new forms of notation can be invented. The play between codification and creation in the language of mini-messages enables young people to play with basic functions, as in any language. They can create cohesion among members but also set members apart, construct community boundaries along with individual space, strengthen shared references, and also produce innovation.

The interplay between a shared glossary and individual uses initially grew out of the constraints of the small size of the mobile phone screen and the limit in the allowed number of characters. However, teens have turned these technical limits into cultural boundaries: they have created an alphabet that defines the peer group membership and the identity of each member.

8.4 Hidden Communication: SMS in Teens' Underground Life

The invention of an ad hoc alphabet is not the only phenomenon that defines the potentially secret nature of sms communications. Certain practices also help to establish this communicative game. The mobile phone's portability and ever-decreasing size make it possible to hold it in one's hand almost hidden from the eyes of others. Typing on the keys is a potentially invisible action. But the absolutely decisive feature is silence. Text messaging makes it possible to completely avoid oral communication, so conversations can take place with no visible signs or sounds.[10]

Adolescents grasped this technology's potential immediately and have employed it in a linguistic game whose stakes have always been relevant in peer culture: secret communication and the construction of an underground life distinct from that of adults. It is a specific phenomenon strictly related to developmental tasks: putting distance between themselves and parents' or teachers' control and constructing an independent world of norms, references, and values. Violation of and resistance to official norms, tricks and forbidden behaviours allow children and teens to construct a group identity, a sense of belonging to a community, and to start taking control over their everyday lives. From the age when children begin whispering to one another and passing notes at school, they continuously use secrecy. Text messaging thus becomes a new, more efficient tool for enacting this process.

Exchange 1

MATILDE: ciao! **sn** la matti!! **cm** va? ieri **t6** persa la performance della susanna!! prima è caduta poi ha cominciato a parlare con la fede ... **nn t** dico. **tvtttb** p.s. ora l'ho vista sul bus! aiuto!! (Hi, it's Matti! How are you doing? Yesterday you missed Suzanne's performance! she fell and then she started talking with Fede ... what can I say. I love you a lot. P.s. I have just seen her on the bus! help!!)[11]

ARIANNA: se l'hai vista vuol dire che 6 già uscita mentre io sn a scuola a fare storia.. mi dispiace essermela persa ... **tvukdb** (If you saw her, it means you are out while I'm still in at school doing history ... I love you a lot.)

Exchange 2

FRANCESCA: ciao! **ke** fate? noi inglese ... che palle ... (Hi! What are you doing? We are in English ... what a drag.)

MARCO: da noi interrogati simo e la maura, lei non gli lascia la parola ... la odio ... è troppo saccente (Here Simo and Maura are doing their orals ... she doesn't let him talk ... I hate her. She is such a know-it-all.)

FRANCESCA: povero! ma dai, io sarei contenta **ke nn m** facessero parlare ... vabeh ... **t** saluto ke spendo **tr** ... **tvtrb** (Poor him! But I would be glad if someone doesn't let me talk ... anyway ... greetings otherwise it costs too much ... love.)[12]

Exchange 3

GIACOMO: ciao bella!! cosa mi dici di bello? io sono a un corso, tu che fai? (Hi, beautiful! What's new? I'm in class, what are you doing?)
MATILDE: sn a scuola e ho appena finito il compito di mate ... credo sia andato di merda va beh (I'm at school, I already finished a math test. I think I did a shitty exam, anyway it doesn't matter.)

Clearly Arianna was in class with her mobile on, because she received a mini-message from Matilda and answered. Francesca and Marco, Giacomo and Matilde were at school, each in different classes. Unbeknownst to their teachers, they contacted each other and told each other what was going on. Through their exchanges, they cemented their complicity and confirmed certain aspects of a shared culture: Being a know-it-all and exhibiting one's knowledge to the detriment of a friend are forms of behaviour that violate peer culture norms. It is much cooler to not know the right answer and let a know-it-all talk in one's place, or to act unconcerned about the results of school tests.

Text messages allow adolescents to whisper in the ear of a person who is not there without letting others know. Thus the ancient practice of passing notes in class has found a new, far more efficient support. Now digital and wireless "notes" can be sent to friends in the same and other classes. The complicity fostered by transgressions of official class rules, friendship links created and maintained through the traditional system of paper notes, can now be developed in a much broader network. Text messages have taken over the functions of secret communications and created new possibilities for teens' underground life in school, namely, the interactive construction of self and community.

Of course, communicating in secret is not the only way of using text messages. But it is perhaps the one that best reveals where and how this new communications technology meshes with the specific features of adolescent culture. Mobile phones and SMS are shaped by pre-existing meaningful practices; they are integrated into everyday contexts and routines and domesticated by adolescents to serve the needs of their social world.

Use of hidden communication and encrypted linguistic codes are major indicators of the mobile phone's role in constructing a community of peers and its underground life. However, the content of messages is another relevant aspect in the construction of a community outside adult knowledge and control. In our fieldwork we were given access to only one in five of Matilde's 340 exchanges over the course of a month. This gap between the messages to which we had access and those that remained off limits for us is a significant, even indirect, field indicator of the role of text messages in the construction of the adolescents' secret world.

8.5 The Thumb Generation: SMS Conversations

When we asked Matilde to gather and transcribe the text messages sent and received by her and her closest friends, the way in which she transcribed them was the first clue that the informants and the researcher did not grasp the formula "text messages sent and received" in the same way:

Exchange 1

MATILDE: ciao bella t va di uscire oggi? risp. (Hi, beautiful! Do you want to go out today? Answer.)

CHIARA: nn posso ... devo fare 1 po d robe x l'esame ke altrimenti nn faccio mai ... intendevi portarmi fuori ancora cn tommy e giulio? magari possiamo doma (I can't ... I have things to do for the test ... otherwise I'll never do them. Were you thinking that we could go out with Tommy and Giulio? Maybe tomorrow?)

Exchange 2

ARIANNA: ciao, cm va? scusa se nn c sentiamo tnt ma x me è 1 periodaccio ... raccontami la storia del ragazzo ke m dicevi qnd eri in francia (Hi, how are you doing? Sorry if we don't talk much but this is not a good time for me. Tell me about the guy you told me about when you were in France.)

MATILDE: io bn ... 1 po preoccupata x l'esame ma bn ... x il raga t racconto qnd c sentiamo xkè x me è brutto cmq nn è successo niente ... e tu? (I'm okay ... a little worried about the test but okay ... we can talk about the guy when we see each other because he is ugly, anyway nothing happened ... What about you?)

ARIANNA: ho litigato cn franco e ilario ... oggi ho detto ke erano 2 stronzi13 ma ho paura d aver fatto una cagata (I had a talk with Franco and Ilario ... today I said they were bastards, but I'm afraid I screwed things up.)

MATILDE: **doma** parlagli ... digli **ke** hai sbagliato, se la pensi cosi! Alla fine loro sono tuoi amici! E con le altre? ceci, chiara, elisa ... (Talk to them tomorrow and tell them you made a mistake, if that's what you think! After all, they are your friends! And with girls? Ceci, Chiara, Elisa ...)

ARIANNA: **tt una merda** ... mi viene da piangere ogni volta che ci penso (It's all fucked up ... I feel like crying every time I think about it.)

MATILDE: che è successo? (What happened?)

ARIANNA: **d tt d +** ... devo studiare **t** racconto **qnd c** vediamo (Even more ... I have to study I'll tell you when we see each other.)

MATILDE: **nn** so **bn cs** dirti. **sl** cerca **d** capire e **d nn** piangere e **c sn tnt** teste di cazzo [xxx] ma **anke tnt** persone **ke t** amano e capiscono e io **t** voglio **tnt bn** (I don't know what to say. Try only to understand and do not cry there are so many shitheads but also people who love you and understand and I love you so much.)

ARIANNA: grazie ... **t** voglio bene ... veramente te ne voglio tanto ... **anke** se forse non sono molto capace di dimostrarlo ... a presto (Thank you ... I love you ... I really love you so much ... even if I'm not able to show you how much ... see you soon.)

MATILDE: **nn t** preoccupare ... va bene cosi. stai tranquilla e cerca di **nn** agitarti che tu vali 10mila volte **ttt** quanti. Baci (Don't worry, it's okay ... take it easy and try not be upset because you are ten thousands times better than the others. Kisses.)

Beyond the use of codes, the content, and the times when the silent exchanges occurred, what surprised us most was the format. Thirty per cent of the "messages" in our sampling consisted of two turns of talk,[14] 25 per cent consisted of three turns, 10 per cent of four turns and nearly a third of five or more turns. It is difficult to imagine an SMS exchange of fourteen turns, but there was one.

We found only one single message, and the way it was transcribed reveals how much it was perceived as an exception.

1. MATILDE: ciao **cm** va? **sn** la matti. volevo ringraziarti **x** ieri sera, **m sn** divertita ma **m** hai fatto anche pensare ... va ben ... **nn t** rompo piu ... baci baci (Ciao, how are you? It's Matty ... I wanted to thank you for last night but you also made me think a lot ... well ... I wont bug you any more ... kisses.)

2. //

As the transcription shows, from the informant's point of view, the lack of a message in return constitutes an official absence (Schegloff 1968). An answer was expected but did not come, and its absence was recorded as an exception, a break in the routine. As usual, anomalies are what reveal the implicit rules of social interaction: a text message sent "requires" one in return. Because a text message makes the occurrence of an expected reply relevant, it serves as the beginning of a minimal interaction. This kind of communication has borrowed the basic structure of conversation: the *adjacency pair*.[15] Obviously, this minimal two-turn format can be extended and can give rise to extremely sophisticated, detailed exchanges.

The way that Matilde interpreted our field request was evidence of how adolescents have transformed the Short Message System into a conversation-like exchange. We had asked her to transcribe and/or count "text messages," but she in fact noted *sequences of messages*. By choosing this method rather than simply transcribing and counting SMSes, Matilda revealed her point of view: the relevant and meaningful unit of analysis in her eyes was not the messages in themselves but the interchange. As we read the text messages among friends in this network, it became increasingly clear that the adolescents were engaged in interactions that, despite the use of writing, reproduced the classical form of conversation: quick, coordinated alternation of turns of talk. Since they had no ready-made term to designate this specific kind of verbal interaction, young Italians have invented one: *messaggiarsi* ("to message"). A literal borrowing of the English word, this verb highlights the conversational nature of the exchanges.

8.6 Text Messaging as an Interactive Phenomenon: Social Organization and Linguistic Creativity

Given such hypertrophy of conventional signs, it was almost necessary to ask the most naïve of questions to our informants: why? Secrecy, creation of complicity, and issues related to identity were certainly good explanations, but they did not seem sufficient. Why was so much linguistic work done for exchanges that were in the end utterly ordinary? Matilde and Chiara had an immediate answer: "You've got to reduce the number of characters." Their explanation was consistent with that advanced by most researchers (Grinter and Eldridge 2001, Cosenza 2002): the technological limitation of 160 characters requires the invention of graphical means and spurs adolescents' linguistic creativity. However, does this explanation account for the communicational norm of reducing characters? More or less, it seemed.

First, this limit seemed to be only hypothetical, at least for our informants. When we asked the young girls if they had ever reached the maximum number of characters, they looked at each other and said, "No, never." They were surprised, as if they had just realized that the technological limitation had never constrained them. Second, they always used abbreviations, conventional signs, and systematic transgressions of spelling rules, even in very short and telegraphic messages. Clearly, the basic rule about "saving signs," which generated all the other graphic rules, was not based on the technological limitation alone. The relevant question then became: What *is* a "short message?"

To gain a deeper understanding of this communicative practice, we once again took into account the way messages were being transcribed in logbooks. As mentioned above, the informant's transcription was a meaningful action: it revealed that text messages were not single linguistic occurrences but rather *interactive phenomena*. They were used and perceived as components of a larger communicative unit; the sequence of the messages rather then the message itself was the relevant communicative event.

Teens have adapted writing to the main constraining characteristic of naturally occurring oral conversation: the turn-taking system. The social organization of any conversation requires an alternation of turns of talk. It imposes a specific timing to the turn-taking and constraints on how the turns are constructed. To achieve the coordination required, pauses between turns have to be relatively short, and the adjacency turns need to link to each other according to rules of cohesiveness. To interact appropriately, participants must follow a certain rhythm and maintain a certain speed in taking their turns. Adolescents simply imposed such constraining interactive features on writing.

To carry on a conversation with text messages, one has to compose, read, and answer messages quickly. Otherwise participants lose the interactive coordination of conversational exchange. The invention of abbreviations and conventions, and re-invention of phonetic, writing provide the rhythm needed for a writing-reading-writing that fits the interactive format of oral conversation.

The radical changes in spelling and grammar depend on the basic rule of this form of communication: reduce the number of written characters. Yet this rule is due less to the technological limits than to the need to maintain the interactive rhythm.[16] When writing smses, adolescents abide by the same principle that regulates their oral interactions: the survival of the fittest (Andersen 2001), where the fittest is often the fastest.[17] Indeed, if the limit on characters was the fundamental reason for this kind of writing, how would we explain the frequent use of dots and repeated exclamation and question marks (for example, "!!" and "!?!")? How would we be able to explain the systematic use of *"ans"* (answer)? At the expressive and pragmatic level of their language, adolescents do not seem to worry about saving characters at all. Rather, they seek, invent, and add symbols that give their written messages the expressive nuances and pragmatic cues that characterize their oral conversations.[18]

The conversational use of SMS, rather than the number of characters available, is thus the engine of teenagers' linguistic creativity and interactive timing. The rule-breaking aspect may also explain adolescents' passionate and frenetic use of this technology-mediated communication: it provides a place where they can legitimately break spelling rules, distance themselves from conventional grammar, and use an encrypted communication system that is increasingly being recognized as a specific language with a strong identity-making function.

Whatever the factors that make teens invent, use, and share this language, SMS writing derives from a vast metalinguistic process. It enables adolescents to process the structure of the language, constantly perfect its morphology, and explore its phonetic rules. By constructing and especially deconstructing spelling and grammar, they investigate the fascinating world of signs and their arbitrary nature and display their communicative competence in using different languages for different contexts and activities. However, there is clearly more at stake.

8.7 Putting Everyday Life into Words: Gossiping in SMS

As we have seen, SMS use by European adolescents has largely conquered the communicational terrain of the land-line telephone and face-to-face conversation. The portability and minimal cost of SMS are suited to specific features of the teen culture and social world such as the crucial role of verbal interaction in constructing and maintaining contact and cohesion among members of the network.

By reading and striving to understand the sequences of short messages recorded by Matilde, we found that the reasons for use anticipated by SMS designers were completely reversed. SMSes were not used for rapid exchanges of urgent or necessary information, nor were they used to systematically reply to a list of received messages. Instead, the partners in the interactions engaged in long conversations about micro-issues and in co-telling stories about events in their everyday lives.

CHIARA: **cm** va? Oggi **m** ha chiamato la tua mamma **x** trovare dei **raga** belli ... e tu che mi racconti? (How are you doing? Your mother called me today she's trying to find some nice boys ... and you, what about you?)[19]

BRUNO: Io so ... quando ha detto belli mi sono proposto, **x** restare nella modestia! Sai che a ino piace la **cla**? Non dirgli che te l'ho detto (I know ... when she said "nice boys" I proposed myself, I'm so modest! You know that Ino likes Claudia? Don't tell him I told you.)

CHIARA: Io so ... me l'ha detto l'ari, ma **qnd** ho kiesto a ino ha detto **ke** era lei **ke** gli andava dietro (I know ... Ari told me, but when I asked Ino, he said that she was the one running after him.)

BRUNO: no, non è vero ... poi oggi gli ho chiesto se gli piace davvero e ha detto che stanno già insieme ... poi dopo abbiamo chiarito!e poi è gelosissimo! **Tv1kdb** (No, it's not true ... today I asked him if he really liked her, and he said that they were already going out ... then after we clarified he is really jealous! I love you so much.)

CHIARA: Boh! ... e tu? Quali sono state le tue ultime conquiste ? sono venute fuori nuove coppie mentre eravamo in francia? (Boh! ... and you? Who have you been going out with lately? Did any new couples get together when we were in France?)

BRUNO: no ... un mortorio!! Nessuno si fa nessuno a parte me!! Skerzo non posso **risp** xche ho la **batt** scarica! Buonanotte!! **Tv1mdb** (No! None at all! No one tries, no one except me! Joke, I can't answer because my battery is dying! Good night!! I love you so much.)

Despite the technological constraints, these adolescents were engaged in a highly complex verbal interaction, through which they shared the events and constructed the norms of their social world: gossip. Its canonical format requires an astonishing interlocking of the speech verbs. One of the partners has introduced the topic of the imminent story and frames it as gossip through the typical tag: "Don't tell him I told you." The verbal interaction then continues following the canonical structure of gossip: I asked someone something who said something.

Gossip always results from an original narrative and grows as new and always up-dated versions circulate in and through subsequent storytelling. Through the construction of the original story and its variations, adolescents turn themselves and others into characters of a never-ending drama. Each time the story is told, it is constantly enriched with details and new characters whose reported speech endorses different perspectives on the events. The telling of such an under-construction story allows speakers to recreate events experienced by the group and to construct a shared collective memory. Nonetheless, the real strength of gossip lies elsewhere: by allowing tellers and co-tellers to express their assessments of actions and characters in the story, gossip becomes a tool for establishing the values and norms of the group (Goodwin 1990).

As it is introduced in the conversation, the original gossip about Ino and Claudia suddenly becomes a scenario in which new characters appear. Arianna and Ino enter the story with their own voices and opinions on the topic at hand; Bruno and Chiara are not only co-authors of the storytelling but also characters of the story told. However, the scenario is even more complicated. As the reported speech confirms, Ino-speaking-to-Bruno is not the same character as Ino-speaking-to-Chiara, even when he is speaking about the same thing, namely, his commitment to Claudia. Out of this multitude of voices, Chiara is trying to construct a "true" version of what happened, which is the unattainable purpose of all gossip.

This language game is a genuine social practice. Through a discourse that reports discourse that reports discourse, adolescents are constantly weaving their network, exerting control over other members of the group, and establishing implicit norms to regulate their behaviour.

In telling and comparing the various and often conflicting versions of what happened, Bruno and Chiara underline crucial dimensions of their peer culture. First, they are confirming the possibility of gendered discourse: a boy does not talk about his commitment to a girl in the same way to female and male friends. In the first case, he plays the role of a Casanova and portrays Claudia as chasing him. In the second case, he portrays the relationship as a completed conquest: he and Claudia are already together. Second, they are establishing what kinds of personal stories have to become collectively known. The formation of couples is a public social event and is part of the knowledge that members share. Third, through this exchange, Chiara and Bruno are also establishing the legitimacy of two well-defined forms of behaviour: being and getting up to date about what is going on.

Clearly, these are social norms that are completely specific to the peer group, that are established and valid among them, and that define a socially hyper-structured world apart. This world apart is mainly constructed in and through everyday talking about everyday events. Indeed, it is by talking that adolescents share experiences, events, and above all, the related cultural meanings.

Gossip and everyday oral storytelling have always contributed to the making of the world of norms, values, and culturally defined appropriate behaviours. This process is now accomplished through a new means: SMS, which is perfectly adapted to discursive construction of a shared culture.

8.8 Verbal Performances: Flirting in SMS

Adolescent social life is characterized by behaviours that are strictly related to the development of social skills and interactive competencies: exploration of the other's availability, trial and error in learning how to approach someone sexually, decoding of ambiguous signs, gradual showing interest in a budding relationship or gently communicating disengagement, and getting closer or creating distance while trying not to lose face. Through such behaviours, adolescents do more than form and break relationships. They explore and recreate their cultural ways of approaching each other and engaging in intimate relationships, constructing and deconstructing social links and relationships. We are thus witnessing a process of socialization in the strict sense, an arena for basic learning, where the main tools are verbal exchanges. Interactions via SMS reveal the extent that the exchange of text messages among young people has not only borrowed the structure of oral conversation but has also taken over some of its basic functions.

Even flirting has found a means of expression in SMS:

Exchange 1

MATILDE: ciao! cm va? Oggi la sara m ha parlato 1 po ... ma tu cosa intendi per storia? (Hi! How are you? Today I talked a bit with Sara ... what does going out mean to you?)

FRANCESCO: ma niente d serio ... sI uscire ... a te andrebbe? (Well, nothing really serious, just going out ... you want to?)

MATILDE: a me molto!! Non vedo l'ora (Me? Sure!! I would love to.)

FRANCESCO: io sn libero anche domani, se vuoi ... (I'm free even tomorrow, if you want ...)

MATILDE: nn I so, te lo so dire poi xkè per ora devo andare a allenamento ... a dopo! baci (I don't know, I'll tell you later, because now I have to go to practice ... See you later! Kisses.)

Exchange 2

ARIANNA: non voglio romperti o disturbarti ma vorrei capire cos'è successo dopo la francia, non dico che **t** devo piacere ma sembra che mi eviti e che ti dia fastidio vedermi ... **risp** (I don't want to bug you or annoy you but I'd like to understand what happened after France. I'm not saying you have to like me but it seems like you are avoiding me and that you don't want to see me ... answer.)

CARLO: non è cambiato niente .. sono sempre lo stesso! **xkè** dici cosi? **tvtb risp** (Nothing is changed ... I'm still the same! Why do you say that? love, answer.)

ARIANNA: dai ... si vede che c'è qualcosa che non va! **Tvtttb risp** (Come on ... it's obvious that something is wrong! Love, answer.)

CARLO: cosa dici!?! Sono sempre io, il coglione che fa l'idiota coi prof! (What are you saying!?! I'm still me, the guy who acts like an idiot with teachers!)

ARIANNA: non dire cazzate ... prima ti comportavi in un modo e ora in un altro e vorrei capire siccome credo di non aver cambiato idea! (Bullshit ... before, you were one way, now you're different, and I want to understand, I haven't changed my mind!)

CARLO: hai ragione, potevo essere più chiaro con te fin da subito! Non è che non mi piaci più, non voglio avere una storia seria ora (You're right, I should have been clearer with you from the start! It's not that I don't like you anymore, it's just I don't want to go steady right now.)

ARIANNA: ce l'hai fatta! **cmq** non ho mai detto di voler una storia seria! Sono contenta che non ce l'hai con me ... la batteria sta morendo. (Good, you said it! Anyway, I never said I wanted to go steady! I'm happy you are not mad at me ... my battery is running out.)

Flirting is a social activity that requires highly sophisticated communicative competence. To flirt effectively one must master not only the language but also speech. Flirting is a verbal performance and requires the actor to manipulate words and silences, choose the right rhythm of verbal exchanges, engage in oblique communication, and balance daring and restraint. All of these features of flirting can be expressed very effectively in oral discourse using intonation, hesitation, pronunciation, pauses, small laughs, and (obviously) gestures and facial expressions when the conversation is face to face. Skilful and measured use of these communication tools is a generally prerequisite of successful flirting.

Flirting can also be carried out through epistolary exchange. The greater leeway in terms of length and delay between reception and response is a specific advantage of letter writing that compensates for the unique possibilities of oral exchanges. In contrast, SMS writing does not entail producing polished texts that convey the nuances of such a subtle verbal performance. It was designed for quick, dry exchanges devoid of any nuances, to convey information rapidly and asynchronously. Introductions or polite formulas are not required: SMS etiquette makes it possible to eliminate everything that is not strictly informative. Yet adolescents have found ways to adapt the system to the intricate game of flirting. Taking advantage of the mobile phone's mobility and constant presence in their hands, they have learned to use mini-messages to respond to others at all times.

The requirements related to the rhythm of words and pauses, intonation, and invitations to the other to speak are met using codified graphics. In the case of flirting, elements such as dots, pragmatic requests indicating that an immediate answer is appreciated, and intonation markers are frequently used and give SMS flirting the involved style that characterizes young people's way of speaking.

The system also has advantages that have no equivalent in other communication systems. Despite the increase in the number of characters permitted per message, the rule that governs SMS writing is still "save characters." This fortuitous requirement creates a strategic space for flirting. It is technologically possible to communicate by writing long messages, but short messages are still the norm. Advancing and retreating thus take place in a very original and efficient way because one's involvement and commitment can be controlled by manipulating the length of one's messages.

The ability to approach and withdraw discursively is not the only interactive game in flirting. Just as crucial is being able to enter or leave the social encounter without losing face. The short message system provides speakers with a means of solving this problem by claiming that one's battery is wearing out or a prepaid card is almost depleted. These are acknowledged and shared constraints, which rids breaking off the exchange of relational connotations. Regardless of its veracity, the statement "my battery is running out" allowed Arianna to end a problematic exchange in a non-threatening way. After learning that Carlo had broken up with her without telling her, she could interrupt the conversation without losing face. Thus even the system's real or supposed technological limitations become strategic resources in the flirting interaction

Young people have grasped the communication possibilities offered by this technology and have created new ones. They have even transformed its technological limitations into communicational resources. Thus, they have adapted SMS to their own social imperatives.

8.9 Teenagers' Techno-Language across Contexts

SMS language is a strong indicator of an emerging operational culture specific to teenagers. Like their choices in music, dress, and sports, this technology-mediated communication has become a kind of badge of their identity. It confirms their membership in specific cultural communities and establishes their distance from their parents' world.

However, the social consequences of young people's creation and use of this techno-language go beyond construction of persona, culture, and community. Indeed, these linguistic practices affect the cultural milieu in a more general manner. In this case, as elsewhere, adolescents are the creators and conduits of linguistic innovations that enter mainstream language, enrich it with new vocabulary, and provide it with new metaphors. While technological language is enriched with everyday metaphors, the reverse is also true. Expressions such as "reload," "reboot," "reformat," and "spam" have come out of the computer environment and the jargon specific to the Internet and entered everyday language, enriching it not only by new words but also by new ways of grasping reality. This process has been driven mainly by adolescents, who have truly spread linguistic innovations spawned by the technological world.

Indeed, their technology-mediated language has transcended the boundaries of their community and been introduced into other communication contexts. Always attentive to signs of cultural innovation, advertisers have quickly grasped the creative aspect of young people's technological language and have employed formulas such as "4ever" and "u2" in their advertising campaigns. In Europe, where SMS is astonishingly widespread among the young, the linguistic inventions of adolescents who constantly "message" have become an extraordinary source for creators. This is more than recognition of a new market or sales strategy: it is also a legitimization of adolescents' linguistic creativity and the diffusion of these innovations. While the concerns of young people's technological practices are characteristic of their mobile phone culture, that culture is nonetheless in osmosis with the surrounding society. Young people's adoption of new communications technologies is thus a permanent laboratory for cultural creation and social changes.

In the preceding chapters we have closely examined adolescents in their social and cultural universes. By following their oral and written conversations on mobile phones, we have seen them act and speak together, create social bonds, coordinate their daily lives through mobile calls, and construct an everyday culture characteristic of their community. However, the mobile phone is not just a means of creating cohesion within a closed community. As interpreters and diffusers of the mobile culture, young people act as social bridges linking different communities of practices in the urban space. By using the mobile phone in both public and private places, they cross the boundaries of the various spheres of their daily life.

How does mobile phone use reflect the sometimes incompatible constraints of the two separate worlds of family and peer group? In the next chapter, we study the role of mobile phone use in intergenerational relationships, where the technology seems to lead to the creation of new cultural models for being a parent and being a child.

Chapter 9

Intergenerational Communication: Changes, Constants, and New Models[1]

Emerging communications technologies express family culture and social organization and even help to produce them.

Many historical, social, economic, and cultural factors are responsible for the radical changes that have made it impossible to answer the question, "What is a family?" We now have a rather exhaustive descriptive framework for new family models and legal and common-sense definitions of what counts as a family today. It is now imperative to always ask "Who composes a family with whom and how?"

While more discreet than most of the factors producing the structural and cultural transformation of what counts as a family, technologies play a role. Beyond their purely functional aspects (they are used to perform tasks, and they make everyday activities and management easier), technologies have roles in the home, require time in order to be used, and, above all, presuppose and develop knowledge and skills. Family management of spaces and times reserved for technologies, such as the distribution of technological knowledge and skills, symbolically embodies power struggles and negotiations concerning family priorities and shared values. This management is a tool for constantly redefining the reciprocal rights and obligations of all family members.

Technologies and their uses within families thus shed light on and strengthen the principal dimensions of family life, as they do cultural models of parent and child, which are always in the process of definition.

In an era marked by the emergence of new forms of communication, many now wonder what it means to be a parent or to be a child. Throughout this book we have seen that it is easy but inappropriate to try to answer such questions by explaining that technologies cause certain forms of behaviour and change certain communicational attitudes. This rather deterministic attitude supposes that we are passive, or mere objects, or even that we are victims of technological manipulation beyond our ken, with no voice in how our actions are managed.

Since what are in question here are always co-construction and redefinition processes that have no initial causes or ontology, we believe that both technological and social determinism should be avoided, and that we should instead take a cooperative approach and consider interaction among human and non-human actors. Even though the features of the technologies we are offered make a series of actions possible, the meaning embodied in their use and their real impact always depend on the way they are integrated into our everyday lives. While technologies may provide new ways of being parents and children, parents and children also suggest new definitions and new ways to use technologies.

In this book we have proposed an approach that is both interactionist and contextualist, a perspective on the way that both parents and children make meaning and give specific significations to the functions that they perform with the technological objects available on the market. While the technologies' features make a specific series of actions possible, the meanings of uses of technology and technology's real effects always depend on the way it is integrated into the family routine.

Some of the preceding chapters shed light on how young people create and construct their culture. In this chapter we look at, within the family context, the variables and constants of authority and parental responsibilities, as well as children's dependence and independence. We are investigating what technology use can tell us about new ways of actualizing the statuses and roles of family members, and about what happens today in the cultural *habitus* of such families. In this way, and through the eyes of their children (often said to belong to the "Internet generation"), we will gain greater understanding of today's parents.

The use of mobile phones for "remote parenting" forces us to reformulate and create new parental models, most often without realizing it. In turn, technologies contribute to our always open-ended and unfinished quest for new definitions of what it is to be a parent or child. The mobile phone's omnipresence in our lives leads us to pay special attention in this chapter to its uses as an intergenerational communication tool routinely employed by family members to communicate *among* themselves, certainly, but also and above all, to communicate *about* themselves, in other words, *about what they are for one another.* Thus we will see that internal family practices reveal various symbolic functions accomplished in and through the use of communication technologies: redefinition of family boundaries and renegotiation of the statuses and roles of family members.

9.1 The ON versus the OFF Generation

According to some studies, we have gone in one generation from an identification (or entrance-into-life) model of adolescence, in which young people reproduce their parents' paths, to an experimentation model.[2] The career paths of young people, and also of those who are less young, can no longer be seen as linear processes. This is a result of increased flexibility and even precariousness of social roles and positions, and a degree of blurring in individual paths. This blurring is also accentuated by the increasingly massive interpenetration of public and private spheres,[3] resulting in part from the entry of many new communications objects into the family home.

Young people today, particularly those under twenty, adolescents and pre-adolescents, are the first generation to have known *from infancy* such a wide-ranging media landscape,[4] if not veritable multimedia environments. Indeed, people born in the 1980s have experienced an explosion of audiovisual technology, multiplication of television stations, and diversification of cable and satellite offerings, as well as the introduction of video-game consoles and home computers for the general public.[5] In the 1990s they also saw the emergence of the Internet and unprecedented deployment of the World Wide Web. Today they are experiencing new changes brought about by interactional mobile technologies, particularly with respect to the growing portability of computers and the miniaturization of telephones and other multi-functional devices.

While our pre-adolescents and adolescents are clearly experts with the new media, we should also note that they have not had to live through any ruptures in social and technological know-how. Unlike adults, they have not generally had to unlearn old ways of doing things and solving certain problems. They have not had to replace obsolete methods with new practices based essentially on codes and calculation (computing) that make possible an ever-growing range of actions from a distance (telematics). New technologies and multimedia have always been part of their framework of experience, in the family, at school, and in social relations.

All these media are thus part of their daily lives, and it seems there is no distinction between old and new technologies: "That is a distinction made by adults, who associate technological ruptures with new technological learning and new social uses."⁶ Unlike adults, young people take NICTs more for granted than as innovations. After all, they were born into the world of NICTs. The emergence of NICTs in the home environment therefore marks a certain transfer of power with respect to technical know-how, and thus social competencies, within the family. Children and parents experience this reality in different ways.

A good illustration of a technological gap in perceptions and aptitudes between children and parents is the clear difference in habits of using the technology. For example, while for young people it may seem completely normal or even natural to own a mobile and to have it turned on all the time,⁷ this is not necessarily true for members of earlier generations. This was the case of Helen, a mother. Asked if she used a mobile phone, she replied, "I'm going to tell you my big secret. I do, once in a while, if I need a phone and it's there – for example, in the car. But most of the time I forget to turn it on ... I forget to turn the mobile phone on. I never think about switching it on."

By bringing very different attitudes into play, NICTs reveal the cultural gap between generations. They thus become an instrument for symbolically defining the divisions between age groups and parents and children. Beyond this separating function, technologically mediated intergenerational actions and practices also become conduits and instruments through which new definitions and parenting models are produced. The new models come into relation with former ones, thereby giving rise to unexpected negotiations among those involved. Once they are integrated into the family routine, NICTs lead parents and children to constantly re-define boundaries for the family institution. They thus help provide a means of achieving the perpetual quest for practices that are consistent with the paradoxes of parental authority over children, who consider themselves and are considered as increasingly free and autonomous subjects, even as they become more economically dependent on their parents.

9.2 Co-Construction of Family Boundaries by Technology

Traditionally, classical media (land-line telephony, radio, television) always had shared uses within the family. They were collective family tools, frequently located in common rooms that made it possible for the whole family to use them, and also for parents to control their use to some degree. The telephone was often in the entrance hall or kitchen, where there was traffic and potentially parental intervention. Radio and television sets were located in the den or living room, where they were used by the whole family at the same time. With the increase in number and refinement of technologies today, there are often not only several televisions but also several computers in a home.[8] Most homes also have several telephones, whether land-line, wireless, or mobile. This creates a new situation characterized by the possibility of individual, private consumption, which was unknown barely two decades ago.

MANON: Now my mother wants to learn how to use the computer. But sometimes [*laughs*] it's in my bedroom. She comes in, and then she tries. But it's like, it's like my conversations are on it. You know, she tries to close them, then she closes them, but they were important conversations.

INTERVIEWER: So it's an advantage to have it in your room, but a disadvantage when your mom wants to use it.

MANON: That's it, yeah. But it's normal, among my friends, it's normal to have a computer in your room. It's like one computer per person.

Owing to their private uses, new communications technologies (mobile phones, pagers, and personal computers) are more individual, and so overturn the collective aspect of the technologies that used to prevail. Their introduction into the home, along with the Internet, email, and chat rooms, is thus part of the changing landscape of the relations between parents and children and contributes to the construction of new forms of intra-and extra-familial interaction.

Children equipped with mobile phones and pagers carry their families with them outside of their homes. The family has become virtual. This in itself modifies children's interactions in other social circles (friends, school, work). While parents can no longer be certain where their children are, they can actualize the family at any time. Personal communication tools are now transforming individuals into "communicating units, hybrid beings that are in two places at once: the immediate environment and that of the virtual space of all potential networks."[9] This leads to new conventional habits and interactions as well as changes in the frames of reference of personal communication.[10] Young people especially seem to have translated the myth of the communicating unit into reality, for their cultural appropriation of mobile technologies means that they are always online, always available (especially for their peers), and always ready to answer calls.

Parents today may wonder whether it might sometimes be more appropriate to communicate with their children using text messages (SMS) rather than vocally on the mobile phone, for example, when they know that their children are with friends and do not want to be interrupted by a call from their parents (because their friends might make fun of them). A text message is more discreet and also might have less emotional weight.

In sum, the borders between family and friends, once clearly delimited, are now fluid and flexible. The mobile phone is perhaps the technology in the home most emblematic of the blurring of individual, family, and social spaces. At the same time it can help us gain a better understanding of the dynamics at work in many families.

Some parents have no trouble accepting that their children use technologies in the family home to communicate with people outside; others have more difficulty understanding that their children's extra-familial social circle mixes with the private family sphere in this way. Thus, while technologies can help to reassert intra-familial links, they can also as children get older signify an opening towards a social network that gives parents the impression that the child is moving away from the family sphere.

Is the family sphere therefore subject to and threatened by "barbarian invasions" – in other words, by flows of communications that are foreign to it? Helen thinks this is the case with her son: "But you know, he's still pushing buttons ... and with the mobile, you can receive calls, there's no longer any hours for receiving calls, you no longer have any privacy, really anyone can call you contact you any time, on the weekend."

For some parents, new technologies amplify children's individualization because they can reduce the time that all members of the family spend together. A number of parents feel nostalgic for the time when family meetings were relatively regular, and periods of communal leisure and exchange ensured the cohesion of the family.

In fact, such nostalgia is not felt only by parents. Young people also spoke to us about their fears about changes in family boundaries as technologies enter the home. Jimmy observes, "It creates distance ... my favourite thing is talking with my family, all sitting around a table ... If I'm in front of the computer, then I'm going to be isolated from everyone because no one likes computers here. My dad, he likes them for their simplicity, but not for games, not for hobbies ... My sister is in her room on the phone, it's like she doesn't exist ... And my dad, with his cell phone, we can't interrupt him when he's working, but that's normal ... My mom is open [available] all the time because she's always there ... Yeah, they [technologies] create distance, for sure."

Nostalgia for times of family togetherness such as at the dinner table resurfaces among both parents and children. Technologies are blamed for changes in the family's ritual structure and loss of symbolic value. Though this discourse may be more mythical than descriptive, it reveals a shared perception. Today the different schedules of family members in combination with communications technologies that place members in different locations do in fact change the ways that families have traditionally constituted themselves as families. Sharing a meal around a table has lost its status. Being accepted at a family's table used to be an honour that has now been lost, though family ties are still created in different ways. New communications technologies, blamed for the loss of certain rites, nonetheless provide new means of performing the still-important function of determining who is a member of whose family.

9.3 Gift and Counter-Gift

A mobile phone often enters a parent-child relationship as a gift from a parent to a child at a time culturally defined as symbolic. Often it demarcates rites of passage. In addition to highlighting the symbolic thresholds between stages of life, this gift is part of one of the most powerful dynamics of construction of social relations: *gift exchange.*

When we speak of the mobile phone as a *gift*, the choice of term is not random. Indeed, gift-giving implies foregoing the right to ask for something in return. It is different from a trade, which postulates a rule of equivalence; a gift must appear essentially free and disinterested.[11] Thus it is clear that it is more revealing to see it as a relational phenomenon (for example, as a phenomenon of the parent-child relation) than to try to understand it using the principles of trade alone. By looking at the phenomenon as a gift, we try to understand the meaning for those involved; in other words, we try to analyse the symbols that begin circulating.

When we advance that social actors involved in a gift system voluntarily seek to move away from equivalence, we do not mean that giving is essentially unilateral. Generally there is in fact a return, since the gift creates a kind of "positive debt" (not an obligation) between those involved.[12] What is important is not to consider the fact of *a return*, but to consider that in this system *the return is not the official end.*

Studies have shown, for example, that many Christmas gifts are intergenerational and given to children, and that they are thus not necessarily governed by reciprocity. By looking at the symbolism of the exchanges for those involved, we in fact see that the pleasure of giving is important. Advertising in the pre-Christmas period often portrays the mobile phone as a valuable item that is pleasant to give and receive. Based on the "pleasure of giving," such advertising strategies are consistent with one of the rules specific to giving, namely, that of apparent non-instrumentality. This kind of discursive circulation of goods suggests the mobile phone as a gift, apparently free of all constraints.

Some of our observations have, however, shown that the mobile phone as a gift in the family very often carries expectations on the part of the giver, which could entail some form of reciprocity, or counter-gift. We may legitimately wonder whether family members among themselves do not apply some laws of exchange more often than one might think in transactions involving technology. For example, in exchange for giving a mobile phone to his or her child, a parent might *expect* to receive increased ability to contact the child anywhere and at any time. As Nathalie explains, "Well, in my case it was like a birthday present, but actually my parents wanted to know where I was or for me to be able to call them. So it was practically a present for them." She laughs.

In this example, we can see that the exchange need not necessarily be material, since what children give to their parents is acceptance of a new form of parenting. There are also cases in which a non-material gift may be the first part of the exchange, for example, when children "give" good behaviour (e.g., good grades) to their parents in order to receive a reward in return. Some communication technologies such as the mobile lead us to believe that a new form of exchange is gradually taking root in families. While in the past socially approved behaviour was rewarded with items of value such as watches, bicycles, and skis, today items with very different capacities are used as currency, such as communications objects like computers and mobile phones.

Mobile phones and pagers encourage the circulation of symbolic goods because they can enter the scenario as counter-gifts from parents in response to gifts given by their children (e.g., good grades). Then they can also be used to provide new counter-gifts, namely, children's agreement to answer their parents when they call. A gift contains meanings that link the giver and receiver, and promotes appropriate ties, allegiances, and norms of reciprocity. Both a gift and a counter-gift engage the identity of the giver (the parent) and the receiver (the child). In the case of a mobile phone given by a parent to a child, the link is *expressed* in the circulation of the object ("I am giving it to you because you are my child"), and could possibly be *actualized* in the return given by the child ("I have a mobile phone so I call my parents often to reassure them").

The parent-child relation is governed by conventions that, naturally, pre-dated the exchange involving technology. However, that exchange constantly reactualizes the conventions. Thus, a mobile phone gift will be used in the parent-child relationship. It will be a means of actualizing the relationship, because it makes it possible for the parties to contact one another at any time.

While we have just examined the act of giving a mobile phone, parents might also wonder about reasons why they might *refuse* to give such a technology to their children. These reasons could go beyond simple economic principles (e.g., the cost of buying and using the item). From parents' point of view, would a mobile phone take away from or add to their relationships with their children? Would it give the children too much freedom, since they as parents would no longer be able to filter outgoing and incoming calls? Would it open the door to interruptions by friends at all hours of the day? Since the gift concerns the identities of the partners, a good reason not to enter into the gift cycle could be that the gift threatens those identities. Could giving a mobile phone to one's child without any expectation of reciprocity endanger the identities at stake in the relationship?

We have seen that by offering a gift that makes it possible to place one another in a state of constant availability, we bring into play the strength of the relationship and the identities of every family member. Considering, as we do, the mobile phone outside of the gift dynamic does not entail proposing a pessimistic vision of family exchanges or human relationships. A mobile phone given with the expectation of something in return is not necessarily a poisoned gift. It is part of relational systems that are essentially unequal and conflict-ridden. The parent-child relation contains dynamics of control and authority that must sometimes come into conflict with those of independence and autonomy. This goes both ways, for while parents may want to control their children, children may also want to exercise some control over their parents. Of course, children's control will take a different form, but it will nonetheless be control, for children may want their parents to be available when they need them, and they may want to limit their parents' control over them.

9.4 Listen to Your Father and Mother, or Your Mobile?

As we have just seen, when a mobile phone (or pager) is a gift or counter-gift, it becomes a concrete and symbolic object that says "we are a family" because it is a physical representation of the permanent link among family members. It does not matter whether it is turned on or off: it becomes the sign of the reciprocal availability of family members. The mobile phone *is* the link, in the sense that it reiterates it. Rather than simply symbolizing the family link, it reproduces it.

As we mentioned at the beginning of this chapter, while it is tempting to look at the family from a traditional demographic or sociological point of view and to speak of changes in family structures (drop in the birth rate, reconstructed families, for example), it may be more interesting to examine another dimension that is often overlooked: changes in parental authority and responsibility. Certain points in history are relevant to this; for example, in the late 1980s, children's rights were recognized, thereby entailing that they were not inferior beings and could have expectations of their parents. Parents thus have responsibilities and duties with respect to their children.

These changes in the status of children have directly and indirectly affected relationships within families. Thus, the whole notion of parental authority and children's autonomy has placed the two parties in a slightly paradoxical situation. We can use this paradox to take a closer look at the role played by technologies or, rather, to ask the real question: what is the role of communications technologies in the dynamics of change of authority, responsibilities, and competencies in the family?

Beyond the most obvious roles and functions, which can be grasped at a primary level (for example, the exercise of control) there is something more profound. Members of a family have more than functional or strictly utilitarian roles. They produce cultures. In other words, they produce cultural definitions of what it means to be a parent, child, or adolescent. The definitions are inscribed in how parents act and how they incorporate technologies into their relationships with their children. Thus we can consider the idea that the mobile phone is a kind of deputy parental authority, though it does not necessarily submit children to their parents' control. Indeed, it seems rather to promote a degree of autonomy among all family members. The change in the notion of authority has also modified the definition of the reciprocal roles of parents and children. However, the forms of behaviour consistent with this new definition are far from established and shared.

We can thus say that the *habitus culturel* specific to the social group known as "the family" is undergoing change. Yet cultural models of parent and child are still being constructed, and these will be the practical translations of what parental authority now means and the form it takes. In question here are parents' and children's statuses and roles.[14] Their transformations are related to changes in the notion of authority, but should also be brought into relation with the blurring of boundaries between the family and society that has resulted from the integration and use of new technologies in everyday life.

Thus, parental and child identities constructed over time are both sources and products of technological and communicational practices, which in turn affect statuses and roles, and deconstruct and reconstruct new models and boundaries.

Is the mobile a tool for control, dependence, *and* autonomy? While the notion of parental control has changed greatly in recent decades, a certain degree of control over children's activities and friendships is still a parental right and duty. Greater when children are very young, it tends to fade gradually in adolescence and as the child becomes more independent and demonstrates the maturity necessary for entry into adult life. Obviously the way in which children are subject to parental rules, which range from relaxed to very strict, can vary enormously from family to family, depending on the family's specific *habitus*.

Nonetheless, being a parent still means exercising some degree of control. This is a legitimate right linked with the duties that come with being a parent. However, if children wish to grow up and become adults, they have to demand and exercise freedom and assert their independence from their parents. We are thus faced with a complex dialectic between the parental duty to exercise control and children's rights to independence and freedom. This dialectic is itself surrounded in paradox because, while children legitimately demand a certain ration of freedom and autonomy, they cannot free themselves completely from the relationship of dependence that links them with their parents and is presupposed by their status as children.

From this point of view it is interesting to observe the tension that can arise between the social control exercised by parents using the mobile phone and the autonomy that young people can or wish to acquire by using the same device. While the mobile phone can be seen as a real instrument of social and parental control, children are nonetheless (at least initially) in a real relationship of dependence with respect to their parents for a whole set of needs and activities.

First, the dependence can be translated into the terms of a gift or counter-gift of a mobile phone to the child, as we noted above. In fact, in terms of the acquisition and everyday use of mobile phones, children's dependence on their parents seems even more obvious when we look at management of the related costs and how this is negotiated.[15]

INTERVIEWER: Generally, among your friends who have mobile phones, who pays?

ALL: Our parents!

MISHAN: Well, I think it is half and half, because teenagers want to have a little independence, so they pay half. But they can't pay for the whole cost, so their parents pay half.

Indeed, as soon as they are able, adolescents want to express their independence and give themselves a degree of freedom by taking responsibility for part of the cost. Yet, particularly as a counter-gift, the mobile phone is nonetheless often subject to strict rules of use set by parents, especially when they are paying most of the related costs.

The mobile can thus play a role in the balance between autonomy and dependence, particularly among pre-adolescents. When parents begin to leave their children home alone for short periods before and after school or on the weekend, the mobile becomes an important tool in strategies adopted to ensure that all is well. By staying home alone, children learn to solve problems on their own but can get help from parents at any time, thanks to the mobile phone.

However, using the mobile in such situations can also increase a child's dependence. On one hand, children may use it too often and so avoid making routine decisions for themselves. On the other hand, parents may call too often or insist on their children calling them, as we see in the following discussion between Louis and his parents, Gerry and Madeleine:

INTERVIEWER: Do you call your parents often?

LOUIS: Well, yes. Even when I'm going to school.

GERRY: Let's say you don't call, it's because we tell you to call ...

INTERVIEWER: Why do you call them, for example?

LOUIS: Well! Sometimes when it's important or something that, uh ...

MADELEINE: But he doesn't call us. We have to insist on him calling us.

GERRY: In fact, it's because we are starting to leave him at home alone a little. So we tell him, "Before you go, you call."

Through control over the technology, parents construct their status and actualize their roles with their children. The way the control is managed redefines the roles of family members. It can take a number of forms, and the way it is perceived varies. For example, children and parents attribute different meanings to the constant contact made possible by the mobile phone. Guy, a parent, sees the mobile and pager as kinds of "umbilical cords" since they provide him with greater contact with his children: "But we also used it, now less, it used to be a lot like an umbilical cord with the kids. The kids could call us ... Now it's less important ... they're nineteen and twenty now. They both have pagers. Bruno, who didn't want one, we twisted his arm to get him to have one, so we could get in touch with him."

In short, parents use the mobile phone to exercise some control over their children. As Pénélope, a parent, explains, they often take advantage of the fact that their children have mobile phones to keep an eye on them, watch over them from a distance, and even control where they go: "Often there are, well, I know some where it's the parents who want to know where their kids are ... It's a form of security for them, like, you know, parents buy it for their kids to give them, to give the kids some freedom, but at the same time the parents can know where the kids are any time."

For parents, the point is not so much to track their children's movements and find out who they are spending time with but to actualize their duties and rights as parents. For example, they want to know that their children are safe and remind them of their commitments and responsibilities as members of the family. Thus, the point is to know more or less where their children are and with whom, what they are doing, and when they are coming home, and to remind their children when they have to be back or scold them if they are late.[16]

Children can perceive the mobile more as a kind of "electronic leash" that allows their parents to contact them at any time.

BARRY: Then after it was what you call ... it becomes a bit like an electronic leash for the mother ...

INTERVIEWER: An electronic leash?

BARRY: For the mother and then so ... it lets her call me all the time and then, uh ... any time.

ANDRÉE (mother): Well, it's true, I like it.

This electronic collar, as it could also be called, can be perceived as a real constraint by creating an obligation to answer. The much-promised freedom offered by the device then becomes paradoxical. A small delay on the part of an adolescent, or a parent's slightest worry, requires a phone call. Children can literally be tracked.

Karine says, "Well, it's because my parents, it's become like they really want to know where I am, so my parents always want to contact me, they're always afraid when I'm outside. When I'm out they can't contact me because there's no phone, when I'm at someone's it's okay but if I go somewhere and I don't call when I'm going, well, they start freaking out, so ... I need one." And Layla exploits another feature of her phone to "prove" she is okay:

LAYLA: Then you say, "Yes, Mom, see my friends," then you take a picture with your phone. It's so that your mom can see that you're really with your friends.
INTERVIEWER: Could you repeat what you just said?
LAYLA: It's because I say to myself, okay, let's say I call my mother, then my mother really wants to know if I'm somewhere or if I'm really with my friends, you take a picture, then you say, "Yes, Mom, I'm with my friends, look."
INTERVIEWER: So you've got proof.
LAYLA: Yeah, I've got proof.

The duty to inform parents is generally well accepted by most young people, as is the fact that their parents can contact them at any time to exercise control:

SOPHIE: It's safer, not just for us, but for our parents too ... Sometimes there are families that are separated; in ours, we're all together, but even so, my mother likes to be able to call me ...
ANTOINE: In that sense, it's sure that it's another advantage, maybe to be able to get more permission to go out because you tell them something like "Hey, you can call me any time, there won't be any problems."
SOPHIE: "If there's anything, I'll call you, Mom, Dad ..."
KARINE: Because some people go out a lot, they have a really big social life, and for their parents, it would help them a little.
INTERVIEWER: To be able to contact them?
KARINE: To contact them, yeah, so the parents won't freak out, so they won't be there going "Aaaack!"

Even though children consider the autonomy and freedom that the device provides as among the fundamental reasons for owning a mobile, they often focus on safety reasons in persuading parents of the need to get one. Children believe that they will be able to go out more often if their parents know that they can contact them any time and anywhere. They often have in mind situations in which their friends have had permission to go out and have become more independent and they give mobile phones an important role in this area. As Laurence says, "When you see, say, all your friends can go out whenever they want because their parents can always call them, well, you wonder if you couldn't have one too, so then you could go out anytime, whenever you want."

Adolescents thus often manage to turn the constraints of remote mothering[17] to their advantage so as to gain some freedom. Calling to warn that one will be late or inform about where and with whom one is are often also opportunities to get an extension or permission.[18]

LAYLA: Why did you get a mobile phone ?

JEAN: Well, one, to communicate, like to have more independence. You know, when your parents tell you, like in a mall, you have something, a means of communicating, to contact you. Like with your friends, let's say we say, "Okay, let's meet like at the movie theatre."

LAYLA: Okay.

CARL: Me, it's about the same too. It's like the parent-child relationship. It's sure that you know if, if you're going to be late, you're on your way, so then you just have to call your parents on your mobile and then you tell them, "I'm coming, I'm about fifteen minutes late, uh, I'm just in front of such-and-such a place, I'm coming," then they say, "oh, okay, that's fine."

Thus the presence of new communications technologies in the family is often part of a hierarchical system of control that can contribute to changes in the exercise of power in the family and in the ways that family members exercise authority.[19] The paradoxical tension between autonomy and dependence obtained through mobile phone use can also be seen on the parents' side. Indeed, it is interesting to note that here parents sometimes find themselves at the mercy of their children, feeling obliged to answer immediately, no matter what they are doing.[20]

For many, acquisition of a mobile phone makes it possible to carry out individual activities and work while knowing that they can intervene with their children from a distance. Such remote parenting seems to give them a good conscience because they feel they can perform their roles as parents at home, and away from it.

For both parents and children, then, the mobile phone allows great flexibility with respect to time and travel. It makes access so easy that it is no longer necessary to work out strategies for contacting one another efficiently. Instead, as with members of the social network, strategies now have to be developed to create quiet spaces and times. Calls that are not answered have to be justified, just as times when the mobile phone is turned off have to be explained. It is in this respect that the mobile phone can be perceived in an ambiguous way by some users. On one hand, it allows one to perform one's obligations without feeling guilty about not being home or with friends, since family and friends can call at any time. On the other hand, it creates expectations that tie the phone owner to his or her family.

9.5 The Mobile Phone: Tool for Transgression?

As we have seen, the acquisition and use of a mobile phone actualizes rights and duties related to the statuses of parent and child. The rights and duties are sometimes difficult to reconcile and can give rise to paradoxical situations. When such situations arise, there is a potential for conflict that resembles classical intergenerational conflict.

PAULA: Well, I didn't want one, it's my mom who gave it to me, but now I don't want it, in a way, because I have it, she calls me and then I'm somewhere, and she says, "Come home right away." You see? It's a bummer.
INTERVIEWER: So, you'd rather not have one?
PAULA: Well, now she calls me less often now.

We have to keep in mind that the resistance children put up against their parents is an integral part of youth culture. By transgressing the norms, rules, and limitations of adult society, young people display membership in their peer group. Their culture thus requires many secrets and experiences be hidden from parents, school, and other forms of authority. Talking to friends late at night, for example, is valued becasue it is disapproved of by parents. Christine describes her sister's behaviour: "Like at night, because we, we aren't really allowed to talk on the phone at night, but she goes into her room. She talks with her friends at one o'clock in the morning, and us, we can't get to sleep."

The mobile becomes a part of this universe of secrecy and mystery, making it possible to establish a parallel network, hidden from parents. Young people can transgress parental authority because parents do not always have means of checking the information their children give them. Despite the existence of some rules, as soon as children own a mobile phone, their parents have little control over where and when they make calls. It is not easy for parents to know whether their children are really where they say they are, or to know and check with whom their children are talking.

Indeed, since young people are more adept at using and mastering communication technologies, they can use them to get around some rules set by their parents.

INTERVIEWER: And which mobile do you use?

DIANE: It depends who you're calling! ... Me, if someone calls me at my parents', I use theirs, but aside from that, I always use mine. But at my parents' I use theirs.

INTERVIEWER: Why?

DIANE: Because my father doesn't know about it!!! [*laughs*]

INTERVIEWER: Your father doesn't know you have a mobile phone?

DIANE: No, he doesn't know.

INTERVIEWER: But if you call him, how would he know?

DIANE: He'd see the number.

MARIO: On the call display!

INTERVIEWER: Why don't you want your father to know you have a mobile?

DIANE: Because I know what he's going to say to me, he's going to say, "Diane, you're wasting your money, you didn't need that." ... The same old song, and so just to avoid making him talk, even when he comes, I make sure it's not out where he can see it ... I leave it in my bedroom or in a drawer, in a cupboard or somewhere he won't see it.

In other situations, adolescents may simply choose not to answer calls from their parents. Evasion of parental control can extend even to lying, as Tania explained.

TANIA: Before I had one, I really wanted one, like I thought I was always going to use it and everything. But now my mother tells me like, "Oh, take a cell phone," but I don't want to because, you know, then she'll be able to call me where, when she wants, and it's not fair ... It's like, I don't really like that. You're with your friends, and then your mother calls you.

INTERVIEWER: So you'd rather not have one? It's your mother who insists?

TANIA: Yeah, but it's really like, uh, to know where I am, if I'm going to be late or something.

INTERVIEWER: So how do you deal with it?

TANIA: I turn it off. [*laughs*]

INTERVIEWER: You take it but you turn it off.

TANIA: Well, I turn it off, yeah, or else I say I was in the subway.

An additional function of the technology enables Sandrine to filter parental control calls:

DELPHINE: On top of that, I don't have call display, so I have no choice but to answer.

SANDRINE: I have call display, you know, when it's someone, let's say I'm somewhere and it's my parents and I don't want to talk to them, I don't want them to bug me, so I don't answer.

Such resistance is not created by technologies such as the mobile phone; rather, it is part of the *modus vivendi* of intergenerational negotiations. The mobile thus enters the pre-existing dynamic of the parent-child relationship. While it obviously does not construct the relationship, it reiterates the relationship and creates new options for managing it.

9.6 Being Free Together

Seen as a tool for articulating family rights and duties, the mobile phone allows parents to discharge some of their control responsibilities while at the same time allowing their children to exercise their right to independence by giving them a degree of freedom. This is not a traditional negotiation with an alternation of incompatible rights, for example, situations involving pure control ("You may not go out") and others pure freedom ("On Saturday night you are free"). The negotiation consists in a balanced sharing of times when each party exercises his or her rights. In this new form of negotiation, the mobile phone makes it possible to exercise incompatible rights and duties simultaneously. It creates the paradox of children going out, thereby gaining greater independence and freedom – but carrying mobile phones, and therefore also being subject to greater surveillance by their parents. When children are at home with mobile phones, they are limited in terms of travel but have free access to their social networks. The technology and the different perceptions to which it gives rise create a new articulation of the rights and duties of parents and children.

What is in question is the articulation of a kind of "being free together."[21] Like new technologies in general, the mobile phone is a medium of communication that through its use can support this kind of claim in relation to identity. This is probably especially true among young people, for whom the mobile phone provides direct access to personal social networks and, up to a certain point, unsanctioned access to parallel (or "underground") social networks separate from the family and its land-line phone, which remains a collective communications tool.

The pertinence of this observation is growing since today's family is characterized by greater autonomy and individualization of its members. Despite this, and there is nothing to lead us to believe that things will be otherwise in the near future, the family still remains an indispensable substrate for the ongoing construction of the identity of all its members.[22] Yet we can see the parallel development of increasing demand from every family member for his or her own identity, an individual and social identity that in some way escapes the rest of the family and is desired as such. One thing is sure: by sometimes weakening and sometimes magnifying this tension, new communications technologies play a growing role in redefining and renegotiating the roles and statuses of members of the contemporary family.

Mobile Communication as Social Performance: New Ethics, New Politeness, New Aesthetics

10.1 Storytelling about Technologies: Urban Legends and Personal Narratives

As technology enters our lives, one characteristic of everyday life is amplified: that of being a practical accomplishment created moment-by-moment by our actions and discourse. In the end, everyday life is a constant cultural work, a process through which individuals produce the meaning of things, their own identities, and the rules of community life.

Beyond the great strategies of designers, promoters, and "experts," beyond the official versions of technology's functions and uses, there is a whole range of tactics belonging to "ordinary people" (De Certeau 1980). Through their everyday discourses and practices related to such objects, they create new meanings, negotiate shared ones, question what is taken for granted, and establish new obvious truths. Thus, through their words and actions, ordinary people play roles in producing new and often unforeseen cultural models of things.

In the course of our research we noticed that over and above technology use, it was discourse *on* technologies that best revealed the process of symbolic creation that characterizes ordinary culture and is manifested in the folds and wrinkles of everyday life. Thus, when we asked people we met in the field to tell us about their experiences with the latest communications technologies, they provided us with a repertoire of stories. More or less based on experience, more or less constructed ad hoc for practical purposes, their anecdotes and narratives often overlapped, referred to, and sometimes contradicted one another. Although highly contextualized, these narratives resembled the collectively shared stories and urban legends that inevitably accompany the entrance and spread of a new technology in social space.

Less odd than founding myths, more important than simple anecdotes, urban legends are contemporary narratives that combine real and fictional elements, and always have a special relationship with one or more historical facts (Renard 1999). They are always produced in two stages: a perhaps banal historical fact or a simple anecdote is identified as the core event of a narrative; this narrative is transformed into a legend when, circulating by word of mouth and sometimes reported in the media, it acquires mythical elements yet is still believed as being about real events by an increasing audience. While traditional legends were situated in dark forests or isolated villages in a mythical past or dreamed elsewhere, while they relied on supernatural forces to create the problem or solve it, so-called urban legends are different. Not only do they take shape literally under our eyes but their urban nature refers explicitly to modernity, of which the city is one of the most important emblems. Urban legends are always presented as rational, realistic narratives, albeit unusual. They never employ supernatural elements. Firmly anchored in modernity, they are created when one or more initial events are reconstructed according to a scenario or an ideal-typical event structure that is already present in the collective imagination.[1] Unconcerned with truth or even plausibility, urban legends both feed on and feed social imagination, and help to create collective ideas about people, things, and events they recount.

Clearly, new technologies are a fertile ground for the emergence of such narratives in that they provide an extremely rich narrative repertoire of "techno-fears," "techno-sicknesses," "techno-solutions," and "techno-heroes." By situating users and technologies in a narrative framework (where, when, how, why), stories about technologies establish reasons for adoption and use, practical values of technologies, and their unexpected role in problem solving.[2] Conveying their narrative truth about technologies, people, and events, these stories help to create the meaning of the technologies and compete to govern their uses in everyday life.

As they are repeated over and over, everyday narratives about communication technologies achieve the status and roles of mythological narratives: they define our relationships to the objects, legitimize certain practices, and make the relationship between humans and technologies seem natural and obvious, when they are in fact essentially cultural.

In their everyday stories, tellers refer to technologies less in relation to their usefulness than in accordance with the socio-cultural values that they convey. Once transformed into a character of a narrative, the technological artifact becomes a focal point where social rules and values reveal themselves. The object is thus a pretext for creating a dialogue among characters carrying on different narrative programs (Greimas 1983). Sometimes complementary, sometimes in competition, such narrative programs converge around the object. Further, their polemic interactions reveal different stances towards the object and its relationships with human actors.

Even the most trivial and circumstantial story always reveals a more general narrative, because through the story the teller proposes models of events, formulates theories about causes and consequences, expresses assessments and judgments on characters and actions, and enlists the participation of listeners or co-narrators in the theory-building activity to achieve a consensual version (Bruner 1990, Ochs, Taylor, Rudolph, and Smith 1992).

In order to grasp the modelling strength of storytelling about emerging technologies, let us look at adolescents' narratives about the entrance of the mobile phone into their lives. What are they thinking about when they talk with one another about mobile phones? To what basic scenario do they refer in their stories, discourse, and comments?

In a group discussion, some adolescents exchange ideas about the various ways that people use their mobile phones. Nathalie suggests a hypothetical example: "You know, like the guy in the bus who's talking on his mobile and then it starts ringing. You know, like it wasn't on!"

This story about fictitious use – someone pretending to talk on a mobile with no listener on the other end – is more than a hypothetical example. It is a variant of an urban legend that belongs to a repertoire of shared stories about mobile phones. There are variants everywhere in ordinary conversations among both adolescents and adults, in both Europe and North America. Generally more elaborate than the one above, the variants are often constructed like personal stories, autobiographical narratives of personally lived experiences. Catherine, Jean-Pierre, and Guillaume extend the "fictitious use" theme:

CATHERINE: Often in the bus, I often take the bus, and there're people talking on the phone but so loud that everyone can hear them, then suddenly their mobile starts ringing. So really they were pretending to talk, and then they take the phone and they're going "Hello?" [laughs] They really pretend to talk so that everyone will notice them, then when the phone rings they're really embarrassed.

JEAN-PIERRE: It's stupid!

CATHERINE: Has that ever happened to you?

JEAN-PIERRE: No, but I have an anecdote I remember. There was a lady, okay, she was just about to give birth, okay, she was having contractions and there was a guy with a mobile phone that my mom saw just before and she goes, "Hey, that guy there has a mobile. Quick, I'm going to talk to him" and all that. She goes up to the guy and then she sees the guy was calling with a toy. It wasn't a real mobile phone, it was a toy.

While Nathalie suggested a hypothetical case without claiming that it happened, Catherine demonstrates greater skill. She constructs a variant of the same narrative that she constructs as true. "I often take the bus," "there're people talking," "Has that ever happened to you?" She uses all the rhetorical devices to set a scene that gives her story a realistic tone. She does not imagine a possible case, but reports a supposed really occurred experience. Jean-Pierre does the same thing: he translates into autobiographical terms another urban legend that has long been circulating in Canada and Europe.

What is interesting about these narratives is not their claimed truth value. However, by reformulating variations of well-known urban legends about mobile phones, young people engage in polyphonic repetition (Bazzanella 1993) and contribute to the construction of a repertoire of shared cultural versions of this technology and its uses. Circulating like historical narratives about trivial events, the stories are claimed to be true, and can thus become arguments used to support theories. In the above cases, young people use them to illustrate one use of mobile phone: displaying it. Their narratives support the thesis that the real reason to have a mobile phone is that it looks cool. However, as Bruner pointed out, stories are also meaningful because they are always chosen among all the other possible and available ones (Bruner 1990). The attention paid to some stories rather than others in the repertoire of urban legends reveals the canonical script of mobile phone use.

Urban legends, whether situated in the street or on a bus, mainly portray mobile phone use as a *social performance*. The same basic scenario surfaces in personal anecdotes. Humorously parodying her sister, Delphine reconstructs a little dramatic sketch describing her sister's use of the technology: "My half-sister, she's seventeen, and she has a mobile phone, and it's like ... just so cool to walk in the street and talk on the phone, and answer 'Yes, hello, how're you? I'm talking on my mobile right now.'"

Charlotte tells almost the same story about her own sister: "I think it's pretty useless because, what does she do? It's like, she calls, she's like in the bus, she's got nothing to do, and she calls us to chat, to pass the time."

Through these two narratives, Delphine and Charlotte are supporting the thesis typical of adolescents who do not have mobile phones, which could more or less be summarized as "Mobile phones are practically useless except for showing that you have one." As Aesop said, when they are out of reach, the grapes must be sour.

What is important to note here is that these individual and apparently anecdotal stories are in fact constructed on the same basic scenario as the urban legends echoed by the other participants. The storyteller's work inherent to narrative of selecting and reconfiguring events (Goffman 1974, Ricoeur 1986) leads Delphine and Charlotte to choose certain events and anecdotes rather than others. They both choose to tell about events that supposedly occurred in the bus or on the street – in other words, in public places. Thus the repertoire of urban legends, like that of personal anecdotes, provides young people with descriptive resources they can use to (re)construct the canonical model of use of this technology. Their narratives are all constructed on the same scenario, the basic structure of which includes:

1. A *location* that is always a public place: in other words, a place through which people pass or in which they live;
2. An *action*, namely, a telephone call;
3. Three *actors*: the caller, the callee, and an audience that is to varying degrees voluntary, listening, or inconvenienced.

Stories about mobile phones have the functions and the modelling power of all narratives. Using the argumentative force and the rhetorical strength of telling "obvious facts," tellers construct and legitimize a canonical version of the events they recount (Herrnstein Smith 1984). For the purpose of reconstructing participants' ways of thinking about mobile phones, the truth value of these narratives is irrelevant. Whether factual or fictitious, constructed ad hoc or historical, these narratives are "exemplar cases" of an underlying model and evidence of a local theory about mobile phone use. The typical scenario thus promoted has no statistical legitimacy but is rather a *folk model* (Quinn and Holland 1987, D'Andrade and Strauss 1992) of mobile phone use, a canonical image based on stories circulating in the community.

The individual anecdotes we have just cited support the show-off theory and consequently portray individuals who intentionally put on a public performance with their mobile phones to look cool. The following anecdotes are somewhat different, in that the social performance is accounted for as unintentional. Nathalie describes what happened to a friend and to her brother:

NATHALIE: One of my friends was going to St Bruno Mall. We live in Longueuil ... She had her mobile and she was listening to music on her earphones really loud. Then she was on the bus. Then at one point, everyone started staring at her, and so she thinks, "Oh no, maybe my music is too loud." So she reduced the volume, she couldn't understand. She kept going, listening to her music. She got there and then I told her, "Hey, we called you, why didn't you answer?" Haaa! The phone rang but she never answered, she had no idea. She never heard it.

ANNE: So everyone was staring at her, and she didn't really understand ...

NATHALIE: Yeah! Well, you know, you say, "Scuse me but your phone's ringing." But no one went and told her, so she was like "ohhh." My brother, when his phone rings, "Ben, your phone's ringing." He's there like, "Oh, it's mine?" "Yeah, it's yours!" [*laughs*] Not used to it ...

Even though these are not cases of showing off, even though the "public" performances occurred without the knowledge of the principal protagonists, the two narratives nonetheless situate the mobile phone in a scenario where there are a number of characters: a caller (the person who made the mobile phone ring), a callee (the phone owner), and an audience made up of fortuitous witnesses (the other passengers on the bus and the person who tells Ben that his phone is ringing). The construction of these individual narratives and urban legends and their circulation illustrate the cultural model of use of this communication technology. It is situated in what Goffman would call a *social encounter*, a radical interpersonal affair.

10.2 Telephone Conversation as Social Performance

As these everyday narratives and urban legends show, the advent of the mobile phone and its widespread use have dramatically changed the cultural frame of telephone conversation and its typical social participation structure. The telephone conversation is no longer socially defined as private talk between two speakers, nor is it the paradigmatic example of a two-party verbal interaction (Hopper 1991). The cultural script of mobile calls presumes an audience somewhere.

Because of the multiplication of the actors involved, it is relevant to analyse mobile calls as social encounters and as multi-party conversations involving both ratified and non-ratified participants (Goffman 1981). More or less concerned, real or imagined, this included third party is no longer an exception (as may have been the case with land-line telephones); the outsider has become the *constitutive rule* of telephone conversation. The simple fact that the third party is assumed to be virtually present even when this presence is not marked on the surface of the ongoing interaction creates constraints and possibilities that affect the conversation. As Goffman has noted, the role of non-ratified participants in shaping the conversation is crucial since in any verbal performance the audience influences the construction of the discourse.[3]

Appropriate or not, subject to social appraisal or not, the mobile telephone conversation involves not only the caller and callee but also bystanders playing the roles of both eavesdroppers and over-hearers (ibid.). Present and spying in spite of themselves, chance listeners, fairly polite spectators of the exchange occurring before their eyes and ears, unofficial participants are part of the basic scenario of every mobile phone conversation. Involuntary participants, whether listening or pretending not to hear, they are present and help make mobile phone conversation a social performance. This cultural script of the telephone conversation defines preferred actions and expected behaviours and establishes the rule determining variations and exceptions.

The mobile phone may not necessarily have changed the way we speak on the phone, but it has changed the way we conceive of telephone conversation. The question is not whether this canonical model has anything to do with statistic frequencies; from an empirical standpoint people indeed use their mobile phones in private places as well, in their bedrooms or elsewhere in their homes, to prevent others from hearing.[4] Typical scripts of social actions emerge less from what people do than from how they account for what they do.

Thinking about mobile phone use as a radical social performance leads people to construct theories about the technology's impact on their lives and those of others. These consequences derive from the cultural model rather than from the empirical uses of mobile phones. The canonical script of mobile conversation makes people think about new tensions in their relations with others, tensions that can strengthen or lead to renegotiation of explicit and implicit social norms.

10.3 New Ethics for New Social Encounters

A major consequence of this cultural model of the mobile phone is that it leads to a social rather than individual interpretation of the technology. It is precisely because mobile phone use is perceived as a public performance that it triggers a reflection on the social effects of that performance, its choreography, and the roles of the various actors involved. Given that an audience is there, since this audience is seen as affected by the phone call and as constructing an image of the user based on his or her use of the mobile phone, the behaviour is no longer an individual affair. Speaking on the phone becomes social and is thus subject to a process of constant assessment.

Despite the fact that it is widespread, the idea that young people use mobile phones in an apparently dissolute and careless manner, even to the point of violating social constraints, is unfounded. Among young people, mobile phone use is anything but anarchical. They leave nothing to chance; even the most infinitesimal details are subject to codes, evaluation, and a critical eye.

In the following excerpt, Jacinthe, Nathalie, and Anna discuss the way mobile phones have changed people's lives. They pause over a typical scenario, mobile phone use at the grocery store. As they discuss the story, the three young people theorize about the consequences of an individual action and explore different aspects of a social performance that affects the other people in the same social surroundings:

JACINTHE: Well, it depends on what they say too.

NATHALIE: Not at all! It doesn't matter! They've got the right to say what they want …

JACINTHE: Sometimes they yell like they're crazy.

NATHALIE: Even if they're not talking on a mobile, someone who yells is irritating.

ANNA: Well, sometimes they're husbands, they call to ask their wives what to buy in the store. If it's important it's okay, but otherwise if they're pretending to talk to someone on purpose to show that they've got a phone, well …

NATHALIE: It doesn't bug me at all, they can talk wherever they want, they can go into the bathroom and talk on their mobile, it doesn't bug me at all.

JACINTHE: But it's also because the principle of a mobile is that you can be called anywhere, but for sure you know sometimes there are people who yell.

NATHALIE: I don't want to bug you, but what is it? It's irritating when people talk really loudly on their mobiles. But when you think about it, anyone talking loudly to anyone else ... even if they're not on the phone ... So really it's not the fact that they're on a mobile ...

JACINTHE: But it's because there are people who have the reflex to talk louder ... like my dad ... It's really stressful, and in the movie theatre, then, you're like "Come on."

Would "conveying emergency information" justify using a mobile phone in front of other people who suddenly find themselves in the position of involuntary listeners? Probably not, for appraising the degree of emergency is subjective. Yet is not the mobile made specifically for that purpose, to let a subscriber be contacted anywhere? Is it the use of the mobile as such that bothers other people or the content of the communication? It is perhaps the volume of the voice or the ring? Vanessa, reflecting with others on the advantages of having a mobile phone, eventually raises the same issue: "I find it ... it's good for emergencies and work, but the disadvantages are that it's expensive and also it can bug the people you're with. Let's say you're doing something and your friends don't want to be bugged by the ring, the person is going to have to go out, and that's going to disturb everybody."

When discussing mobile phone use, at least paradigmatic use, young people constantly define and redefine the conditions of its appropriateness and wonder about what is right, what is wrong, and why. Mobile phone use thus becomes a subject of polemic discussion, the ethical issues it raises prompting them to explore the social ethics of everyday life.

It is possible to establish a typology of uses that young people consider appropriate and inappropriate. However, this would be only an empirical question, since such judgments change depending on personal experience, circumstances and what is at stake in the conversation. What is particularly interesting is not so much the details about what is considered appropriate but the reflection on the social dimension of individual behaviour.

The young people below are thinking about the appropriateness of official rules that regulate mobile phone use at school:

ADRIEN: In your schools, are you allowed to have mobiles in class or in the building?

CAROLINA: Not in class, but in the school building, yes.

MARTHA: Us, neither in class nor in school.

VALÉRIE: It's the same for me.

ADRIEN: The same as for Martha?

MARTHA: Like, at school you can't walk and talk, that's for sure!

CAROLINA: But some do!

VALÉRIE: If you go into the school, if you've got one, you've got to turn it off.

CAROLINA: Yeah, you've got to turn it off during class.

MARTHA: It's not allowed, but some people don't do it.

ADRIEN: What do you think about those rules?

MARTHA: I think they're okay, it's like ... you're in your class, if everyone had a mobile in class, the teacher might be talking and everyone would be talking on the phone ...

CAROLINA: Maybe if it was something urgent, you never know, but I think it might be okay ...

MARTHA: Never!

CAROLINA: But I think that at that age ...

MARTHA: I think that a pager that vibrates, a pager that vibrates so there's no sound, no disturbance, nothing – like that, you look, and then at break time you go. Otherwise you tell the teacher, "I'm going to the bathroom," then you go call because if you say, "It's urgent, I'm going to go call," then it'll get confiscated for sure because it's not allowed in class.

The school rules are strict prohibitions (in class you cannot talk on the mobile phone or receive calls) that strongly limit individual freedom. Contrary to what one might imagine, the young people find the idea perfectly appropriate. They reconstruct the logic of such prohibitions and agree with their necessity. Even though they explore the possibility of certain violations of the basic rule, that rule remains. By talking together about mobile phone uses, they reveal their awareness of the basic principle of community life: individual interests and freedom end where those of others begin. The basic script of mobile phone use that underlies all their narratives forces them to hold two points of view simultaneously: that of the user and that of the other. The other limits personal space and action. However, their reasoning becomes more complex since the other involved is not just the involuntary audience – it is also the person with whom the called is talking when the mobile rings.

Carolina describes her response to being put in this situation: "Sometimes you're talking with someone and then, you know, it rings, then they start talking, talking, talking, and you say, "Hellooo, I'm here!" but he keeps talking. I don't like that." Who has priority in this kind of situation?

Whose rights should be given precedence? Those of the partner in the face-to-face conversation or those of a ghost participant⁵ who interrupts? The latter also has rights, new rights created by the object: the right to be able to reach those with mobile phones at any time. As the discussion continues, the reflection on ethical consequences of mobile phone use becomes more articulate:

CATHERINE: But if someone really needs to get in touch with you –

JEAN-PIERRE: Yeah, yeah, who really wants to talk to me, well, I'm going to answer anyway ...

CATHERINE: Would it bug you to be interrupted right now – that's the question.

JEAN-PIERRE: It depends, it depends where, it always bugs me but I'm going to answer just to be polite, I'm going to answer, I'm not going to just leave the person waiting.

GUILLAUME: If I'm in a restaurant or at the theatre I don't answer, but aside from that I do. It's just politeness.

CATHERINE: And would you like it if someone trespassed on your private life by calling you often, in a place where you can always be reached?

ELISSA: If there's somewhere I don't want to be bothered, well, I can always turn the mobile off. So if I turn the phone off, no one'll be able to reach me.

CATHERINE: But sometimes you forget, and sometimes I turn it off but it turns itself back on and then people call and it's embarrassing ...

When thinking about how and when to use a mobile phone, it is not enough to simply consider the audience's point of view, for there are two other people involved: the caller and the callee. The break in the flow of the social interaction also affects the person who has been called. The mobile phone's ring can produce that most social of emotions: embarrassment. Is there an easy solution to this "social violation?" One need only turn off the mobile or refuse to answer. But when exploring this solution, these adolescents find that it is not necessarily the best because it does not take into account the rights of the person calling.

To answer or not to answer one's mobile becomes an ethical question involving at least three actors and their needs, desires, rights, and obligations. Striking a balance among the often incompatible rights of the caller, the callee, and the involuntary audience is not easy. Young people explore the need to negotiate and construct rules to reconcile sometimes conflicting perspectives. It is fascinating to see that, beyond the new practices introduced into their everyday lives by the new technology, one of the unexpected results is a debate on social ethics. Faced with the theatrical performance embodied in all public uses of mobile phones, young people reflect on the difficult and always precarious equilibrium between individual and collective concerns. Even though they explore this problem in a perfectly circumstantial manner, they nonetheless weigh difficult issues such as respect for the other, the need for shared rules in social life (such as in the classroom), the possibility of violating rules (like keeping one's mobile on), and the inevitability of punishment.

The exchanges among young people about mobile phone use become a veritable laboratory of social thought. They explore and grasp the intersubjective dimension of social life, and taking an intersubjective perspective into account is the foundation of all ethical reasoning. As soon as the mobile phone becomes not only an object of use but also an object of discourse, it is transformed into a tool for constructing culture in the broad sense; it unleashes social thought and new awareness of the other.

10.4 Politeness Rules: Manners for Mobile Use

When a new technology appears in everyday life, one of the problems it raises is that of politeness. Uses that are pretty much inscribed in the technology itself have to be put into practice, and social norms governing such practices may not yet exist. Mobile phones are a typical example. Since there were no pre-established codes, the first regular uses became real social laboratories for constructing rules of politeness. Cultural meetings in public places, for instance, play a pedagogical role in defining the social uses of this technology: in theatres, movie houses, and churches, announcements ask people to turn off their mobile phones. This is a reminder that this code is not yet shared or internalized.

Far from calling for deregulated mobile phone use, teenagers participate in the social construction of politeness rules and in developing a social consensus on such a code. In a completely consistent manner, their reflection on the ethical dimension of mobile phone use blends and changes into thought on the codes that should regulate that social performance. Etiquette and politeness rules are indeed pragmatic solutions to almost everyday ethical micro-problems. From good manners to the most codified protocols, codes of etiquette are cultural buffers that prevent and absorb most social offences deriving from individual action. In Goffman's terms, they are *situational ethics* (Goffman 1981, 132).

CAROLINA: I think sometimes it's a bit show-offy, yeah. They could go out or turn down the volume. It bugs me, it bugs me when a person starts talking like that. But if it's in the bus, they can't go out, but they could at least, they could lower the tone, or talk fast and say, "I'll call you back later" but not continue ...

MARTHA: That's it, call back later, maybe.

ADRIEN: Well, you, if you had a mobile, would you talk in the bus?

CAROLINA: I don't think so.

MARTHA: It's the same thing.

ADRIEN: But how would you react if someone came up to you and said, "Talk quieter, you're bothering me"?

CAROLINA: Well, I'd call back later.

VALÉRIE: Me, as soon as I have a mobile, I talk ... like we said, like, I'm going to try not to talk louder, it's something I don't like when others do it.

ADRIEN: And do you feel embarrassed to talk when you're in a public place with other people who are going to hear your conversation?

MARTHA: No, it depends on what kind of conversation, who you're going to be with. If you're talking with friends, you don't care, but if it's someone intimate, well ... They could go out or turn down the volume, talk fast and say, "I'll call you back later."

These young people are formulating hypothetical norms for regulating mobile phone use in public. Their judgments do not refer to mobile phone use as such but to the conditions of the performance. Beyond the solutions suggested in each case, it is indeed the rules of etiquette that are in question. This specific type of social rule is designed mainly to govern behaviour in public so that it meets expectations and thus attains legitimacy. This is exactly what the young people are doing: they are theorizing about the need for shared norms for a collectively regulated practice.

Below, four adolescents talk about the fact that some people buy mobile phones to look cool. Assoum revisits the issue:

ASSOUM: You keep going on about style. What do you mean by "style"?

ANTOINE [laughing]: Being more modern!

SOPHIE: But some people have mobiles just to show that they are really cool. Like smoking, it's like "Yo!" I think it's stupid but some are like "Hey, I'm cool, yo, I've got a cigarette, I've got a mobile." It's the same thing: "I feel older, I've got a mobile, a pager, look at me everyone," and they put it here.

NASSER: Then there's also like maybe his mobile is newer than mine, he's going to say, "Hey, yours is really ugly," just to say, "Check mine out, it's nicer and smaller."

ANTOINE: Or else also attract attention, really, say ... like when your phone rings you put the volume on max and you let it ring, yeah, then everyone turns around and they see you have a mobile ... It depends on the context, it really depends on the context, that's for sure.

These conversations clearly delineate the crucial threshold excess. Excessive display of the object, tone of the speaker's voice, number of rings, volume, desire for the smallest or most colourful model: all extremes are criticized as ridiculous, impolite, and ultimately inappropriate. While negotiable and dependent on the context, there is something that makes a difference that these young people try to assess. As always, appropriate behaviour is not a question of what one does but how. The issue is to possess this know-how and demonstrate the ability to perform the action according to a minimal choreography of personal behaviour in public. Intimate conversation, loud talking, and high-volume ringing should not intrude excessively in public. Young people seem deeply concerned by a quest for etiquette for imposing forms and limitations, thresholds, and conditions to prevent personal and intimate life from being exposed inappropriately. Here too what is really interesting is not what young people consider impolite but the fact that they engage in reflection on politeness and the need for etiquette to define forms of situational ethics. This level of reflection is part of young people's technological culture.

The skills needed to communicate using a mobile phone are not limited to mastery of a particular grammar and lexicon. They also cover social aspects and norms that govern use of phones in public places. Knowing how to talk on a mobile also means knowing when, where, and especially how. In this respect, the most highly criticized form of behaviour is trying to "look cool." Like a person who displays his wealth, technological social climbers over-display their objects and assume that this will enable them to acquire the most highly desired social status: coolness. Their mistake in social grammar does not concern what they own or what they do but rather measure, manners, and ways of dealing: they lack of etiquette knowledge. Technological social climbers do not see the subtle threshold that flips the social meaning of a form of behaviour and transforms it into its opposite. Unknowingly, they cross the invisible line that separates ownership necessary for being part of the group from ownership that situates them outside the group of those who know how to act the right way.

By thinking about these issues, teenagers demonstrate not only their level of communications skills but also their extreme sensitivity to social rules of behaviour. As we have seen, they are severe judges of their own behaviour and that of others in public. By grasping the fine line between appropriate and inappropriate uses and by highlighting the importance of etiquette in defining identity, they participate in the process of defining communicative and social skills related to the use of new technologies.

10.5 Biomorphism or Sociomorphism? Embodying New Communication Technologies

The human body has always been subject to processes of culturalization. Physical manipulations involving shape, posture, and size, and socio-cultural interpretations involving attribution of meanings, values, and roles to the body, transform it into a text in and through which actors write and read their identities and those of others.[6] More is involved than individual identity. One's own body (Merleau-Ponty 1945) is marked by personal as well as collective history; it relates the past, indicates the present, and allows the future to be glimpsed; it broadcasts social and cultural belonging. Clothing, accessories, fitness and body-building practices, makeup, and disguises have always submitted the body to codes of shared aesthetics. A patchwork of appliquéd objects, subject to all sorts of modifications, the body thus enables the individual to be part of a society, community, and group. A somatic business card, it tells us who we are and who we want to be in the eyes of others.

As anthropologists have noted, the body is a *social skin* (Pandolfi 2001), a cultural artifact that strongly connects self and community. This theoretical framework underlines the aesthetics of communication techno-objects. Here we are referring to aesthetics in its etymological sense: *aísthesis,* a category defining the domain of perceptions and sensations. It includes tactile and visual sensations, of course, but also the perception of self in society. Being comfortable, feeling sure of oneself, and having the feeling that one is protected give one advantages. These are mental representations, psychological reactions, that are nonetheless based on the tactile sensation of having an appropriate object and considering oneself properly equipped, safe from lack or need. Designers are well aware of the porous membrane between the physical and the psychological. An object's shape has to not only meet biomorphic requirements but also, and more importantly, sociomorphic requirements.

Yet the process through which culture creates the body is always being renewed. Changes in the aesthetics of the body in public are always temporary. What does culture ask us to show or hide today? Are we supposed to display tension or relaxation? Should our hands be free or constantly engaged in carrying or manipulating something? A new aesthetics of the body has helped public-health campaigns against smoking. Not smoking is less a question of health than the adoption of a new choreography of social encounters. Ways of holding a cigarette – the hand gestures involved in lighting one, the two fingers gripping it – are simply no longer in style.

Designing an object's shape in accordance with sociomorphic concerns is thus something that has to be done over and over again, for while the morphology of the physical body is almost unchanging, its morphology as social skin is not. The only way to control the embodiment of culture is through anticipation. Designers suggest and impose on the body its next form and change by inscribing a simulacrum of the user's body into the object's shape. As some have pointed out, the process of anticipation always runs the risk of resulting in a "stereotype of perception" (Marrone 2002, 26): the sensations that an object is supposed to induce are planned from the beginning, inscribed in its design, and valid for everyone in any circumstance. The same would apply to the user's body, in which the visible form and even movements would be dictated by the aesthetics of the object.

The idea of needs and values being determined by the market and manufacturers is not new. We would never have needed portable telecommunication objects if no one had designed them, and mobile phone aesthetics would never have developed to such extremes if there had been no mobile phone to carry around. However, despite any design determinism, the relationship between the shape of an object and its user's lifestyle is circular.

As mobile phones have become smaller, their aesthetic value has changed; now invisibility is desirable. We will probably have to wait until miniaturization reaches its limits to realize that a too-small mobile phone is impractical. Suddenly a new aesthetic will be proposed and, it may once again become attractive to display the object, and its beauty will again be related to harmony between its design and ease of use. An object's form thus determines the cultural forms of its use and the aesthetics of the user's body, but the opposite is also true: forms of use and the user's body can impose new aesthetics on the object.

What makes this interplay fascinating in the case of some technologies is the new links between the object's form and function and the subject's own body. While all designed objects take biomorphism into account and reflect ergonomics, most provide for an alternation between junction with and separation from the body. Chairs, knives, pens, and computer keyboards are designed to operate in harmony with the body and reduce feelings of strangeness and otherness. However, they do not claim to create permanent links with the user's body. Inversely, because they are designed to be mobile and portable, the latest avatars of distance communication tend to integrate themselves with the owner's body in the strict sense. The total and constant integration of the body and object defines more prosthetics than the "necessary" clothing accessories. The object becomes part of the body in the same way as its biological parts. According to McLuhan's well-known formula, it is on us and with us, in our hands as an expression of ourselves.

The mobile phone is an extension with a unique intrinsic property: it enables us to connect here and elsewhere, the present and the absent, the self and others. It allows us to escape from a here that we share with others and talk with someone who is elsewhere. As an object that users want "stuck on them," it thus poses an aesthetic problem. This new body part must integrate with the user's shape, movements, and actions while complying with the fuzzy, changing nuances of social aesthetics. In short, such objects require us to reformulate the representation of the physical self in public. It is certainly no accident that teenagers, strict judges of social appearance who are very aware of their bodies, are fully engaged in the quest for aesthetics in the mobile phone.

10.6 New Aesthetics or New Self-Perceptions?

The mobile phone is perhaps the only new communication technology that poses the problem of aesthetics in relation to one's physical-self image. This technological object is perceived as a visible part of one's body that nonetheless has its own shape, colours, dimensions, and textures, which can integrate with the body harmoniously, or not. It is precisely the fact that integration may be impossible or partial that allows aesthetic reasoning.

Anne sums this up in her contribution to a conversation on the role of mobile phones in constructing one's self-image in public:

ANNE: So to avoid having a negative image when you've got a mobile, you have to hide it?

NATHALIE: No. But there's like a grey area. You know, if you're wearing a shirt that's a little short and you've got your mobile hooked on, it shows, you know, it's fine. But if you overdo it ... it's like anything.
ANNE: It can show, but you shouldn't display it, is that it?
[...]
NATHALIE: You just shouldn't overdo it, that's all, there's always a limit, it's like anything. You know ... like some wear their pants a little low because it looks cool, you know, having loose pants. But on some people it's really like a garbage bag dragging on the ground, you're like bleah, it's not good either, you know. It's like if you overdo it, it's not good.

A discussion about moderation and one's degree of freedom with respect to politeness turns into a reflection on individual aesthetics. Nathalie uses the classical aesthetics paradigm and advocates a balance of shapes. This balance would guarantee a quasi-natural integration of the technological prosthesis with a clothed body. The issue is thus not framed in terms of "hiding the prosthesis," for that would be only the symmetrical opposite of displaying it. Instead, both are governed by the logic of excess and over-statement. The analogy with wearing pants only highlights the aesthetical paradigm in question: beauty excludes excess because beauty *is* moderation. Like a pair of pants, a mobile phone is a visible part of the body in public. For the body to satisfy aesthetic criteria, it has to be free of all excess and inappropriate shapes. And since the mobile phone is conceived as a visible prosthesis of the body, its shape and colours also become subjects of aesthetic reflection.

Catherine asks whether design has an effect on choosing a mobile: could it influence someone's decision to buy one? Jean-Pierre says, "Yes, yes, the design. For example, a rounded mobile, and someone who likes round shapes is not going to buy a completely cubic mobile, a little square one – 'Oh, I've got a little plastic cube in my pocket.'" As Guillaume says, the mobile "has to match the rest of your clothes."

Harmonious integration with the body seems as necessary as it is diffi-cult to achieve.[7] A mobile phone should be a "natural" component of the physical person, but in fact it is not, at least not for those who are not yet accustomed to the prosthesis.

The mobile phone poses a problem of *in-corporation* in the strict sense of the term. If we take this word in its metaphorical sense, this is nothing new: all technologies require a process of domestication into users' practices and systems of meaning. In the mobile phone's case, incorporation is not only metaphorical. On the contrary, this communication technology requires a return to the problem of incorporation in the literal sense because it is the body in its whole physical dimension that is the primary context of its reception. Its size, shape, and design require physical domestication. Integration in accordance with aesthetics of balance and moderation can succeed only if it is based on a new perception of self, for it is the mental image of one's own body that first must integrate the prosthesis as one of its parts. The mobile phone thus requires a new cognitive image of the physical self that integrates a biological body with a technological object.

The process is not evident, for, beyond biomorphic design and ergonomics, the feeling of strangeness can be eliminated only through the most ancient of practices linking humans and objects: use. This is probably what explains why those who do not have mobile phones or are new users see them as non-integrated and even apparently non-integratable prostheses. However, those who are used to them adopt the opposite point of view. For example, in Italy and Northern Europe, adolescents' discourse indicates that the mobile is seen as an integral part of the body, an object that adapts to its shape perfectly and follows its movements naturally (Cosenza 2002). Indeed, one need only observe how children with mobile phones act and move to confirm the extent to which mobile phones are parts of their bodies. According to the classical pattern of evolution, culture has inscribed new patterns on the bodies of these young people. At least in these countries, the technology has reformulated the paradigm of people's actions and movements in the space of half a generation.

The question is not whether and where the object is integrated or not, since the answer would be only empirical and necessarily dependent on individuals and contexts. In fact, the question must shift; we must go beyond the difference between achieved and envisioned integration. What makes the phenomenon interesting is the fact that the mobile phone creates and even imposes a problem of physical integration, and generates questions about the aesthetic aspects of a person. As a visible part of one's own body, it inspires reflection that goes far beyond the quest for formal beauty to reach that of a new perception of the self. Thus, this new communication technology requires less creative effort from industrial designers than it does from users, who have to perform a cognitive change. They have to reformulate their images of their bodies and integrate the new "organ."

10.7 Between Globalization and Localization: A Few Conclusive Notes

Comparison of uses of mobile communication technology with the discourses about such uses reveals that the objects fit perfectly into one of the categories formulated to grasp and systematize the complexity of object-oriented postmodernity: that of globalized objects (Semprini 2002).

This category encompasses contemporary objects that have four distinctive features:

1. Mobility: they are designed to travel with people wherever they go.
2. Proximity to the user's body: they have to meet *aísthésic* criteria, because they purportedly provoke sensations.
3. Usefulness and fun: they perform certain functions but can also be perceived as fun everyday toys.
4. Regressive aesthetics: their shape, colour, and texture are meant to evoke an original blend (ibid.).

As Semprini points out, considered as a whole, globalized objects create an image of a possible world characterized by relatively basic features. It is an easy, reassuring world where leisure and pleasure seem to cover every task, even the most tedious. No pressure, no stress, no feeling of commitment – all fear of guilt and concern for responsibility towards others is erased or even rejected by the world vision inscribed in such objects. Consistently and consequently, the actors who are supposed to live in that everyday world are represented as free of constraints, masters of time and space, proud of their health and beauty, ready to undo social ties that never bind them anyway, and able to situate themselves outside of any cultural conformity (Semprini 2002, 55–6). Obviously these images are nothing but meanings inscribed in objects, representations of a possible world and of social actors whose primary features would be lightness and disengagement. Trans-contextual and thus a-contextual, these meanings are only potential. It is in and through the process of contextualization, through users' adoption and actions, that those virtual meanings possibly become actual. Sometimes users' tactics and practices reverse them and change the sense inscribed in globalized objects. When actors adopt the objects for their situated practices, when they localize, domesticate, and assimilate them in living contexts, they can suddenly reverse prior meaning. This is indeed the process we observed in our research on adolescents and their mobile phone use.

As we have seen, young people have established a veritable permanent laboratory of social inquiry about mobile phones and their uses. Far from referring to a world free of concern for others, far from projecting the users into a world where space and time are under individual control, far from placing people in a world free of social and cultural constraints, mobile phones become a means of creating and enlightening the social ties of the self.

Mobile phones have done much more than change people's communications habits, lifestyle, intergenerational relations, and peer community rituals. They have amplified the perception of the Other as a subject analogous to the self, a source of possibilities but also limitations, a primary pillar of the radically intersubjective architecture of social life.

As a globalized object, the mobile phone's design and engineering embody a plan in which the user is free and social links are simply optional. Yet in the concrete context of use and associated discourse, this meaning gives way to its opposite: at least among young people, mobile phones open up a world where the Other becomes a presence affecting the self and its narrative program.

Whether trying to avoid bothering an involuntary audience, respecting the person with whom one is speaking when a ghost participant interrupts, or designing new forms of etiquette, young people seem to see the use of this communication technology in terms of compliance with intersubjective ethics.

The cultural model developed by users can abruptly reverse the typical meanings of globalized objects. Far from referring to a simulacrum of a nomadic individual free of all constraints, mobile communication technologies evoke a context that is constantly defined by the presence of the Other.

As a social performance, mobile phone use requires constraints, rules, and shared practices. As we have seen, mobile communication devices create the need for rules of politeness and produce new awarenesses of how others see us. They are used to control commitment of members to a group; they allow for moment-by-moment storytelling by lovers; they create communities sharing ways of interacting; they mark the cultural distance between parents and children. In any of these cases, emerging mobile communication technologies amplify the meaning of relationships, the subject's intersubjective dimension, and his or her deep roots in a social and cultural context.

From this point of view, and according to our informants' practices, the hybrid techno-human intended by industrial designers is anything but an actor free of constraints or responsibilities towards others. On the contrary, the technology seems to have produced a new awareness of others as analogous to the self and a new awareness that it is only by crossing their respective perspectives that the relationship to the technology can become a way of life.

Notes

Chapter 1

1 In the following chapters we give examples of the process of assigning new meaning to everyday times and places.
2 We discuss new technologies and intergenerational relationships in chapter 9.
3 In chapter 10 we explore the social consequences of this break in face-to-face interaction.
4 In chapter 8 we look at examples of the "secret language" that young people use to communicate by mobile phone.
5 We will develop this concept in greater detail when we discuss inter-generational differences in terms of how family borders have changed (chapter 9).
6 See chapter 10 concerning new ethics and etiquette.
7 The weight of advertising discourse in the circulation and construction of social ideas about NICTs is the topic of Chapter 4.
8 The following quotes were gathered in a project called "Zero NICT" with graduate students, which required that they abstain from using any new information and communications technologies for a full week. A similar experiment called "Zero Information" was done with under-graduate students and required a complete "information blackout" of mass media.
9 Quoted from the "Zero NICT" project.

Chapter 2

1 From a radically ethnomethodological-constructionist perspective, the cultural models that organize everyday life in intersubjectively shared ways are seen as constructed moment-by-moment by the ways people

participate in social events (Garfinkel 1967). Adopting a bottom-up analytical perspective, the constructionist approach conceives the structures and the meanings of social action as products of the creative process of culture-making through everyday actions and discourses. Of course, this radically bottom-up view may be counterbalanced by the cognitive perspective on *cultural models* (D'Andrade 1984, D'Andrade and Strauss 1992). From a more top-down perspective, the cognitive approach sees the cultural models as prototypical, language-based scripts of events that work as frames of reference for inference-making and as guides for appropriate, understandable and accountable actions. From a phenomenological perspective, both processes need to be taken into account. People are seen as creative social actors engaged in constructing the meaning, sense, and social organization of their world. This process is conceived as radically embedded in and possible because of the cultural frames and material resources available in the world where people live (Gergen and Semin 1990).

2 The next chapter specifically describes this process.

3 Assoum is one of the informants actively involved in our ethnographic study of the multiple roles of the mobile telephone in adolescent life. See chapters 5, 6, and 7.

4 "By conditional relevance of one item on another we mean: given the first, the second is expectable" (Schegloff 1968, 1083).

5 This phenomenon is described in greater detail in chapter 3.

6 The notion of reflexivity is strictly related to Giddens's introduced the concept of "duality of structure" (Giddens 1979, 1984) that takes into account the process of mutual construction between practice and social structure.

7 Bourdieu's notion of *habitus* refers to a similar process. The cultural capital each individual inherits defines the boundaries of his or her ways of thinking and acting.

8 The process of domestication of technologies by adolescents that imposes specific traits of their culture will be discussed in chapter 7.

Chapter 3

1 See chapter 2.

2 See chapter 1.

3 The preceding chapter sketches out some of the consequences of this migration, for example, changes in the signified of the objects themselves depending on whether they are closer or further away.

4 See chapter 2.

5 Chapter 9 on intergenerational relations explores in greater detail the

idea of transformation of the private and public spheres in the family home.

6 This was the "Zero NTIC" project referred to in chapter 1.

Chapter Four

1 The original French version on which this chapter is based was written with the collaboration of Flavie Langlois Caron. We would like to express our gratitude to Bell, Rogers AT&T, Fido, Telus, and Vodafone for allowing us to reprint their ads.

2 Here we are obviously referring to Barthes's notion of "myth" (1957).

3 Examples include a television ad by Rogers AT&T and one by LG, both broadcast in fall 2003. Our *corpus* of Canadian advertising includes ads broadcast to French-speaking and English-speaking Canadian audiences. Some of these are excellent examples of regionalized messages and even localization of a product that circulates globally. By using certain cultural and linguistic clichés, they target Quebeckers, who see themselves differentiated from Canadians, and vice versa, as communities with special cultural features.

4 Nokia ads 1995 to present.

5 Solo Bell Mobility 2004.

6 We discuss this feature specific to young people's culture and its relationship to their mobile phone uses in Chapter 7.

7 In chapter 5 we will see that parody is a form of discourse characteristic of adolescents.

8 It seems the reception of this Canadian advertising campaign, broadcast from 2003 to 2005, had a very positive effect on the company's sales. The images are taken from the following sites: http://www.radio-canada.ca/nouvelles/Index/nouvelles/200310/01/002-BELL-UPA.shtml, and http://lcn.canoe.com/lcn/economie/nouvelles/archives/2003/10/20031001-125332.html

9 We study the fascinating world of SMS in chapter 8.

10 LG–Solo, Bell television ad, fall 2003.

11 Site www.Rogers.com.

12 For example, in 2002, 76 per cent of Italians aged fourteen to seventeen owned a mobile phone, compared with only 35 per cent of Canadians aged twelve to seventeen (BBM 2002).

13 Fido television ad, December 2002.

14 Telus print ad, fall 2003.

15 Telus print ad, fall 2003.

16 Vodafone Omnitel television ad, fall 2002.

17 Bell print ad, fall 2002.
18 Rogers AT&T print ad, fall 2003.
19 Rogers AT&T print ad, summer 2002.
20 Fido television ad, fall 2003.
21 Telus print ad, fall 2003.
22 Fido television and print ads, fall 2003.
23 Loblaw television ad, summer 2003.
24 Winners television ad, fall 2003.
25 Yoplait television ad, fall 2003.
26 Heineken television ad, fall 2003.

Chapter 5

1 Doxa Report, *Junior 2005*.
2 According to Mauss's theory of the gift (Mauss 1950), this term refers to a specific dynamic of social exchange and its structuring function. In contrast, the word "present" refers to the material object chosen to perform this function. The present can vary (depending on the group, historical period, market, etc.) but its function (gift) remains constant. On the gift's dynamic as a transaction in contemporary society, see Bloch and Buisson 1991, Godbout and Caillé 1991, Dosse 1995, Godbout 2000.
3 For an analysis of the mobile phone as an object that satisfies the conditions of "gift exchange" among peers and family members, see chapters 7 and 9.
4 Everything being equal (in terms of economic level, cultural circle, and place of residence), it seems that belonging to a specific age group plays a major role in choice and use of manners of speaking (Eckert 1988). This does not mean that different groups of adolescents use the same slang or adopt the same ways of speaking. The language of young people varies from one group to the next. However, it maintains a relative internal consistency and certain differences in relation to other social groups, such as adults.
5 For an analysis of adolescents' gossip through SMS, see chapter 8.
6 See among others, Taylor and Harper 2003; Ling and Yttry 2002; Kaseniemi and Rautiainen 2002; Green 2002; Riviére 2002; Caronia and Caron 2004.
7 The distinction between "etic" and "emic" was created by the linguistic anthropologist Kenneth Pike in analogy with linguistic distinction between phonetic and phonemic analysis.
8 Even in this case, prudence is required. For example, there is a line of sociological thought that, reasonably, suggests drawing the line between

adolescence and adulthood at the time when the child leaves the family home. In some cases, this would mean that adolescence lasts until age thirty.

9 Our privileged informants were asked to fill a logbook to record information related to their mobile phone uses. Their notes on who called whom, when, why, where, and with whom, and our interpretation of field materials, were then jointly interpreted to attain a better understanding of the context of the recorded conversations. This long explanation comes from one of the first sessions of work with Assoum.

10 Building upon Bachtin theory, the dialogic turn in social sciences sees ethnographic practices as dialogues and the ethnographic text as a polyphonic construction in which different voices should appear. See Clifford and Marcus 1986, Clifford 1988 and Van Maanen 1988.

11 Antoine and Sophie were young francophone Canadians. Nevertheless they typically used some English expressions or anglicisms as is common for adolescents of this linguistic community. To respect the richness and the living quality of our data, we chose to report the conversations in the original language. For an analysis of the code switching and the different languages spoken by these adolescents living in a North American metropolis, see chapter 6. For a guide to transcription conventions used here and elsewhere in the text, see p. xi.

12 In English in the original.

13 This statement was written in the logbook in which young people were supposed to briefly note why they used their mobile phone each time they used it.

14 See chapter 7 for an analysis of the many links between technologies and the culture specific to young people.

15 The analysis of the syntactic rules governing the social organization of conversation has been at the core of the first empirical studies of conversation analysis (CA): Schegloff 1968, Sacks, Schegloff, and Jefferson 1974, Schegloff, Jefferson, and Sacks 1977. For a critical examination of CA, see Goodwin and Heritage 1990.

16 See, among others, Schegloff 1979, 2002; Hopper and Chen 1996; Hopper and Koleilat-Doany 1989; Hopper 1991, Houtkoop-Steenstra 1991, Zimmermann 1984, 1992.

17 Empirical studies on social uses of mobile phones mainly rely upon users' accounts of their communicative practices (gathered through focus groups or individual interviews) and participant observation. While great analytical attention has been paid to text messages and other forms of written technology-mediated communication (Grinter and Eldridge 2001, Grinter and Palen 2002, Riviére 2002, Violi 1998, Violi and Coppock 1999), there seems to be a lack of ethnographically

grounded conversation analysis of oral exchanges through mobile phone.

Chapter 6

1 Our fieldwork concerned naturally formed groups of urban teenagers of different ethnic and linguistic backgrounds living in a North American metropolis. While some spoke mostly French, most spoke English, and many were bilingual. According to the standards of sociolinguistics and ethnography of communication, in this chapter we transcribe teenagers' mobile conversations in the original language or languages spoken by participants: English and French. Since the chapter is dedicated to the social and cultural meanings of people's ways of speaking, forms of talk, blending of languages and code switching, this convention is unavoidable. However, we add a translation in standard English to make available the conversations or turns of conversation that were not in English.

2 As linguistic anthropologists have pointed out, transcription is a complex activity of representing events according to the theoretical approach of the analyst and his or her aims. Transcripts are always a compromise among the richness of naturally occurring conversation, the aim and the theoretical approach of the analyst, and the readability of the transcript itself (Ochs 1979, Duranti 1997). To maximize the readability of our transcripts, we adopt a very light version of the conventions for the transcription of naturally occurring conversation. For conventions used in text, see p. xi.

3 "I've got super good tickets," "three kilos of deodorant, three kilos of gel," "we're going to rent it, man, it's great!" are other examples of teenagers' hyperbolic language we found throughout our corpus.

4 Instead of using predefined linguistic categories to analyse our corpus, we adopted a more grounded approach. Taking advantage of the linguistic, cultural, and age differences of the researchers, we analysed the conversations according to each researcher's categorization of the discourse as typical French or English Canadian, typical teenagers' speech, or expert jargon. The hypothesis was that specificity and typicality of everyday forms of talk are not inherent characteristics of language but rather are judgments that largely depend on the speaker and listener. At least to a certain extent they are "evident" for people who do not share them. The stranger or more unfamiliar a variation, linguistic register, or lexical domain sounded, the more likely it would be to be identified as specific to a category of speakers. Conversely, the less an item was identified as specific by a researcher, the more likely it was to correspond to

his or her typical speech pattern. Differences in ascribing items to specific categories were then cross-analysed to gain a grounded understanding of the conversation's linguistic heterogeneity.

5 Code switching is a recurrent phenomenon in the conversations among these urban North American adolescents, who shift between French and English on a regular basis. For a cultural analysis of this phenomenon, see section 4 below.

6 Information about the context of the conversation (where, when, in front of whom, with whom, etc.) came from the logbook.

7 Contemporary ethnography no longer tries to resolve the paradox of the observer: that of claiming to observe how people live when they are not being observed. It also does not consider the presence of the researcher and recording instruments as biases that must be controlled because they would alter the claimed authenticity of behaviour considered natural. Given the context-dependent and interactive roots of every form of social behaviour, it is impossible to conceive of behaviour that is "authentic" or unbiased by context and interaction. Similarly, it is impossible to imagine completely artificial behaviour – in other words, behaviour created entirely by the context and unrevealing of the actors themselves. Contemporary ethnography assumes that individuals' reactions to the presence of researchers and recording instruments are social interactions in themselves. Situated and culturally specific, such behaviour is thus integrated in researchers' data and is treated as a valuable source of information.

8 At least since the 1970s, the varieties and heterogeneity of the languages used in multiethnic societies have been studied both from a linguistic and sociological point of view. See Hymes 1971, Gumperz 1982.

9 According to Goodwin (1990), an operating culture is the set of knowledge, practices, and language needed to participate in an activity and to mutually coordinate with other participants. It is an underlying body of references shared by the members of a community of practice that allows them to interact appropriately in locally situated actions. Describing the culture of a group as a monolithic entity is thus a misleading practice, because individuals have access to different operating cultures (ibid., 9).

Chapter 7

1 Drawing on Gilbert Ryle's notion, Geertz (1973) defines "thick description" as a text that represents both "actions-in-context" and the meanings these actions in context have for the social actors involved. Interweaving the ethnographer's "experience distance concepts" with

the informant's "experience near concepts," a thick description tries to convey the multiple possible interpretations of social reality.

2 While we have already proposed an analysis of the role of mobile phones in creating the meaning of social contexts and events (chapters 2 and 3), the following pages take us to the heart and into the details of adolescents' daily life. Their practices and words illuminate their everyday spaces and reveal their interpretations of those spaces.

3 For a discussion of the role of mobile phones in trans-generational relations, see chapter 9.

4 See chapter 2.

5 Adolescents explain some uses and their preferences for some technologies by framing them as "cool." "Coolness" can be considered a specific feature of young people's culture (Danesi 1994).

6 Chapter 5 describes the use of hyperbole as a feature of adolescents' language.

7 As we will see in chapter 8, in many European countries the opposite situation prevails.

8 The sign "::" is a convention to indicate a stretched-out pronunciation of words that expresses how fatiguing it is to perform the actions the words refer to. The ways some words are pronounced and the use of some abbreviations can be seen as a sign of "linguistic laziness" that is perfectly consistent with the cultural laziness we are describing.

9 The category "laziness" does not exclude "coolness"; both belong to the repertoire of cultural reasons that adolescents use to account for their technological mediated activities. See chapter 5.

10 For a discussion of the circularity of the relationship between the "competences" of a technological object and those of the social actor, see chapter 2.

11 See chapter 4 for an overview of advertising discourse.

12 In ethnographic research, data collection methods and informants' subjective reaction to them are considered "data" per se. They are crucial interpretative resources for investigation and analysis.

13 For a discussion of the manipulative tendencies of technology, see chapter 2.

14 This is an approach to use that is specific to this generation's culture. As we saw in chapter 3, the reasons adults adopt mobile phones have different foundations. In general, intergenerational differences are based on different ways of viewing communication and related tools. See chapters 3 and 9.

15 We will not describe this aspect in greater detail because we have already talked about adolescents' preference for leaving the phone on and the social meanings associated with uses that contradict this

"restrictive rule." In fact this is a typical example of the "urgency of communication" explored in chapters 1 and 3.

16 The notion of "prototype" comes from cognitive psychology and accounts for what the actor sees as an "exemplary case" of a category of events or actions. It is often a more or less detailed scenario or image that refers to a cultural model, not to a statistical average.

17 The ethnographic hypothesis about this prototypical model of mobile phone use comes from and is grounded in our previous research (Caronia and Caron 2004).

18 Chapter 10 explores the consequences of this prototypical model of use, with an explanation of the social construction of new ethics and etiquette and the ways NICTs have led to the creation of a social reasoning.

19 Despite the standards of ethnographic studies on language and since this chapter is dedicated mostly to topics and contexts of teenagers' mobile calls, we choose here to translate those conversations (or parts of them) that were not in English. We hope that the well-known limits of translating naturally occurring conversations may be counterbalanced by an easier reading of the transcripts.

20 See chapter 6.

21 The linguistic markers of the ethnic and linguistic background of the two speakers are more evident in the original French conversation. However, the phenomenon applies to all the adolescents we encountered, whether they speak English or French. Ways of speech always mark social identity, ethnic and cultural background, and national belonging (Gumperz 1982).

22 For an analysis of storytelling in everyday life and the notion of "living narratives," see Ochs and Caps 2001.

23 In the following pages we closely examine this adolescent-specific way of using mobile phones.

24 On the narration of stories as a means of constructing everyday life, see Ochs and Capps 2001.

25 Like "vegging" and "doing nothing," "hanging out" is one of the cultural categories that adolescents use to organize and interpret their daily lives. It involves loitering or lingering and accounts for teenagers' typical way of spending time in public spaces such as shopping centres and around school.

26 For an analysis of the gift-giving exchange between parents and children, see chapter 9.

27 This image clearly refers to Foucault's central metaphor of prison as a panoptikon that draw on Bentham's principle that power must be visible and unverifiable (Foucault 1981).

28 The role of mobile phones in the parent-child dynamic is be discussed in chapter 9.

29 See chapter 4 for analyses of the social discourses that accompanied the introduction of the mobile phone into social milieus.

Chapter 8

1 At least in Italy, voice-calling on mobiles is mostly reserved for parents. However, even in such cases adolescents quickly invented a system of communication to avoid spending money. Before companies introduced inexpensive or even free-of-charge plans for one-to-one calls, adolescents would make their parents' phones ring according to a code that meant "call me."

2 The volume of exchanges through SMS is perhaps one of the most striking differences between mobile phone use by adolescents in Europe and North America. European teenagers were the earliest and most prolific users of SMS (Grinter and Eldridge 2001).

3 Similar to natural groups' social structure, the group comprised core members whose links were strong and who were in touch on regular basis, along with more peripheral members. It is indeed through the use of SMS that the social structure of this peer group was constructed: who called whom and whom they spoke about were also ways to define moment-by-moment membership and reciprocal links.

4 In our fieldwork we adopted and combined the main methods of ethnographic research. We crossed data coming from researchers' naturalistic observations and field notes, logbooks, recorded linguistic material, and informal interviews with our informants about their practices and recorded texts messages.

5 Matilde is the pseudonym of a girl who had just turned fourteen and, like most of her friends, had received a mobile phone for her eleventh birthday (the average age young Italians receive their first "*telefonino*"). In Italy in 2000, mobile phone ownership among adolescents aged fourteen to seventeen was 76 per cent.

6 Ethnographic research on adolescents has specific constraints (Fine and Sandstrom 1988). For example, the researcher has to find a balance between investigating the peer culture and respecting the secrecy towards adults that is one of this peer culture's most salient features. In our case we had to establish a form of contract that officially assumed the possibility of secrecy. Matilde was therefore asked to transcribe at her discretion as many SMS exhanges as possible. However, she was also asked to tell us the total number of messages. This enabled us to establish a trusting relationship based on respect for a specific cultural

feature (secrecy) and also to gain an overview of the role of sms in maintaining that cultural feature. In effect, we had access to one out of five of her messages (sixty-five transcribed out of 340 sent and received).

7 While this form of interaction may seem to be secondary to the data gathered, in ethnographic research the data collection process is a datum in itself that requires rigorous analysis, on a par with the information gathered. This is all the more true since it is often through such actions in the field that "natives" show researchers the frameworks through which they organize, represent, and interpret their own practices.

8 The secret nature of this form of communication has been noted by other researchers using other methodological tools, such as interviews (Grinter and Eldridge 2001, Rivière 2002) and analysis of corpora of messages removed from their speech context (Cosenza 2002). The ethnographic approach makes it possible to go beyond the declarative level specific to interviews and to the linguistic analysis of the forms and functions of decontextualized communication. Analysis of practices *in vivo* illustrates the frames of reference underlying actions used by the subjects in their everyday lives. According to grounded theory (Glaser and Strauss 1967), categories of action are *in* action, which is where the researcher must seek them.

9 This recurrence of rules governing texting makes it possible for friends with minimal competency in one another's mother tongues to exchange messages. The fact that these operations are shared across languages can be explained by a basic principle of this form of communication: reduce the number of written characters to maintain the rhythm of oral interaction.

10 Here we have an excellent example of the ambiguous nature of technologies. Because of its shape, size, portability, and communicational functions, the mobile phone lends itself to two different forms of use: secret use and (as we saw in previous chapters) displayed use. While advertising discourse seems to target mainly the latter (see chapter 4), adolescents have grasped this functional polymorphism and employ both forms of use strategically.

11 According to the standards of ethnographic approaches to language study, we transcribe the original texts in the original language, adding a translation to make their content accessible. Obviously there is some risk of loss of features specific to these groups of adolescents. English-language smses are, of course, not the same as those in Italian. An English sms version of the exchange would be: MATILDE: *z matty hru? yestrda u msd suzannes performance she fel & thn she strtd tlkn w fede. wot cn I sa. tc. P.S. jst saw her on th bus!* 911!!/ ARIANNA: *if u c*

her ur out, im stil in cls doin history. tc tlk2ul8tr. For examples of English-language SMSes, see http://www.transl8it.com/cgi-win/index.pl.

12 FRANCESCA: ciao wrudg? wer n eng. Zzz/ MARCO: thr skng qz to simo &maura. Maura dont lt him tlk. I h8 her. shz such a brain!!/ FRANCESCA: por hm! bt id b :-) if she ddnt lt me tlk. gtg cul sry spndn 2% mch.

13 Like the language of North American adolescents, that of Italian adolescents is full of swear words that have lost any etymological meaning and have acquired, through use, pragmatic meanings related to identity and membership.

14 In a conversation each intervention is considered a turn of talk, even if it is an acknowledgment of reception or silence.

15 Schegloff and Sacks 1973.

16 Many authors have pointed out the hybrid nature (between speech and writing) of computer-mediated communication. See Baron 1999, 2000, Violi 1998, Violi and Coppock 1999, Garcea and Bazzanella 2002. For an analysis of this aspect in mini-message exchanges, see Rivière 2002.

17 On characteristics of adolescents' speech, see chapter 5, part 2: "Linguistic Creativity and Cultural Innovation."

18 The only technological limitations that make a significant difference are the life of the battery and how much credit remains on the prepaid card. These factors do not affect the length of the message but rather the duration of the *"messaggiarsi."* One in ten of the interactions Matilde transcribed for us ended with an explicit reference to one of these two reasons.

19 As in most conversations, participants share background knowledge that ensures their mutual understanding: Bruno's mother's job was to cast attractive young male actors in commercials.

Chapter 9

1 The original French version on which this chapter is based was written with the collaboration of Mathieu St-Onge.

2 Galland 1999.

3 See chapter 1.

4 Jouët and Pasquier 1999.

5 Hersent 2003.

6 Galland 1999, our translation. (The French original is "C'est là une distinction d'adultes qui associent les ruptures technologiques à de nouveaux apprentissages techniques et à de nouveaux usages sociaux.")

7 See chapter 8 for a discussion of young people and the "ON" culture.

8 See chapter 3.

9 Guillaume 1994, our translation. (The French original is "Cellule

communicante, un être hybride qui appartient à deux espaces en même temps, celui de l'environnement immédiate et celui de l'espace virtuel de tous les réseaux potentiels.")

10 See the next chapter, in which we will discuss ethics and mobile phones.

11 Godbout 2000.

12 Beyond any dual and therefore "trade" theory of the gift suggested by Mauss (1950), a number of authors have highlighted the fact that the essence of the "gift" as defined by Mauss is the giving-receiving-reciprocity triad. Receiving and especially "knowing how to receive" marks the area of negotiation between the giver and the receiver. The "reciprocity" obligation is thus not inscribed in the gift as such but in the "giving-accepting" interaction. By accepting the gift, the receiver can choose to engage in "counter-giving." The interval between giving and counter-giving is, according to Bourdieu, proof of the gratuitous nature of the gift. Indeed, Mauss's theory of the gift lends itself to both an interpretation that focuses mainly on the compelling dimension according to which there is no free gift (Dosse 1995) and an interpretation that highlights the gift's degree of gratuitousness in relation to trade (Godbout 2000).

13 Godbout 2000.

14 "Status" should be understood to refer to a social position and rank in the family that can change over time. "Role" means a model of conduct that prescribes a set of forms of behaviour in relation to a status, in other words, the practical translation of the rights and duties related to the status. This is the dynamic aspect of status.

15 Martin, 2003.

16 Ibid.

17 Rakow and Navaro 1993.

18 Martin, 2003.

19 Heurtin 1998.

20 Martin, 2003.

21 De Singly 2000.

22 Ibid.

Chapter 10

1 Renard (1999) identifies two other types of changes involved in the creation of "legends:" in addition to resulting from a reconstructed event, a legend can originate in an exaggerated or displaced event. Whereas it may also arise from the conjunction of a number of simultaneous transformations (that is, an event could be exaggerated, displaced, and reconstructed all at once), we are assuming that the urban legends

about mobile phones are mainly reconstructions of events that connote myths that are already present in people's social and collective imagination. Of course, such reconstructed events could also be displaced or exaggerated.

2 Obviously such stories also, and even often, provide reasons not to adopt (and to not use) technologies and create arguments for non-use. They are nonetheless ordinary ways to create the meaning of technologies.

3 According to Goffman's analysis of social encounters, the presence of bystanders and overhearers "should be considered the rule, not the exception" (1981, 132.)

4 As we have seen in previous chapters, this is even truer among adolescents who use their mobile phones to create personal oasis and as a strategy for constructing a private space in the public area of the family. See chapters 7 and 8.

5 As we suggested in chapter 2, the mobile phone's entry in the public arena has created a new character in social encounters: the ghost participant.

6 Advertisers are notable users of the body as a medium for discourse on identity. See examples of this in chapter 4.

7 Fortunati (2002) also notes this challenge raised by mobile phones: integration with the body or clothing is not always harmonious, which leads the author to question the very idea of portability.

Bibliography

Andersen, G. 2001. *Pragmatic Markers and Linguistic Variation: A Rele-vance-Theoretic Approach to the Language of Adolescents*. Amsterdam/Philadelphia: John Benjamins Publishing.

Appadurai, A., ed. 1986. *The Social Life of Things*. Cambridge: Cambridge University Press.

Attali, J. 1994. *Le Revenu Français*. http://www.attali.com (accessed 11 July 2006).

Augé, M. 1992. *Non-lieux: Introduction à une anthropologie de la surmodernité*. Paris: Éditions du Seuil.

Baron, N. 1999. "History Lessons: Telegraph, Telephone, and E-mail as Social Discourse." In *Dialogue Analysis and the Mass Media*, edited by B. Naumann, 1–34. Proceedings of the International Conference Erlangen, April 2–3. Tubingen: Niemeyer.

– 2000. *Alphabet to E-mail: How Written English Evolved and Where It's Heading*. London: Routledge.

Barthes, R. 1957. *Mythologies*. Paris: Éditions du Seuil.

Baudry, P. 1999. "La fragmentation identitaire." In *Vers une citoyenneté simulée: Médias, réseaux et mondialisation*, edited by S. Proulx and A. Vitalis, 163–81. Paris: Éditions Apogée, collection Médias et Nouvelles Technologies.

Bazzanella, C. 1993. "Dialogic Repetition." in *Dialoganalyse 4*, edited by H. Loffler, 285–94. Tubingen: Max Niemayer.

Benjamin, W. 2000. "L'œuvre d'art à l'époque de sa reproductibilité technique." In *Walter Benjamin Œuvres 3*, edited by W. Benjamin, 67–113. Paris: Gallimard.

Bercelli, F., and G. Pallotti. 2002. "Conversazioni telefoniche." In *Sul dialogo*, edited by C. Bazzanella, 177–92. Milano: Guerini.

Bloch, F., and M. Buisson. 1991. "Du don à la dette: La construction du lien social familial." *Revue du MAUSS* 11: 54–71.

Boden D., and H.L. Molotch. 1994. "The Compulsion of Proximity." In *Now/Here: Space, Time and Modernity*, edited by R. Friedland and D. Boden, 257–86. Berkeley: University of California Press.

Boltanski, L., and E. Chiapello. 1999. *Le nouvel esprit du capitalisme*. Paris: Gallimard.

Bonneville, L. 2001. "Temporalité et Internet: Réflexion sur la psychologie du temps à la lumière des pratiques domiciliaires." *COMMposite V2001.1*. http://commposite.uqam.ca/2001.1/articles/bonnev2.html (accessed 11 July 2006).

Bruner, J. 1986. *Actual Minds, Possible Worlds*. Cambridge, Mass.: Harvard University Press.

– 1990. *Acts of Meaning*. Cambridge, Mass.: Cambridge University Press

Cairncross, F. 1997. *The Internet in the Death of Distance: How the Communications Revolution Will Change Our Lives*. Boston: Harvard Business School Press.

Caron, A.H., and C. Berre. 1995. "Diffusion de la technologie visuelle 'Videoway' à l'aube de l'autoroute électronique." In *Repenser la télévision*, edited by F. Guglielmelli, 321–40. Paris: Association Télévision et Culture.

Caron, A.H., L. Giroux, and S. Douzou. 1985. "Diffusion et adoption des nouvelles technologies: Le micro-ordinateur domestique." *Canadien Journal of Communication* 11, no. 4: 369–89.

Caron, A.H., and L. Caronia. 2000. "Parler de télévision, parler de soi: Une étude sur la mise en discours des pratiques médiatiques au foyer." *Communication* 20, no. 1: 123–54.

– 2001. "Active Users and Active Objects: The Mutual Construction of Families and Communication Technologies." *Convergence: The Journal of Research into New Media Technologies* 7, no. 3: 39–61.

Caronia, L. 2002. *La socializzazione ai media. Contesti, interazioni e pratiche educative*. Milano: Guerini.

– 2005. "Mobile Culture: An Ethnography of Cellular Phone Use in Teenagers' Everyday Life." *Convergence: The Journal of Research into New Media Technologies* 11, no. 5: 96–103.

Caronia, L., and A.H. Caron. 2004. "Constructing a Specific Culture: Young People's Use of the Mobile Phone as a Social Performance." *Convergence: The Journal of Research into New Media Technologies* 10, no. 2: 28–61.

Castelain-Meunier, C. 1997. "The Paternal Cord: Telephone Relationship between 'Non Custodian' Fathers and Their Children." *Reseaux* 5: 161–76.

Cheshire, J. 1987. "Age and Generation-Specific Use of Language." In *Sociolinguistics: An Introductory Handbook of the Science of Language and Society*, edited by U. Ammon, N. Dittmar, and K. Mattheier, 160–67. Berlin: Mouton de Gruyter.

Cicourel, A. 1992. "The Interpenetration of Communicative Contexts: Examples of Medical Encounters." In *Rethinking Context: Language as an Interactive Phenomenon*, edited by A. Duranti and C. Goodwin, 291–310. Cambridge Mass.: Cambridge University Press.

Clifford, J. 1988. *The Predicament of Culture*. Cambridge, Mass.: Cambridge University Press.

Clifford, J., and G.E. Marcus, eds. 1988. *Writing Culture: The Poetics and Politics of Ethnography*. Berkeley, Los Angeles: University of California Press.

Cosenza, G. 2002. "I Messaggi SMS." In *Sul dialogo: Contesti e forme dell'interazione verbale*, edited by C. Bazzanella, 193–207. Milano: Guerini.

D'Andrade, R. 1984. "Cultural Meaning Systems." In *Culture Theory: Essays on Mind, Self, and Emotion*, edited by R.A. Shweder and R. LeVine, 88–119. Cambridge: Cambridge University Press.

D'Andrade, R., and C. Strauss, eds. 1992. *Human Motives and Cultural Models*. Cambridge: Cambridge University Press.

Danesi, M. 1994. *Cool: The Signs and Meanings of Adolescence*. Toronto, Buffalo, London: University of Toronto Press.

Davis, F. 1992. *Fashion, Culture and Identity*. Chicago: Chicago University Press.

De Certeau, M. 1980. *L'invention du quotidien: Arts de faire*. Paris: UGE.

– 1984. *The Practice of Everyday Life*. Berkeley: University of California Press.

Dosse, F. 1995. *L'empire du sens: L'humanisation des sciences humaines*. Paris: La Découverte.

Douglas, M., and B. Isherwood. 1979. *The World of Goods: Towards an Anthropology of Consumption*. Harmondsworth: Penguin.

Duranti, A. 1997. *Linguistics Anthropology*. Cambridge: Cambridge University Press.

Eble, C. 1996. *Slang and Sociability: In-Group Language among College Students*. Chapel Hill: University of North Carolina Press.

Eckert, P. 1988. "Adolescent Social Structure and the Spread of Linguistic Change." *Language in Society* 17: 183–207.

Fine, G.A., and K.L. Sandstrom. 1988. *Knowing Children: Participant Observation with Minors*. Newbury Park, Calif.: Sage.

Fischer, H. 2001. *Le choc du numérique*. Collection "gestations." Montreal: VLB éditeur.

Fortunati, L. 2002. "Italy: Stereotypes, True and False." In *Perpetual Contact: Mobile Communication, Private Talk, Public Performance*, edited by J.E. Katz and M.A. Aakhus, 139–69. Cambridge: Cambridge University Press.

Foucault, M. 1981. "The Order of Discourse." In *Untying the Text: A Post Structuralist Reader*, edited by R. Young, 48–78. Boston: Routledge & Kegan Paul.

Galland, O. 1996. "L'entrée dans la vie adulte en France. Bilan et perspectives sociologiques." *Sociologie et sociétés* 28, no. 1: 37–46.
– 1999. "Une génération sacrifiée?" *Sciences Humaines* 23: 20–1.
Garcea, A., and C. Bazzanella. 2002. "Discours rapporté et courrier électronique." *Faits de langue* 1: 233–46.
Garfinkel, H. 1967. *Studies in Ethnomethodology*. Englewood Cliff: Prentice Hall.
Geertz, C. 1973. *The Interpretation of Cultures*. New York: Basic Books.
– 1977. *Local Knowledge: Further Essays in Interpretive Anthropology*. New York: Basic Books.
Gergen, K.J. 2002. "The Challenge of Absent Presence." In *Perpetual Contact: Mobile Communication, Private Talk, Public Performance*, edited by J.E. Katz and M.A. Aakhus, 227–40. Cambridge: Cambridge University Press.
Gergen, K.J., and G.R. Semin. 1990. "Everyday Understanding in Science and Daily Life." In *Everyday Understanding: Social and Scientific Implications*, edited by G.R. Semin and K.J. Gergen, 1–18. London: Sage.
Gergen, K.J., and M.H. Gergen. 1991. "From Theory to Reflexivity in Research Practice." In *Research and Reflexivity*, edited by F. Steier, 76–95. London: Sage.
Giddens, A. 1979. *Central Problems in Social Theory: Actions, Structures and Contradiction in Social Analysis*. Berkeley: University of California Press.
– 1984. *The Constitution of Society: Outline of the Theory of Structuration*. Cambridge: Polity Press.
Glaser, B., and A. Strauss. 1967. *The Discovery of Grounded Theory*. Chicago: Aldine Publishing.
Godbout, J.T. 2000. *Le don, la dette, l'identité: Homo donator vs homo oeconomicus*. Montreal: Boréal.
Godbout, J.T., and A. Caillé. 1991. "Le don existe-t-il (encore)?" *Revue du* MAUSS 11: 11–32.
Goffman, E. 1959. *The Presentation of Self in Everyday Life*. Garden City: Doubleday.
– 1967. *Interaction Ritual*. Garden City: Doubleday.
– 1974. *Frame Analysis*. Cambridge, Mass.: Harvard University Press.
– 1981. *Forms of Talk*. Philadelphia: University of Pennsylvania Press.
Goodman, N. 1978. *Ways of World Making*. Indianapolis: Hackett.
Goodwin, C., and J. Heritage. 1990. "Conversation Analysis." *Annual Review of Anthropology* 19: 283–307.
Goodwin, M.H. 1990. *He-Said-She-Said: Talk as Social Organization among Black Children*. Bloomington: Indiana University Press.
Gras, A., B. Jorges, and V. Scardigli, eds. 1992. *Sociologie des techniques de la vie quotidienne*. Paris: L'Harmattan.

Green, N. 2002. "Qui surveille qui? Contrôler et rendre des comptes dans les relations de téléphonie mobile." *Réseaux* 20 (112–13): 249–74.

Greimas, A.J. 1983. *Du sens 2: Essais sémiotiques.* Paris: Seuil.

Grinter, R. and L. Palen. 2002. "Instant Messaging in Teen Life." In *Proceedings of the ACM Conference on Computer Supported Cooperative Work.* New Orleans: ACM Press.

Grinter, R., and M.A. Eldridge. 2001. "Y do tngrs luv 2 txt msg?" In *Proceedings of the Seventh European Conference on Computer Supported Cooperative Work,* edited by W. Prinz, M. Jarke, Y. Rogers, K. Schmidt, and V. Wulf, 219–38. Dordrecht: Kluwer Academic Publishers.

Guillaume, M. 1994. "Le téléphone mobile." *Réseaux* 65: 27–34.

Gumpert, G., and S.J. Drucker. 1998. "The Mediated Home in the Global Village." *Communication Research* 25, no. 4: 422–39.

Gumperz, J., ed. 1982. *Language and Social Identity.* Cambridge: Cambridge University Press.

Haddon, L. 1992. "Explaining ICT Consumption: The Case of the Home Computer." In *Consuming Technologies: Media and Information in Domestic Spaces,* edited by R. Morley and E. Hirsch, 82–96. London: Routledge.

Hafner, K., and M. Lyon. 1999. "Le temps du mail: Écrit instantané ou oral médiat." *Sociologie et sociétés* 32, no. 2: 154–5.

Hennion, A., and B. Latour. 1996. "L'art, l'aura et la distance selon Benjamin ou comment devenir célèbre en faisant tant d'erreurs à la fois." *Les cahiers de médiologie* 1: 234–41.

Heritage, J. 1984. *Garfinkel and Ethnomethodology.* Cambridge: Polity Press.

Herrnstein Smith, B. 1984. "Narrative Versions, Narrative Theories." In *On Narrative,* edited by W.J.T. Mitchell, 209–32. Chicago: University of Chicago Press.

Hersent, J.-F. 2003. *Les pratiques culturelles adolescentes.* Paris: BBF 3: 12–21. http://www.enssib.fr/bbf/bbf-2003-3/02-hersent.pdf.

Heurtin, P. 1998. "La téléphonie mobile, une communication itinérante? Premiers éléments d'une analyse des usages en France." *Réseaux* 90: 37–50.

Hopper, R. 1991. "Hold the Phone." In *Talk and Social Structure: Studies in Ethnomethodology and Conversation Analysis,* edited by D. Boden and D.H. Zimmerman, 217–31. Berkeley and Los Angeles: University of California Press.

Hopper, R., and C. Chen. 1996. "Languages, Cultures, Relationships: Telephone Openings in Taiwan." *Research on Language and Social Interaction* 29: 291–313.

Hopper, R., and N. Koleilat-Doany. 1989. "Telephone Openings and Conversational Universals: A Study in Three Languages." In *Language,*

Communication and Culture, edited by S. Ting-Toomey and F. Kevizing, 157–79. Newbury Park, Calif: Sage.

Houtkoop-Steenstra, H. 1991. "Opening Sequences in Dutch Telephone Conversations." In *Talk and Social Structure: Studies in Ethnomethodology and Conversation Analysis*, edited by D. Boden and D.H. Zimmerman, 232–50. Cambridge: Polity Press.

Hymes, D., ed. 1971. *Pidginization and Creolization of Languages*. Cambridge, Mass.: Cambridge University Press.

Iori, V. 1996. *Lo spazio vissuto*. Firenze: La Nuova Italia.

Jauréguiberry, F. 1998. "Lieux publics, téléphone mobile et civilité." *Réseaux* 90: 73–83.

Jouët, J., and D. Pasquier. 1999. "Les jeunes et la culture de l'écran: Enquête nationale auprès des 6–17 ans." *Réseaux* 90-3: 25–102.

Kasesniemi, E., and P. Rautiainen. 2002. "Mobile Culture of Children and Teenagers in Finland." In *Perpetual Contact: Mobile Communication, Private Talk, Public Performance*, edited by J.E. Katz and M.A. Aakhus, 170–92. Cambridge: Cambridge University Press.

Katz, J.E., and M.A. Aakhus, eds. 2002. *Perpetual Contact: Mobile Communication, Private Talk, Public Performance*. Cambridge: Cambridge University Press.

Kopytoff, I. 1986. "The Cultural Biography of Things: Commoditisation as Process." In *The Social Life of Things: Commodities in Cultural Perspective*, edited by A. Appadurai, 64–91. Cambridge: Cambridge University Press.

Labov, W. 1972a. *Language in the Inner City: Studies in the Black English Vernacular*. Philadelphia: University of Pennsylvania Press.

– 1972b. "Rules for Ritual Insults." In *Studies in Social Interaction*, edited by D. Sudnow, 120–68. New York: Free Press.

Lally, E. 2002. *At Home with Computers*. Oxford: Berg.

Landowski, E. 1989. *La société réfléchie: Essais de socio-sémiotique*. Paris: Éditions du Seuil.

– 2002. "Dalla parte delle cose." In *La società degli oggetti: Problemi di interoggettività*, edited by E. Landowski and G. Marrone, 39–44. Roma: Meltemi.

Latour, B. 1992. *Aramis, ou l'amour de techniques*. Paris: la Découverte.

– 2002. "Una sociologia senza oggetto? Note sull'interoggettività." In *La società degli oggetti: Problemi di interoggettività*, edited by E. Landowski and G. Marrone, 203–29. Roma: Meltemi.

Lave, J., and E. Wenger. 1991. *Situated Cognition: Legitimate Peripheral Participation*. New York: Cambridge University Press.

Lindström, A.B. 1994. "Identification and Recognition in Swedish Telephone Conversation Openings." *Language in Society* 23, no. 2: 231–52.

Lindstrom, L. 1992. "Context Contests: Debatable Truth Statements on Tanna (Vanuatu)." In *Rethinking Context: Language as an Interactive Phenomenon*, edited by A. Duranti and C. Goodwin, 101–24. Cambridge: Cambridge University Press.

Ling, R., and B. Yttri. 2002. "Hyper-Coordination via Mobile Phones in Norway." In *Perpetual Contact: Mobile Communication, Private Talk, Public Performance*, edited by J.E. Katz and M.A. Aakhus, 139–69. Cambridge: Cambridge University Press.

Livingstone, S. 1992. "The Meaning of Domestic Technologies: A Personal Construct Analysis of Familial Gender Relations." In *Consuming Technologies: Media and Information in Domestic Spaces*, edited by R. Silverstone and E. Hirsch, 113–30. London: Routledge.

– 1996. "La signification des technologies domestiques: Une analyse des constructions mentales individuelles dans les relations familiales entre les sexes." *Réseaux 79*. http://www.enssib.fr/autres-sites/reseaux-cnet/79/03-livin.pdf (accessed 12 July 2006).

Livingstone, S., and M. Bovill, eds. 2001. *Children and Their Changing Media Environment: A European Comparative Study*. London: Lawrence Erlbaum.

Lynch, M. 1993. *Scientific Practice and Ordinary Action: Ethnomethodology and Social Studies of Science*. Cambridge: Cambridge University Press.

Marrone, G. 1999. *C'era una volta il telefonino*. Roma: Meltemi.

– 2002. "Dal design all'interoggettività: Questioni introduttive." In *La società degli oggetti: Problemi di interoggettività*, edited by E. Landowski and G. Marrone, 9–38. Roma: Meltemi.

Martin, C. 2003. Représentations des usages du téléphone portable chez les jeunes adolescents." Paper submitted to the Tenth Colloque bilatéral franco-roumain: Supports, dispositifs et discours médiatiques à l'heure de l'internationalisation, 28 June–3 July, CIFSIC, University of Bucharest.

Mauss, M. 1950. *Sociologie et Anthropologie*. Paris: Presses Universitaires de France.

Merleau-Ponty, M. 1945. *Phénoménologie de la perception*. Paris: Gallimard.

Ochs, E. 1979. "Transcription as Theory." In *Developmental Pragmatics*, edited by E. Ochs and B.B. Schieffelin, 43–72. New York: Academic Press.

– 1986. Introduction. In *Language Socialization across Cultures*, edited by B.B. Schieffelin and E. Ochs, 1–13. New York: Cambridge University Press.

– 1988. *Culture and Language Development: Language Acquisition and Language Socialisation in a Samoan Village*. Cambridge: Cambridge University Press.

Ochs E., and L. Capps. 1996. "Narrating the Self." *Annual Review of Anthropology* 25: 19–43.

– 2001. *Living Narrative: Creating Lives in Everyday Storytelling.* Harvard: Harvard University Press.

Ochs, E., C. Taylor, D. Rudolph, and R. Smith. 1992. "Storytelling as a Theory Building Activity." *Discourse Processes* 15, no. 1: 37–72.

Ohl, F. 2001. "Les usages sociaux des objets: Paraître 'sportif' en ville." *Loisir et Société* 24, no. 1: 111–36.

Pandolfi, M. 2001. "Body." In *Key Terms in Language and Culture*, edited by A. Duranti, 11–14. Malden, Mass.: Blackwell.

Plant, S. 2000. On the Mobile: The Effect of Mobile Telephones on Social and Individual Life. http://www.motorola.com/mot/documents/0,1028,333,00.pdf (accessed 11 July 2006).

Pronovost, G. 1996. "Les Jeunes, le temps, la culture." *Sociologie et sociétés* 28, no. 1: 147–58.

Quinn, N., and D. Holland. 1987. "Culture and Cognition." In *Cultural Models in Language and Thought*, edited by D. Holland and N. Quinn, 3–42. Cambridge: Cambridge University Press.

Rakow, L., and P. Navarro. 1993. "Remote Mothering and the Parallel Shift: Women Meet the Cellular Phone." *Critical Studies in Mass Communication* 10, no. 2: 144–57.

Rampton, B. 1995. *Crossing: Language and Ethnicity among Adolescents.* London: Longman.

Renard, J.-B. 1999. *Rumeurs et légendes urbaines.* Paris: PUF.

Ricoeur, P. 1986. *Du texte à l'action. Essais d'herméneutique 2.* Paris: Seuil.

Rifkin, J. 2000. *L'âge de l'accès: Survivre à l'hypercapitalisme.* Montreal: Boréal.

Riou, N. 2002. *Pub Fiction.* Paris: Éditions d'organisation.

Rivière, C. 2002. "La pratique du mini-message: Une double stratégie d'extériorisation et de retrait de l'intimité dans les interactions quotidiennes." *Réseaux* 20, nos. 112–13: 139–68.

Rogers, E. 1983. *Diffusion of Innovations.* New York: Free Press.

Sacks, H. 1972. "On the Analysability of Stories by Children." In *Directions in Sociolinguistics: The Ethnography of Communication*, edited by J.J. Gumperz and D. Hymes, 325–45. New York: Rinehart & Winston.

– 1984. "On Doing 'Be Ordinary.'" In *Structures of Social Actions*, edited by M. Atkinson and J. Heritage, 413-429. Cambridge: Cambridge University Press.

Sacks, H., E. Schegloff, and G. Jefferson. 1974. "A Simple Systematics for the Organization of Turn-Taking for Conversation." *Language* 50, no. 4: 696–735.

Schegloff, E. 1968. "Sequencing in Conversational Openings." *American Anthropologist* 70: 1075–95.

– 1972. "Notes on a Conversational Practice: Formulating Place." In *Studies in Social Interaction*, edited by D. Sudnow, 75–119. New York: Free Press.

– 1979. "Identification and Recognition in Telephone Conversation Openings." In *Everyday Language: Studies in Ethnomethodology*, edited by G. Psathas, 23–78. New York: Irvington.

– 2002. "Beginnings in the Telephone." In *Perpetual Contact: Mobile Communication, Private Talk, Public Performance*, edited by J.E. Katz and M.A. Aakhus, 284–300. Cambridge: Cambridge University Press.

Schegloff, E., and H. Sacks. 1973. "Opening up Closing." *Semiotica* 8: 289–327.

Schegloff E., G. Jefferson, and H. Sacks. 1977. "The Preference for Self-Correction in the Organization of Repair in Conversation." *Language* 53, no. 2: 361–82.

Schutz A. 1967. *The Phenomenology of Social World*. First published, 1932. Evanston, Ill.: Northwestern University Press.

– 1962. *Collected Papers*. Vol. 1. The Hague: Martinus Nijhoff.

Semprini, A. 1995. *L'objet comme procès et comme action*. Paris: L'Harmattan.

– 1996. *Analyser la communication: Comment analyser les images, les médias, la publicité*. Paris: L'Harmattan.

– 2002. "Oggetti senza frontiere." In *La società degli oggetti: Problemi di interoggettività*, edited by E. Landowski and G. Marrone, 47–60. Roma: Meltemi.

Semprini, A., ed. 1999. *Il senso delle cose: I significati sociali e culturali degli oggetti quotidiani*. Milano: Franco Angeli.

Silverstone, R., E. Hirsch, and D. Morley. 1992. "Information and Communication Technologies and the Moral Economy of the Household." In *Consuming Technologies: Media and Information in Domestic Spaces*, edited by R. Silverstone and E. Hirsch, 15–31. London: Routledge.

Singly de, F. 2000. *Libres ensemble: L'individualisme dans la vie commune*. Paris: Nathan.

Steier, F., ed. 1991. *Research and Reflexivity*. London: Sage.

Taylor, A.S., and R. Harper. 2003. "The Gift of the Gab?: A Design Oriented Sociology of Young People's Use of Mobiles." *Computer Supported Cooperative Work* 12 no. 3: 267–96.

Van Maanen, J. 1988. *Tales of the Field: On Writing Ethnography*. Chicago: University of Chicago Press.

Violi, P. 1998. "Electronic Dialogue between Orality and Literacy: A Semiotic Approach." In *Dialogue in the Hearth of Europe*, edited by Cmejrkovà et al., 263–70. Tubingen: Nyemeir.

Violi, P., and P.J. Coppock. 1999. "Conversazioni telematiche." In *La conversazione: Un'introduzione allo studio dell'interazione verbale*, edited by R. Galatolo and G. Pallotti, 319–64. Milano: Raffaello Cortina Editore.

Weilenmann, A., and C. Larsson. 2001. "Local Use and Sharing of Mobile Phones." In *Wireless World: Social and Interactional Aspects of the Mobile Age*, edited by B. Brown, N. Green, and R. Harper, 99–115. Godalming and Hiedleburg: Springer Verlag.

Weissberg, J.-L. 1999. *Présence à distance: Déplacement virtuel et réseaux numériques: Pourquoi nous ne croyons plus la télévision*. Paris: L'Harmattan.

Willis, P. 1990. *Common Culture: Symbolic Work at Play in the Everyday Cultures of the Young*. San Francisco: Westview Press.

Wilson, T.P. 1991. "Social Structure and Interaction." In *Talk and Social Structure: Studies in Ethnomethodology and Conversation Analysis*, edited by D. Boden and D.H. Zimmerman, 22–43. Berkeley: University of California Press.

Zimmerman, D.H. 1984. "Talk and Its Occasion: The Case of Calling the Police." In *Meaning, Form, and Use in Context: Linguistic Applications*, edited by D. Schiffrin, 210–28. Washington, D.C.: Georgetown University Press.

– 1992. "The Interactional Organization of Calls for Emergency Assistance." In *Talk at Work*, edited by J. Heritage and P. Drew, 418–69. Cambridge: Cambridge University Press.

Zimmerman, D.H., and D. Boden. 1991. "Structure-in-Action: An Introduction." In *Talk and Social Structure: Studies in Ethnomethodology and Conversation Analysis*, edited by D. Boden and D.H. Zimmerman, 3–21. Berkeley: University of California Press.

Index